British Planning and
Nationalization

BRITISH PLANNING

AND

NATIONALIZATION

BY BEN W. LEWIS

o CBd may '52

NEW YORK

The Twentieth Century Fund

PUBLISHED IN GREAT BRITAIN BY

George Allen & Unwin Ltd.

MANUFACTURED IN THE UNITED STATES OF AMERICA
BY THE HILDRETH PRESS, BRISTOL, CONNECTICUT

Foreword

EVENTS IN GREAT BRITAIN have always been of great concern to the United States—more so, usually, than happenings in any other foreign country. A common heritage of blood, language and political institutions has, of course, bound us very closely to the British in spite of our many friendly differences. The access to power of a Labor party in Great Britain, pledged to a socialist program radically different from our economic theory and practice, naturally had profound repercussions in this country. These were vastly intensified as the Labor government proceeded to fulfill its pledges to institute over-all economic planning and to nationalize the basic industries of Britain.

Obviously it is far too early to pass any final judgment on British planning and nationalization. But it is none too soon to describe, for the benefit of the inquiring American public, what the Labor government did and at least to summarize the initial operations of the nationalized industries.

To this end the Fund commissioned Professor Ben W. Lewis of Oberlin College to visit Great Britain, gather what information he could within the time at his disposal, and to write a brief reconnaissance report of his findings for American readers. These are included in the present volume.

While he was in Great Britain Dr. Lewis talked with government officials, political leaders of all parties, economists, and leading figures in labor and business circles. He also, of course, delved deep into the published sources of information both here and abroad.

Since Dr. Lewis wrote his report the Labor government has been defeated in the General Election of October 1951. But, as he points out in his preface, this detracts little, if at all, from the value of his report. The record of Labor's six years of planning and nationalization is still of supreme

importance in judging present-day Britain and its future—
especially because it seems most unlikely that the new
Conservative government will do much in the way of
denationalization.

The Fund hopes that this brief summary of recent British economic history will help Americans to comprehend
what has happened there and its implications—for Great
Britain, and for the United States in its relations with Great
Britain, our closest foreign friend and ally. The Fund
deeply appreciates Dr. Lewis' contribution to a better
American understanding of the situation.

EVANS CLARK, *Executive Director*
The Twentieth Century Fund

330 WEST 42D STREET
NEW YORK 36, N. Y.
DECEMBER 28, 1951

Author's Preface

THIS BOOK EXPLORES a number of selected areas in which, since 1945, the Labor government of Great Britain has undertaken positively to control the economic life of the nation. Chapter 1 is concerned with the operation of Britain's formal economic planning machinery. Chapters that follow deal with nationalization, town and country planning, distribution of industry, the national health service, housing and agriculture. The projects reviewed do not cover the entire range of activities undertaken by the British government to supersede or correct the processes of the free market in an effort to obtain more complete and better use of economic resources or better division of the economic product. They do constitute the bulk of the total program, however, and they are fully illustrative of its character. If they differ from other projects not considered here at length, it is largely in the fact that they are more thoroughgoing or novel, and, hence, more controversial.

Chapter 1 mentions price control, rationing and exchange control only in passing. These involve little that is new or instructive. The chapters on nationalization are concerned primarily with the major programs—coal, transportation, electricity and steel. The Bank of England, gas, telecommunications and civil aviation are mentioned only briefly. I have allowed the discussions of health, housing, and town and country planning to represent Britain's overall program in the social services (which include, in addition, national insurance, pensions, welfare services and special provision for the young, the old and the handicapped) and education, which have come to be among the least controversial of government activities. In treating the efforts of the government to promote economic development other than by nationalization, I have by-passed the development-council device and the recent monopoly legislation in favor of the more positive approach displayed in the case of agriculture and the distribution of industry.

This study does not purport to be an exhaustive full-blown inquiry into the subjects under discussion. In the case of each selected project I have attempted primarily to tell what has happened and what is now happening—to set out the main lines and phases of structure and operation in their historic and contemporary setting. I have tried, as well, to identify the principal issues raised by the projects and to indicate something of current British opinion on those issues.

I have relied heavily upon published materials for my information and I am acutely aware that the book lacks the "atmosphere" and "feel" that would be necessary if it pretended to be a complete study or to advance confident and seasoned judgments. I have attempted severe restraint in appraisal. The record to date is short and will permit only the most speculative of conclusions. In any event, competent judgments would require longer and more intimate contact with Britain's government, industry and people than I have enjoyed. I realize, however, that scientific objectivity is more frequently sought after than attained by those who write on controversial economic-political subjects. Hence, so that the reader may allow for any inadvertent bias that may color my presentation, let me be the first to say that I have much sympathy for what the Labor government is trying to do.

I am grateful to the authors and publishers who have permitted me to quote directly from their publications. I am particularly indebted to *The Economist* and *The Times* (London) upon which I have relied heavily for information, analysis and comment. Friends in British universities, industries and the government have been extremely generous in providing information and offering helpful suggestions. The Twentieth Century Fund made possible an exploratory trip to Great Britain in June and

July 1949; and Evans Clark, the Fund's Executive Director, J. Frederic Dewhurst, the Fund's Economist, and the Fund's editorial staff have all been most helpful and encouraging at every stage. I owe a special debt of gratitude to Adolf A. Berle, Jr. for encouragement and assistance in planning the study and getting it under way.

BEN W. LEWIS

OBERLIN, OHIO

POSTSCRIPT

The manuscript for this book was completed and sent to the press only a few days before Prime Minister Attlee's call for the General Election of October 25, 1951. The text has not been altered as a consequence of the outcome of the election. No change in the factual account, or in the analysis of interpretation, seems to be required. To be sure, a Conservative government has now begun to pick up and deal in its own way with the several projects instituted by Labor; but, just as Labor's six postwar years in office involved a growth from, and not a break with, the past, the years ahead will see no fundamental break with 1945–1951. The new government may discontinue one of Labor's programs (nationalized steel) and may modify others, and its administration of some of the programs will be characterized by restrained enthusiasm. Irrespective of parties and governments, however, large-scale nationalization and peacetime planning are almost certain to be continued indefinitely as integral features of the British economy. The six years of nationalization and planning treated in the pages that follow are significant in themselves and as a closed period; they are even more significant for their bearing on the years immediately ahead.

B.W.L.

CONTENTS

TABLES

British Planning and Nationalization

CHAPTER I

Economic Planning

ECONOMIC PLANNING (or what is now called economic
planning) in Great Britain is concerned with the task of
fitting the nation's resources to Britain's imperative economic needs. The pattern—broad, tentative and shifting—
is drawn and redrawn by the government; and the devices
for directing the flow of resources to meet its requirements
range from persuasion and exhortation to licensing of private economic activity and government investment and
purchasing. The object is to employ the national resources
in what the government deems the best interests of the
nation as a whole, the balanced satisfaction of vital needs.

Two needs—payments for imports and domestic investment—are specially urgent. The life of Great Britain depends on imports of food and materials. Payment for these
imports, following the economic and physical damage
wrought by World War II, has demanded a major read-
justment in British production and trade. Wartime destruction, together with the postponement forced by the
war in the maintenance, expansion and modernization of
capital equipment—factories, machinery, shops and houses
—has transformed Britain's ordinary peacetime requirements for capital expenditures into demands of formidable
proportions.

In the nature of the case, governments everywhere today
engage in "planning" in a limited sense and degree. Their
expenditures and their taxation and budgetary programs
are so large in scale as necessarily to affect materially the
character and conduct of all economic activity within their
range. No government, even in carrying on its ordinary
operations, can be "neutral." It must act with an awareness

of effects, and to this extent, at least, with purpose and design, whether it characterizes its actions as "planning" or "budget policy" or simply "administration."

The British have been drawn extensively into planning in this sense by reason of their broad programs of nationalization, social services and housing, which have involved the government increasingly as a direct participant in the economic arena. Beyond this, however, they have used deliberately the opportunity thus afforded to employ budgetary and fiscal programs as major instruments for carrying out government policies involving broad areas of the economy.[1] In addition, the government has undertaken to continue into the postwar period (although until very recently at a declining rate) much of the apparatus of government economic decision-making and control that during World War II was substituted by general consent for the processes of the free market.

British Planning Born of Necessity

Although planning by the Labor government has an ideological basis, it is important to keep in mind that British planning in 1945–1951, with its accompanying controls, is eminently pragmatic, born of hard, immediate necessities. It springs from shortage of resources in the face of insistent demands and pressures that no government conscious of its responsibilities could safely ignore.

Britain has lost much of its wealth at home and abroad in two world wars; British capital equipment and productive and commercial techniques have been falling behind in world competition; long-standing inadequacies and inequities in the domestic economy demand correction. The international economic position of the nation, long a source of affluence and power, now exposes it to

1. In his Budget speech before the House of Commons, April 18, 1950, the Chancellor of the Exchequer characterized the Budget as the government's "most important control and as the most powerful instrument for influencing economic policy." *Parliamentary Debates* (Hansard), House of Commons, Vol. 474, col. 40.

the vagaries of foreign economic conditions and policies—international trade, essential to existence, has had to be remade and redirected overnight. Britain needs to construct, to repair, to enhance the health and well-being of the people, to export, to rebuild and maintain national defense, and to live from day to day; the resources from which these needs are to be supplied are very limited. Britain is experiencing inflation and fears depression. These are the forces and conditions responsible for the appearance of planning (British brand) and its acceptance by the British people at this juncture in their history.

Government planning and controls were not inevitable, of course, even under these circumstances, but reliance upon positive governmental measures rather than acquiescence in the operation of the impersonal mechanism of the free market is easy to understand. Britain has been in an economic emergency since the close of World War I, and the pressures were increased and sharpened by the physical destruction and economic consequences of World War II. Emergencies generate positive, collective action. The British people—even British "socialists"—do not take kindly to restraints on their liberties,[2] but the restraints involved in British planning have their roots in shortages that are known and acknowledged. When everyone knows that there is less than usual to go around and to do with, it is natural to embrace a contrived program that purports to spread the impact of the shortages "fairly" and to move the limited resources directly into broad uses generally accepted as representing the national interest.

Labor pronouncements have made much of planning; the explicit programing and control of the nation's overall economic life are certainly more congenial to a Labor than to a Conservative government. It is difficult to be-

2. Amusing support for this proposition will be found in the strictures delivered before the Electrical Development Association by Lord Citrine, chairman of the "socialist" British Electricity Authority, on the delays, red tape and frustrations experienced by the Authority in its attempts to secure authorization for capital expansion. *The Economist*, April 29, 1950, pp. 957–58.

lieve, however, that any government, regardless of its political complexion, would have found it possible, since 1945, to modify or lessen appreciably the cautious, tentative, almost hopeful efforts to budget the nation's resources in major categories that have constituted the British planning program to date.

Coalition Government Had Plans

Planning to meet the economic problems of the peace was undertaken by the Coalition government even before the end of the war, but the major problem foreseen at that time was unemployment. The 1944 White Paper on employment policy set forth measures of government action designed to cope with transitional unemployment consequent upon war-end readjustments, and to provide for the general, long-term maintenance of demand and of employment. It declared:

The Government accept as one of their primary aims and responsibilities the maintenance of a high and stable level of employment after the war. This Paper outlines the policy which they propose to follow in pursuit of that aim.[3]

The document anticipated the "transitional" difficulties of shortages, inflation and misdirected production. It stated flatly that rationing, price controls, subsidies, the encouragement of savings and control of the flow and direction of investment would all have to be continued, and that broad priorities (with accompanying licenses, allocations and labor controls) would have to be established in order to insure the necessary increase in exports, the provision of mass necessities rather than luxuries, and the production of capital goods for industrial rehabilitation. The White Paper warned:

It cannot be expected that the public, after years of war-time restrictions, will find these proposals altogether palatable; and the Government have no intention of maintaining war-time

3. *Employment Policy*, Cmd. 6527, H.M.S.O., May 1944, p. 3.

restrictions for restriction's sake. But they are resolved that, so long as supplies are abnormally short, the most urgent needs shall be met first.[4]

Nonetheless, from the vantage point of 1944, these problems were regarded (perhaps hopefully) as transitional, and the consideration given to them in the White Paper was brief and general. It is significant, then, that seven years later the "short run" has lengthened out indefinitely; unemployment has been troublesome only in the "depressed areas"; and the planning engaged in by the successor to the Coalition government is still very largely related to scarcities and to heavy demands now swollen by new preparations for defense. The most acute and immediate phases of demobilization and retooling for peace have been accomplished and remobilization is again under way, but Britain has suffered throughout from limited supplies, and the anticipated lack of jobs that prompted the "forward look" in 1944 has yet to materialize.

THE NATURE OF BRITISH ECONOMIC PLANNING

Economic planning in Great Britain is somewhat less pretentious, detailed and precise, and also more limited and less effective in determining actual British economic conduct, than has been supposed by those who have not examined it at close range.

The first of the annual Economic Surveys, presented by the Prime Minister to Parliament in February 1947, opened with an illuminating statement of the government's position on the need for and nature of British economic planning.[5]

"The object of economic planning," said the *Survey*, "is to use the national resources in the best interests of the nation as a whole. How this is done must depend upon the economic circumstances of the country, its stage of political development, its social structure and its methods of government." The *Survey* stated that the £8.5 billion worth

4. *Ibid.*, p. 9.
5. *Economic Survey for 1947*, Cmd. 7046, H.M.S.O., pp. 3–9.

of goods and services produced annually by Britain's 20 million workers with the aid of vast capital equipment and materials drawn from the markets of the world must be directed to the satisfaction of five main national needs: (1) defense; (2) payment for imports; (3) capital equipment and maintenance; (4) personal consumption; and (5) public services. These are claims upon the nation's work; if more is taken to satisfy any of the claims, the other claims must suffer; if less than full use is made of the nation's resources, fewer total requirements can be met. There will always be an excess of requirements over resources, but, as a result of wartime destruction and interruption, certain basic needs assume an unusual importance. "The gap between resources and requirements will in the end be closed by some of the requirements being left unsupplied. But if the process of closing the gap is left to chance [i.e., the market], some vital requirements are sure to be squeezed out by the less essential."[6] It is the task of economic planning to effect the balance.

It was the theme of the *Survey* that there is an essential difference between totalitarian planning which employs compulsion in order to subordinate individual desires and preferences to the demands of the state, and democratic planning which proceeds in a manner designed to preserve the maximum possible freedom of choice to the individual citizen. Britain's highly complex industrial system is a result of over a century's steady growth; the decisions determining production are dispersed among thousands of organizations and individuals; the public is accustomed to a wide range of choice; and since Britain's existence depends on imports, its exports must compete successfully in world markets and its industry must be readily adaptable to changes in those markets. It follows that British planning must be highly flexible. The government is developing a long-term plan for each of the nation's basic industries and services—coal, power, steel,

6. *Ibid.,* p. 7.

agriculture, transport and building—and it intends, as part of its economic plan, to see that these programs are advanced and kept in proper relationship to each other and to the whole economy.

Chief Elements of the System

The system of economic planning which the government is undertaking, continued the *Survey*, has the following chief elements:

(i) An organisation with enough knowledge and reliable information to assess our national resources and to formulate the national needs.

(ii) A set of economic "budgets" which relate these needs to our resources, and which enable the Government to say what is the best use for the resources in the national interest.

(iii) A number of methods, the combined effect of which will enable the Government to influence the use of resources in the desired direction, without interfering with democratic freedoms.[7]

It was recognized that over the economy as a whole, in peacetime, the government's control of production, distribution and consumption must be exercised by measures far less drastic than those employed in time of war. The government may provide a framework and may set goals or targets in major categories, but the making of detailed day-to-day decisions is the task of individuals and individual firms. Consultation, persuasion and agreement are the principal instruments of democratic planning. The main emphasis in Britain must be on short-term planning; it is not possible, because of major uncertainties primarily in the international field, to prepare a plan even for the next five years with sufficient precision to enable it to serve as a useful guide to industry and the public.

The following excerpts from the memoranda submitted to the Organisation for European Economic Co-operation

7. *Ibid.*, pp. 5-6.

throw additional light on the government's conception of economic planning:

Any programme of economic planning must be in the nature of a broad strategical plan sufficiently flexible to meet unpredictable and rapidly changing events. It is not possible to establish firm and definite plans which would bind the United Kingdom economy to a pre-determined course of action so far ahead as 1952–53 or even eighteen months hence. . . . The United Kingdom national programmes set out to define the general objectives which the country will seek to follow. No other method of programming is possible in a democratic community. For, quite apart from the unpredictable impact of external events, policies can be fulfilled only if they gain the voluntary co-operation of the people as groups and as individuals. . . .

Detailed conclusions cannot be drawn from these forward estimates about the pattern of the standard of living to be attained or about the exact distribution of production at home or of our trade overseas. The figures are illustrative of the nature and relative scale of the problems that on present evidence seem likely to arise, the possible solutions, and the points upon which special effort will have to be concentrated. . . .

Economic planning in the United Kingdom is based upon three fundamental facts: the economic fact that the United Kingdom economy must be heavily dependent upon international trade; the political fact that it is and intends to remain a democratic nation with a high degree of individual liberty; and the administrative fact that no economic planning body can be aware (or indeed ever could be aware) of more than the very general trends of future economic developments. Many of the assumptions about the future on which plans must be based are profoundly uncertain and many economic events are wholly outside the control of any one nation; many can only be partially influenced by international agreements, and those such as the effect of the weather on the crops are beyond human control. Even in purely domestic economic matters the means of control which can be effectively used within a democracy are limited. Underlying economic uncertainties there is the factor of political stability in the world at large.[8]

8. *European Cooperation*, Cmd. 7572, H.M.S.O., 1948, pp. vi, 1.

British planning thus is designed, in a period of con-spicuous shortage and unusual demand, to supplement and partially to supersede the forces of the free market in determining priorities in the use of resources. In a measure it sets targets; in a measure it undertakes direction; in a measure it attempts to forecast results. It assumes that under prevailing conditions, as in time of war, certain economic goals are so clear, so well understood and so generally ac-ceptable that the government may speak for the nation as a whole in requiring their achievement. A small minority of individual demands which, if allowed free operative ex-pression, would impair the national program may appro-priately and in the name of democracy be overridden.

The program does not purport to be inspired. It is hesi-tant and tentative; its goals melt easily into predictions, and its predictions into hopes. Its objectives and elements are broad: It is concerned that scarce steel shall go into factory buildings (as into battleships in time of war) rather than into dog tracks; it is not concerned that the factory build-ings shall be painted gray rather than blue. It operates in full awareness that any planning program that taxes unduly the patience of the electorate will be self-defeating—and knows that both the broad impact of the program and the personal irritations it causes keep it constantly on the de-fensive.

The Labor government may be confused in its concept of planning. It may be attempting to mix elements which simply cannot be combined in a single program.[9] It may be naïve in its hopes and expectations, but the nature of its intent cannot fairly be questioned. It is attempting to com-bine a free democracy and a planned economy, and where operating experience demonstrates that elements of the two

9. See J. H. Jewkes and E. Devons, "The Economic Survey for 1947," *Lloyds Bank Review,* April 1947, p. 1. For an authoritative reitera-tion of the concept and principles of democratic planning expressed in the *Economic Survey for 1947,* see the Budget speech by the Chancel-lor of the Exchequer, April 18, 1950, cited in footnote 1.

are mutually exclusive, planning is subordinated to freedom.

THE PLANNING MACHINERY

The machinery of planning had its inception in the war years, and has evolved, planlessly, into a curious mixture of old-line and newly created elements. There is, first and foremost, the Cabinet itself—the final authority for all plans and arbiter of all disputes arising from otherwise irreconcilable claims of the several ministries and departments.

The two principal Cabinet committees concerned with economic planning are those on Economic Policy of which the Prime Minister is chairman, and the Production Committee under the chairmanship of the Chancellor of the Exchequer. The Economic Policy Committee has responsibility for formulating general economic policy, and the Production Committee for detailed recommendations on such matters as major capital developments, the siting of important factories, the investment programs, the Economic Survey, etc.[10]

Service Units of the Cabinet

The Cabinet has two service units whose planning roles are important—the Central Statistical Office and the Economic Secretariat (or Section). The first of these was established in 1940 to collate statistical data bearing upon the entire range of government economic interest and responsibility, to expand the statistical service and to make it more available both within its own four walls and to the public. The agency that was to become the Economic Section of the Cabinet Office began to take shape in 1939, when a small group of prominent economists was brought into the service of the Cabinet. The function of the Section, as it has developed under able guidance, is to furnish economic answers and, upon occasion, economic "advice" to the ministers. It is solely a "staff" office, and the emphasis of its work is objectively economic rather than political or administra-

10. *The Economist,* January 21, 1950, p. 118.

tive. It has representatives on many of the interdepartmental committees, however, and works closely with the Economic Planning Staff which, with no economic section of its own, draws heavily upon the Economic Section for economic analysis.

Economic Planning Staff

In September 1947, the Cabinet was enlarged to include a Minister for Economic Affairs, whose task was to coordinate all economic policy, including the programs of the principal economic departments or ministries. Within two months, Sir Stafford Cripps, the Minister for Economic Affairs, was appointed Chancellor of the Exchequer, and the recently created ministry was absorbed into the Treasury. Sir Stafford Cripps, in his dual capacity, occupied the key post in the planning organization.[11]

The Economic Planning Staff and its head, the Chief Planning Officer, report to the Chancellor of the Exchequer. The Staff was established in May 1947. Its function is

to *initiate* thought and action in general economic matters of vital importance to the nation and to coordinate the use of economic resources. . . . The Planning Staff is advisory; it has no executive status. The Cabinet, Cabinet Committees, Ministers and their Departments continue to be responsible for all actual decisions and for their implementation. The Planning Staff has, however, the personnel, the expertise and the access to facts which give it the capacity for a combinational planning of resources appropriate to given sets of objectives.[12]

11. Following the 1950 General Election, the government appointed a Minister of State for Economic Affairs "to give some additional relief to the Chancellor of the Exchequer from the growing pressure of business which has resulted from his dual responsibility both for financial business and for the coordination of economic policy." *The Times* (London), March 1, 1950. The first appointee to the new post was Hugh Gaitskell, former Minister of Fuel and Power. Later, when upon the resignation of Sir Stafford Cripps, Gaitskell was made Chancellor of the Exchequer, the post of Minister for Economic Affairs was left unfilled. *The Times* (London), October 20, 1950.

12. *Post-War Britain, 1948–1949,* Central Office of Information, London, 1948, p. 54.

Economic Planning Board

The planning organization embraces, as well, an Economic Planning Board, to advise the government on the use of economic resources, on both a long-term and immediate basis. It consists of officials drawn from the Planning Staff, the Treasury and other departments, and representatives from private industry and the labor unions, under the chairmanship of the Chief Planning Officer. The institution of the Board

. . . associates management and labor continuously with the Government in the consideration of planning problems as a whole. The Government is thus able to receive and take into account in good time the views of industry, while industry is in a better position to understand the problems confronting Government.[13]

Departments and Interdepartmental Committees

Government departments and interdepartmental committees make up an important part of the planning machinery. During the war, a system of "sponsoring" was developed, under which each industry or sector of the economy was assigned to a department whose task it was to entertain and weigh the problems and claims of its industries and to represent them in government economic councils. The departments and the industries they sponsor are, broadly speaking, as follows:

. . . the Board of Trade is responsible for the consumer goods industries, e.g., clothing, textile goods, and leather, paper, and wooden goods; the Ministry of Supply for the capital goods industries, e.g., iron and steel, chemicals, engineering and aircraft; the Ministry of Transport for roads and railways and, jointly with the Admiralty, for shipbuilding; the Ministry of Fuel and Power for coal, gas, electricity and oil; the Ministry of Works for building and civil engineering. The administration of the housing programme is the responsibility of the Minister of Health, as are the country's water supplies. The Minis-

13. *Ibid.*, p. 54.

try of Food is responsible for the purchase, import, distribution and manufacture of foodstuffs, while the Ministry of Agriculture is responsible for the import of animal feeding-stuffs, agricultural production, forests and fisheries.[14]

The departments thus perform a dual role in peacetime planning: in their executive capacity it is their task to put plans into action, but it is from their knowledge and experience that the facts and prospects and programs for Britain's industries are made available for incorporation into a national plan.

Interdepartmental committees, with members drawn from interested departments, the Planning Staff, the Economic Section and the Central Statistical Office, complete the structure. The committees are "functional . . . they attempt to translate the projected programmes of the Departments, and of the various sectors of the economy which they 'sponsor' . . . into the principal categories of economic planning; e.g., the balance of payments, production, imports, exports, manpower, and above all the capital investment programme."[15]

Planning Staff Is Central

The Economic Planning Staff occupies the central position. The Staff is divided into an Internal and Coordinating Section and an External Section, each headed by an Undersecretary. The group is small; it consists of men drawn mainly from the government service and the universities, who know government machinery and who have some facility for negotiation. Much of its success has depended and will continue to depend upon personalities and ease of contact. The agency is characterized by its own members as a "coordinating" element—a catalyst or solvent. It does not evolve and impose; it coordinates. It is on the lookout for gaps and inconsistencies in the programs of the ministries.

The pressure for the establishment of the Staff came, not from the ministers, but from the permanent officials of the

14. *Ibid.,* p. 55.
15. *Ibid.,* pp. 54–55.

departments who felt the need for a group with time and facilities to assume responsibility for coordinating department programs and proposals. Lack of such activity had led earlier to difficulties, particularly in the allocation to the departments of more resources than were actually available for distribution. But it must not be overlooked that, under the Labor government as always, the departments are "sovereign"—they are in no sense servants of the Planning Staff.

The functions of the Economic Section of the Cabinet Office and of the Economic Planning Staff have sometimes been confused by outsiders, although there is no evidence of internal confusion. The two groups work in close proximity and their members are continuously in professional and personal contact. The prime function of the Economic Section, however, is to give economic advice to the Cabinet (including the Planning Staff as an agency of the Treasury performing an over-all service for the economic ministries), whereas the prime function of the Planning Staff is to negotiate, guide and reconcile departmental programs and claims in the economic sphere.

Nature and Purpose of Controls

The nature of the controls employed by the government has been indicated earlier in this chapter. On this matter the government is explicit, and the record supports its professions. The *Survey* describes these controls as follows:

The apparatus of Government controls is used to guide the economy in the direction which is indicated by the plan. Over an important part of the national economy, the Government can exercise direct influence. The level of Government expenditure approved by Parliament, and the expenditure of other public authorities, determines the amount of production of a wide range of goods and services, e.g., education, public housing, supplies for the Armed Forces; the policies of the socialised industries and services have a substantial effect upon the whole economy, and are ultimately subject to Government control. The Government's fiscal policy can exert indirect influence over the course of production. There are now a large number of direct controls, the purpose of which is to allocate scarce resources of all kinds between the various applicants for their use —rationing, raw material controls, building licensing, production controls, import licensing, capital issues control, etc. Other controls again, such as price control, influence the course of production by limiting profit margins.

This control apparatus, taken as a whole, can have a substantial effect upon the course of the national economy. But the controls cannot by themselves bring about very rapid changes or make very fine adjustments in the economic structure. To do this, they would have to be much more detailed in their application and more drastic in their scope. Indeed, the task of directing by democratic methods an economic system as large and complex as ours is far beyond the power of any Governmental machine working by itself, no matter how efficient it may be. Events can be directed in the way that is desired in the national interest only if the Government, both sides of industry and the people accept the objectives and then work together to achieve the end.

. . . Under democracy, the execution of the economic plan must be much more a matter for co-operation between the Government, industry and the people, than of rigid application by the State of controls and compulsions. The Government must lay down the economic tasks for the nation; it must say which things are the most important and what the objectives of policy should be, and should give as much information as possible to guide the nation's economic activity; it must use its powers of economic control to influence the course of development in the desired direction. When the working pattern has thus been set, it is only by the combined effort of the whole people that the nation can move towards its objective of carrying out first things first, and so make the best use of its economic resources.[16]

So far as the control of *industry* is concerned, every product of British industry is assigned to a "sponsoring" government department or ministry. If a firm (or group of firms or an entire industry) is in need of equipment or materials, or if it desires to issue capital shares, or to build or to export or

16. *Economic Survey for 1947*, pp. 8–9.

import, its first task is to obtain the approval and the active support of its sponsor.[17]

A firm may not issue securities without permission from the Capital Issues Committee (Treasury);[18] it may not build without a license from the Minister of Works, the Board of Trade and the local authority; it must receive its allocation of scarce industrial goods and raw materials from the ministry or committee in charge of the items involved; its project will be appraised in the light of the manpower situation as viewed by the Minister of Labor, and of his recommendations. It may produce (i.e., it will receive its necessary allocations) only if its product is deemed sufficiently important to the national economy; it may import or export only by license, although it may be required as a condition for receiving its allocations to produce a certain proportion of its

17. "Since the war . . . one department or another has become 're-sponsible' for every industrial product . . .

" . . . the department is both the servant and the master. It offers to the firms . . . advice and information, help in preparing applications for import licenses, currency allowances, building licenses, and for Treasury permission to raise loans, guidance on alternative sources of materials, and a great many other things. On the other hand, it is the first authority asked for an opinion on the advisability of granting an application, and if it says no the chances of its being overridden are small indeed . . . [Probably its most important function] consists in the opportunity it provides for informal discussion and for the exchange of information between industry . . . and the Government . . . on their respective needs, desires and difficulties. The Government is enabled to know what can and what cannot be done; industry is encouraged to feel that in the end its own aims and those of the Government are at least capable of reconciliation, and to fall in, without being compelled to, with a policy which it itself has helped, by its information and expressions of opinion, to formulate." "Government and Industry," *Planning*, September 18, 1950, p. 49.

18. The Committee consists of seven members, "experienced in finance and industry," appointed by the Treasury. The Committee meets weekly, but its staff of some ten civil servants is available on all business days. The Committee is concerned "with the purposes and amounts of proposed issues, but not ordinarily with the terms on which they are offered . . ." "Government Control Over the Use of Capital Resources," *Midland Bank Review*, August 1950, pp. 1–7.

output for the export market. Firms may be required to produce certain types of goods. In connection with all these regulations there is much in the way of informal negotiation and persuasion that precedes the taking of formal action, and frequently makes it unnecessary for formal action to be taken.

There are, of course, the over-all and indirect controls that the government exercises through the medium of taxes, public expenditures and budget surpluses, as well as through government bulk purchases of materials and supplies for resale and through the investment, purchasing and production programs of the nationalized industries.

Consumers jointly with sellers meet controls in the form of point rationing and maximum prices.

The controls exercised today in Great Britain, however extensive they may appear to people fortunate enough to live under conditions of peacetime plenty, are almost exclusively of the restrictive or conditioning type; positive orders to individual persons or firms are virtually nonexistent. Individuals or firms *may not do* certain things; they may do certain other things only upon complying with stated conditions; and their individual choices are certainly made in an atmosphere charged with government influence. Nonetheless, the bulk of economic activity is free from government dictatorship; the government has in fact employed positive directions only in a handful of cases. It has required certain (utility) goods to be made—as a condition for making other goods—and it has ordered a few workers into particular employment, but these assertions of power have been exceptional.

Throughout the government and its departments—and not least of all, in the Planning Staff itself—there has run a strong sentiment in favor of removing price, rationing and allocation controls at the earliest moment when supply conditions might make such a move feasible. The "ring fences" around coal mining and agricultural labor were abolished late in 1949; in March 1950, the entire Control of Engagement Order dealing with the labor market was revoked, after months of progressive relaxation.[19] The allocation of steel, with the exception of sheet and tin plate, was abandoned in May 1950.[20] Rations of particular goods have been increased or decreased in keeping with supply development, and certain goods have been removed entirely from the rationing lists. The rationing of sweets was discontinued in the spring of 1949, but events proved that the move was premature and, at the insistence both of suppliers and consumers, sweets rationing was reinstated within a few weeks. The situation in late 1950 was summarized authoritatively in these terms:

> The number of direct controls remaining is much smaller than is commonly thought, and of those which do remain several are retained partly for their indirect use—the allocation of softwood, for instance. There are still a few cases where the total output of an industry is limited, or where the whole or a proportion of its output is classed for export only. The rationing of materials has largely ceased, as has consumer rationing and the control of labor, and fuel rationing is now of diminished importance.[21]

19. *The Times* (London), March 10, 1950. The following table, from P. D. Henderson and Dudley Seers, "1949: Forecast and Fact," *Bulletin of the Oxford University Institute of Statistics,* January and February 1950, p. 33, is instructive:

	October 1947–March 1948	April 1948–September 1948	October 1948–March 1949	April 1949–September 1949
Directions under Control of Engagement Order (1947)	19	10	0	0
Directions to remain in coal	258	90	67	42[a]
Directions to remain in agriculture	104	25	17	10

a. A further 24 directions were issued in October 1949 alone to coal miners, indicating a stiffening after the decline in coal employment had set in.

20. *The Times* (London), May 23, 1950.

21. "Government and Industry," p. 46. See the "Survey of Existing Controls," *Labor and Industry in Britain,* British Information Services, December 1950, pp. 165–66, and "Price Control in Britain," *ibid.,* March 1951, pp. 16–22. The government's direct controls have been based largely on emergency wartime legislation which provided for renewal of the powers after December 1950, by vote of Parliament, on a year-to-year basis. The King's speech of October 31, 1950, included

It is ironical that only a few weeks later, and just as the people of Britain were beginning to enjoy their highest postwar level of economic well-being, the tightening world situation made it imperative once more to channel scarce resources into a huge rearmament program—thus setting the stage for the reimposition of the familiar array of wartime restrictions.

THE ECONOMIC SURVEY

The nearest approach to a formal "economic plan" in Britain is the *Economic Survey* published annually by the government in February or March.[22] A description of the *Survey*, together with an account of the process by which it comes into being, will give further indication of the character of British planning.

Active work on the *Survey* for the following year is begun each fall by a working party under the chairmanship (most recently) of the Head of the Economic Section. The working party consists of representatives from the Economic Section, the Central Statistical Office and the Planning Staff, and, from time to time, representatives of departments concerned with matters immediately under consideration. Representations on behalf of particular industries and interests are made by the "sponsoring" department, and interdepartmental committees present tentative programs covering such segments of general economic activity as imports, exports and investment.

the statement that "legislation will be introduced to make available to my Ministers, on a permanent basis but subject to appropriate Parliamentary safeguards, powers to regulate production, distribution and consumption, and to control prices." The Amendment moved by the Opposition, "regretting" the proposed legislation (it would give the government a "blank cheque") was defeated, 299–289. *The Times* (London), November 8, 1950. See *The Economist*, November 11, 1950, p. 721; November 18, 1950, p. 793; and November 25, 1950, p. 865, for a thorough discussion of the issues involved in permanent legislation of this type.

22. *Economic Survey for 1947,* Cmd. 7046, H.M.S.O.; *for 1948,* Cmd. 7344; *for 1949,* Cmd. 7647; *for 1950,* Cmd. 7915; *for 1951,* Cmd. 8195.

Each department works out the total claims for manpower, materials, equipment and finance that it is willing to support on behalf of the industries or agencies it is sponsoring. Each is concerned with its "clients' " construction programs, and with the amount, make-up and direction of their projected outputs. Many of these estimates, of course, indicate output of materials for other industries or departments. The coal industry and the power industry, under the Ministry of Fuel and Power, and the steel industry, under the Ministry of Supply, are claimants for manpower and equipment and materials; they are also providers of resources for other industries and for each other. Estimates of available manpower come from the Ministry of Labor, and are set over against the manpower requirements of each industry.

Interdepartmental committees on investment, import programs, import licensing, exports, ECA and the like, present estimates and recommendations. The Central Statistical Office furnishes estimates of national income and expenditure. The foreign exchange statement, comparing income requirements with prospective income from exports, provides the basis for the import program and the export target. The investment statement compares estimates of requirements for capital equipment and maintenance with materials available to industries producing equipment (building and engineering), with the portion of the production of the engineering industry that can be diverted to home needs from the export market, and with the funds available for financing capital work.

From all of this, the working party makes up a tentative draft for discussion by a committee consisting of the permanent heads of the economic departments, chaired by the permanent secretary of the Treasury. Here the claims are pressed anew and in the light of the developing picture of the total situation. From the discussion a clearer, tighter program emerges. Differences are reconciled, except in extreme cases, and the resulting proposals are handed on to the Economic Planning Board. This agency, under the chair-

manship of the Chief of the Planning Staff, and with three
representatives each from industry and labor, together with
the permanent secretaries of the Board of Trade, the Treasury and the Ministries of Labor and Supply, gives final
advice on the content of the *Survey*. It then remains for the
ministers themselves, chaired by the Chancellor of the Exchequer, to iron out any remaining differences, to choose
between any alternative courses which may have been sent
up from below, and to give final approval.

The *Survey*, its contents thus processed and determined,
is then returned to the Planning Staff, to be rewritten as a
public document. It is published shortly before the Budget
speech, and the ensuing debate in Parliament is on the
Survey as well as the Budget.

The *Survey* itself—a document of some 35 to 60 pages—
may be characterized as a "snapshot" of the British economic scene as of a moment of time. It is a statement of
what has happened during the preceding year, and, in the
words of the *Survey for 1947*, "a broad pattern of national
work at which the Government considers the nation should
aim. It is a framework, not a blueprint." The *Survey* an-
nounces broad goals and targets for the "current" year,
already two or three months old by the time the *Survey* is
published. The estimates and aims, since they appear formally for public guidance, are not to be treated lightly or
casually disregarded, but they constitute neither a commitment by the government nor a strait jacket for British economic activity, either private or public. The *Survey* brings
the government's estimates, predictions, hopes and targets
all together, once a year, for over-all scrutiny and analysis.

But policy-making and policy-adjustment are continuous, and as the year progresses the government departs on
occasion from its *Survey* position in line with changing conditions and altered convictions. The making of the *Survey*
facilitates the reaching of broad, over-all decisions. As a
public statement, the *Survey* is far more precise and definitive than, say, a political party platform; on the other hand,
it is in no sense a "master plan."

The Economic Survey for 1949

A recent *Survey*—1949—may be taken as typical in form
and content.

Summary of 1948

It begins with a three-page summary of events in 1948
compared with the record of 1947. (Tables later in the
Survey enable a comparison of results in 1948 with the
targets and forecasts presented in the *Survey* for 1948.)
Although the labor force increased by only 2 per cent, industrial production as a whole rose by 12 per cent above
the 1947 level. There were substantial increases in coal and
textile production, even though the targets were not quite
reached. Steel production exceeded even a substantially
raised target.

At the outset of 1948, revised plans were made, designed
to reduce the rate of investment below the mid-1947 rate
in order to divert resources into the export markets. As it
happened, however, the receipt of ERP aid and the increase
in steel production made it possible to revise the revised
program, and actual investment in 1948 proved to be greater
even than in 1947. During 1947, the volume of building
work in hand had run ahead of building labor and materials; in 1948 the balance was restored—the number of houses
under construction fell, while the number completed rose.
An increased number of factories was completed in the Development Areas. Productivity in the building trades was
improved through additional supplies and a more balanced
program.

Britain's overseas trade position improved during 1948.
The volume of imports increased over 1947 by 4 per cent
whereas exports (the largest in volume since 1929) rose by
25 per cent. The pattern of trade was gratifying, since it
reflected a lessening dependence upon dollar sources for
imports, and, with few exceptions, a surpassing of export
targets straight across the board. The terms of trade (ratio
of prices of exports to prices of imports) deteriorated over

the year; nevertheless, in the latter half of the year exports and re-exports were sufficient to pay for over 90 per cent of imports, compared with about 70 per cent in 1947. The balance of invisible payments was greatly improved, and the overseas deficit for the year was estimated provisionally at £120 million—an improvement of over £500 million in a single year. There remained, however, a grave deficit in Western Hemisphere payments—the worst danger spot in the economy.

The increase in real national income during the year was sufficient to counterbalance the drop in net receipts of goods from abroad, so that, despite the increase in exports, the British had more real resources to enjoy at home than in 1947. "Thus the expansion in total output, combined with the measures taken in concert by Government and people to make the best use of these resources, did much in 1948 to restore our balance of payments and to improve our capital equipment without sacrifice to the standard of living."[23]

Inflationary pressures were kept under control: employment was high and wage rates rose moderately; retail and wholesale prices remained stable from the spring to the end of the year. The cooperation of industry and labor, combined with the large budget surplus, served to offset the inflationary effects of the reduction in overseas deficit and the rise in home investment.

To sum up, "1948 was a year of substantial progress in nearly every part of the economic life of the United Kingdom," but "In terms of dollars we are still not paying our way. Sustained efforts to solve the hard core of our economic difficulties are still required."[24]

Program for 1949

Part II of the *Survey* sets out the government's program and estimates for 1949, under the headings Production, Investment, Balance of Payments, Manpower, and National Income and Expenditure.

23. *Economic Survey for 1949*, p. 5.
24. *Ibid.*, p. 5.

It points out that the *rate* of improvement achieved in 1948 can hardly be duplicated in 1949 and later years. Output during 1947 was disorganized and delayed by the fuel crisis, and 1948 was the first postwar year in which, after reconversion (reorganization, rebuilding, restocking), physical output really began to match productive capacity. The period of rapid expansion in much of the economy is drawing to a close. The *Survey* notes also that many of the programs cannot be presented with precision because of uncertainty as to the amount of ERP aid that will be forthcoming.

A target of between 215 million and 220 million tons is set for coal (deep-mined and open-cast)—figures that must be reached if necessary increases in home consumption and in coal exports are to be realized. The problem here is tied up with more regular attendance by workers, greater output per man-shift and an increase in the number of faceworkers —matters actively under consideration by the National Coal Board and the National Union of Mineworkers.

There will be some increase in the production of electricity resulting from the commissioning of new plant (only about half of the new plant estimated for 1948 was actually ready for use during the year), but the tremendous growth in consumption, which places impossible peak demands upon productive capacity, will continue to make load spreading necessary.

Steel production has been most gratifying, but there must be a continuing expansion of capacity and output. By 1953–1954, a domestic output of 17.5 million ingot tons should be reached. There will be increased production in 1949 from new blast and steel furnaces, but there will be limiting factors in the form of scarce imported raw materials. In the most favorable circumstances the industry output for 1949 should be between 15.25 and 15.5 million tons of ingot steel, but the increase will not be spread evenly over all steel products.

In similar fashion, the *Survey* deals with the production

of other basic commodities—raw materials, textiles and agricultural products.

Discussion turns next to the general scale of the proposed investment program and the principles underlying its distribution. The government's intention to maintain a large investment program is declared, together with the ancillary proposition that this will call upon the community for self-restraint in limiting present consumption in order to release the necessary resources. Timber and steel are likely to be limiting physical factors. Softwood is still imported largely from North America and the scale of possible imports will be contingent on export earnings and ERP aid.

The division of total steel supplies in 1949 is planned at 60 per cent for home investment, 30 per cent for exports and the rest for defense and consumer goods. "There is no simple and final answer to the problem of the right balance between the claims of home investment and those of exports." Further, much of home investment must go not to new projects but to maintenance and replacement. ". . . it is the Government's intention, while maintaining investment in the social services at the 1948 level, to increase to the maximum investment in those industries and basic services where increased output will, directly or indirectly, assist the balance of payments, and, more particularly, serve to increase dollar earnings or reduce dollar expenditures."[25]

A table showing gross fixed investment by principal industries and by types of investment, gives an estimate of £985 million for construction and £770 million for plant in 1949, as against comparable figures of £825 million and £640 million for 1947, and £915 million and £720 million for 1948. Explanation in the text accounts for variations among industries.

Turning to the balance of payments, the *Survey* sets an over-all export index target of 150 for 1949 (1938 = 100), against a performance of 109 in 1947 and 130 and 143 in the first and second halves, respectively, of 1948. The limi-

25. *Ibid.*, p. 15.

tations on increased exports are identified as manpower shortages, claims of the home market, trade barriers erected by other countries and high British selling prices. The index of 150 is broken down by commodity groups.

Imports projected for 1949 show only a slight increase. Uncertainties in the terms of trade, together with the stiffening of international competition, make precarious the most carefully prepared forecasts. The surplus of invisible receipts over payments is predicted at £35 million for January–June 1949 as against £16 million and £82 million for the two halves of 1948. There follows a carefully reasoned discussion of, and predictions relative to, the balance of payments on current account, and the long-term dollar problem.

The discussion of manpower, with over-all and particularized estimates, is of interest for the attention given to manpower in defense, recruitment policies for particular industries, and for the statement, "The Control of Engagement Order was effective in enabling large numbers of workers to be guided into essential work during 1948 without the interference with individual freedom which the widespread use of powers of direction would entail. Only 300 directions had to be issued during the year while 576,000 placings were made in the essential industries granted priority in the supply of labour."[26]

Forecast of National Income

The discussion of national income and expenditure sets out in round figures a forecast of these accounts for 1949, on the basis of the programs and estimates earlier described. "These calculations cannot claim to give more than a broad illustration of the tendencies at work."[27] Total resources

26. *Ibid.*, p. 30. Under the Control of Engagement Order (October 1947) workers in certain categories and within certain age limits are required to report to an employment exchange when out of work. They are free to accept jobs only in "essential" industries.

27. *Ibid.*, p. 34. The discussion and data on national income and expenditure occur on pp. 34–41 of the *Survey*.

available in 1949 for use at home are set down at £10,900 million, as compared to figures of £10,105 million for 1947 and £10,620 million for 1948. (See Table 1.)

TABLE 1

DOMESTIC EXPENDITURE ON GOODS AND
SERVICES AT MARKET PRICES, 1947–1949
(*In Millions*)

Expenditure	1947	1948	Forecast for 1949 at End 1948 Prices
Personal	£ 7,465	£ 8,004	£ 8,200
Government	2,069	1,914	2,040
Gross capital formation	2,040	2,352	2,330
Subsidies	434	515	515
Less indirect taxes	−1,903	−2,165	−2,185
	£10,105	£10,620	£10,900

Source: *Economic Survey for 1949*, p. 35.

Consumption figures are discussed in detail by principal categories; it is estimated that government expenditures will increase by some £125 million, largely by reason of central government expenditures on the health service.

Gross capital formation is estimated at about the 1948 level. The combined capital account is shown in Table 2.

It is pointed out that the government surplus of £427 million in 1948 represents a change of £768 million since 1947, and that in the fight against inflation this surplus had to counterbalance the fall in the deficit in the balance of payments and the rise in gross home investment. Despite the success of this operation, it is still too early for the removal of price controls, and the hoped-for increase in labor mobility has not yet developed. There has been a gratifying response to the government's appeals for restraint in wage negotiations and in the distribution of profits. It is hoped that in 1949 the combination of government surplus and

TABLE 2
COMBINED CAPITAL ACCOUNT, 1947–1949
(In Millions)

Sums Set Aside	1947	1948	Forecast for 1949 at 1948–1949 Tax Rates	Capital Formation	1947	1948	Forecast for 1949 at End 1948 Prices
Current surplus of public authorities	£ –341	£ 427	£ 415	Gross capital formation at home	£2,040	£2,352	£2,330
Transfers to private capital account	306	179	185	*Plus* external investment (foreign balance)	–630	–120	—
Additions to company tax reserves	40	50	45				
Depreciation allowances	750	825	900				
Undistributed profits	405	540	575				
Personal savings a	250	211	210				
Total sums set aside	£1,410	£2,232	£2,330	Total capital formation	£1,410	£2,232	£2,330

Source: Economic Survey for 1949, p. 39.

a. The figures of personal savings are balancing items: that shown for 1949 is not a forecast, but depends upon the assumptions made about the other items.

public savings will be sufficient to pay for the investment program. The *Survey* states:

This discussion shows that the evils of inflation can be avoided only through the co-operation of the Government and the nation as a whole. The Government is steadying prices by subsidies on essential goods and by direct control. It is also saving through a Budget surplus. Similarly, employers and employees must exercise restraint on prices, dividends and wages; and everyone must save through the National Savings Movement or in other ways. These are the necessary conditions for economic and social stability.[28]

Major Objectives

Part III of the *Survey* summarizes the paramount objectives for 1949: (1) the expansion of exports to Canada and the United States; (2) the expansion of "our steadily rising production, especially in the key industries of coal, steel, textiles and agriculture"; (3) the reduction of costs, particularly of exports, and improvement of quality of products; and (4) continuance of the battle against inflation "with all the weapons used successfully in 1947 and 1948."[29] With reference to productivity, it is pointed out that the greater part of the task of shifting productive resources to meet the profound changes in the country's postwar position has been achieved (except for the shift necessary to overcome the dollar deficit), and that the first stage of increasing peacetime output as a whole has also been successfully passed. The period of normal progress lies ahead, and this involves more and better capital equipment, and the "development of efficiency by greater skill, energy and adaptability." The government can help, but "the problem is primarily one for industry. . . . *Our recovery will never be complete unless we can develop a keen and adventurous spirit in management, and a readiness to welcome new and improved methods by labour.*"[30]

28. *Ibid.*, p. 41.
29. *Ibid.*, p. 42.
30. *Ibid.*, pp. 43, 44.

The program for 1949 calls for increased exports, the maintenance of a large investment program and the use of more resources for defense and the social services. This means a heavy demand for resources and the consequent danger of inflation and instability.

The fight against inflation, as projected in *Survey* statements that bear the quality of appeals and exhortations much more than that of orders and directions, entails individual and group restraints in the matter of prices, dividends and wages, and increase in personal savings. Government measures to prevent inflation are promised.[31]

The Outcome as Reviewed in 1950

Part I of the *Survey* for 1950 presents the government's review of actual developments in 1949, for comparison with the prospects and tasks it had set out twelve months earlier. Detailed information, enabling comparisons to be drawn within particular sectors of the economy, appears in Part III.[32]

Total production increased steadily throughout the year, and generally throughout the economy. The index of industrial production, covering industries accounting for roughly half of the national income, was more than 6.5 per cent higher during 1949 than in 1948; and the evidence indicated that the increase in production was largely an increase in output per man.

Granting that evidence on general changes in productivity is crude at best, the *Survey* still felt that "it is probable that output per man-year in business enterprises increased by nearly 4 per cent compared with the increase of 2.5 per cent assumed in the National Income forecasts in the last *Survey*. In the industries covered by the index of production the increase seems to have been about 5.5 per cent."[33] The

31. *Ibid.*, pp. 44–46.
32. See *Economic Survey for 1950*, Part I, "Development in 1949," pp. 3–10; and Part III, "Production, Investment and Consumption," pp. 23–35.
33. *Ibid.*, p. 3.

Survey pointed out that much of the increase was due to the conspicuous performance in a few industries:

The chief reasons for the rise in productivity in these industries seems to have been more skilled work and better management, together with continued improvement in supplies and stocks of raw materials and components. It is also probable that the investment of the postwar years began to show results in output per man in 1949. Finally, partly as a result of the publicity campaigns organised by the Government, employers and the Trade Unions, both managements and workers became more conscious of the importance of higher productivity in present economic circumstances. The development of joint consultative machinery has encouraged interest in this subject at the factory level, while confidence in the continuance of full employment has resulted in a greater readiness on the part of the two sides of industry to adopt improved methods of work and incentive schemes of payment.[34]

The *Survey* for 1949 had predicted some increase in the gold and dollar deficit of the sterling area in the first half of 1949; it had been unwilling to hazard a forecast for the second half of the year, and its attitude toward the whole problem had been one of hope rather than of confidence or determination. Events proved that the hope was not solidly based: "the deterioration was much greater than was expected."[35] Purchases by the United Kingdom in the dollar area were no greater than forecast, but dollar expenditure by the rest of the sterling area grew beyond expectation; and the dollar earnings of the sterling area fell rather than continuing to rise as had been hoped.

A falling off in industrial activity in the United States brought a reduction both in sales and prices of primary products exported by the sterling countries; and "widespread expectation that the pound would have to be devalued led sterling area importers to anticipate, and foreign importers to delay, purchases and payments."[36] Gold and

34. *Ibid.*, p. 4.
35. *Ibid.*, p. 4.
36. *Ibid.*, p. 4. Others have suggested that "in any attempt to ana-

dollar reserves, already low, were drawn upon heavily, and confidence in sterling was progressively weakened. Emergency measures were adopted. United Kingdom purchases from the dollar area were sharply reduced and at a specially convened meeting, Commonwealth Finance Ministers agreed to recommend comparable actions to their governments. Nonetheless, the loss of reserves continued, and devaluation of the pound from $4.03 to $2.80 was reluctantly decided upon.

The spectacular reduction in the sterling area gold and dollar deficit that followed (a deficit of $31 million in the fourth quarter of 1949, as compared with $539 million in the third quarter) was recognized as due in large measure to temporary and nonrecurring factors, and the *Survey* made no attempt to predict the permanent effect of devaluation. By the end of the year, however, more than three fifths of the loss of reserves during the summer crisis had been recovered. During 1949 continued progress was made in economizing in dollar imports even though total imports were advancing. Compared with 1947, dollar imports were a third lower in volume; nondollar imports were a third higher.

The *Survey* was happy—or at least not displeased—over the national income and the balance of the economy in 1949. Gross national product (at market prices) rose by over £500 million to a total of £12,834 million, and was supplemented by a £70 million surplus of imports over exports to bring the total resources available for domestic use to a figure of £12,904 million. On the expenditure side, personal consumption accounted for £8,402 million, and government current expenditure for £2,037 million; leaving £2,465 million for gross capital formation (to be compared with

lyze the reasons for the *debacle* of mid-1949," the following factors at least must be considered: "(1) the persistence of inflationary pressure at home; (2) the United States recession; (3) the policies of other members of the sterling area, and changes in the sterling balances; (4) the results of the low rates quoted for sterling in several foreign exchange markets; and (5) the effect of expectations that the pound would be devalued." See P. D. Henderson and D. Seers, *op. cit.*, p. 23.

a corrected figure for gross capital formation of £2,590 million in 1948).

The government continued during 1949 to recommend deflationary bank credit and capital expenditure policies to banks and bankers. Bank credit expanded only slightly; and on several occasions the attention of bankers was called to the need to exercise restraint and care in financing capital expansion.[37]

Unemployment continued low throughout the year, averaging about 300,000 (about 1.5 per cent of the number of insured employees). Total money expenditure ran "at an excessively high level" in 1949, and the government moved in the fall to reduce investment and government spending. There were indications late in the year that, apart from government action, the pressure of demand was beginning to ease. Consumers shifted their buying, and, while prices rose on the average, some prices were reduced. "This implies that during the course of 1949 the amount which consumers were willing or able to spend did not increase so quickly as supplies available."[38]

ECONOMIC PLANNING

In considering the experience of 1949, two questions stand out as bearing on the nature of the Economic Survey and the status of economic planning in Great Britain—(1) how much of 1949 was the *Survey for 1949* able to foresee,

37. "In April, 1949, the Chancellor of the Exchequer issued a further memorandum of guidance to the Capital Issues Committee, . . . stressing the importance of giving preference to increases of capacity designed to overcome shortages of basic materials, to projects which were likely to increase exports to, or save imports from, hard currency countries on a substantial scale, to the promotion of technical developments and practices, and to proposals which would yield marked and immediate reductions in costs. As on former occasions, the principles laid down in this memorandum were brought to the notice of the Bankers, in order that their policy in the matter of credit facilities should continue to conform with that of the Capital Issues Committee." *Economic Survey for 1950,* p. 7.

38. *Ibid.,* p. 8.

and (2) how much of 1949 did the government direct or influence? In short, how much of the operation of Britain's economy is actually anticipated or planned?

How Good Was the Forecast?

Comparison of the detailed results with the detailed forecasts or targets for 1949 shows several hits or near-misses, and several misses of substantial degree. The target for coal output was 215–220 million tons; actual output was 215.1 million tons. Coal for home consumption was set down at 198–200 million tons, and for export and foreign bunkers at 17–20 million tons; actual results turned out to be 195.3 million tons and 19.3 million tons respectively.[39] The forecast for production of steel ingots and castings was 15,250–15,500 thousand tons, the results, 15,553 thousand tons; for exports of finished steel, 1,600 thousand tons, the results, 1,735 thousand tons; and for the supply of finished steel to the home market, 10,500–10,700 thousand tons, the results, 10,471 thousand tons.[40] Estimates of probable consumption of selected raw materials in 1949, admittedly provisional, proved in practically all cases to be high;[41] and the estimates for textile output and exports were high in some instances and low in others.[42] In the case of agriculture, livestock production made better progress than crops. Indeed, with the exception of sugar beets, almost all the main crop acreages were below target and less than the area sown in 1948–1949. Crop yields generally were high, and in some cases offset the fall in the area sown, but the wheat crop was below that for 1948–1949. Flocks and herds of almost all kinds of livestock increased steadily, and the output of livestock products in many cases exceeded the program.[43]

The estimates of distribution of manpower in 1949 also were low in certain major categories and high in others.[44]

39. *Economic Survey for 1949*, p. 9; *for 1950*, p. 24.
40. *Economic Survey for 1949*, p. 9; *for 1950*, p. 25.
41. *Economic Survey for 1949*, p. 11; *for 1950*, p. 25.
42. *Economic Survey for 1949*, p. 11; *for 1950*, p. 28.
43. *Economic Survey for 1950*, p. 26. For details, see *ibid.*, p. 27.
44. *Economic Survey for 1949*, p. 32; *for 1950*, p. 31.

The forecast for personal consumption expenditure for 1949 amounted to £8,200 million, as against an actually attained figure of £8,402 million, the estimates for individual categories of expenditure being high in some instances and low in others.[45] Comment has already been made on the fact that the growth in productivity in 1949 was considerably in excess of the rate of increase assumed in the *Survey* for 1949.[46]

How Far Was Control Effective?

The comparisons just outlined will serve to indicate the nature of the Survey, and to answer those who are tempted to look upon the Survey as a program for the rigid containment and direction of the British economy.[47] One of the dis-

45. *Economic Survey for 1949*, p. 37; *for 1950*, p. 34.
46. See p. 32.
47. For a more complete comparison of Survey targets with actual performance, see P. D. Henderson and D. Seers, *op. cit.* These authors have the following to say (pp. 7–8) about the technical qualities of the Survey:
"The work of anyone trying to compare current performance with the targets set in the *Economic Survey* is . . . greatly complicated by differences in units and coverage between the statistics used in the Survey and those currently available to the public. . . . to leave such obstacles in the way of those trying to assess development is quite incompatible with the Government's oft-declared reliance on public co-operation. The effectiveness of the Survey as a 'working pattern' for the year's economic activity must be greatly reduced by the inability of the public to see exactly what progress is being made and thus what extra efforts or modifications in direction are required.
"The lack of official adjustment to programmes is also rather odd. There have occasionally been revisions of targets, particularly for exports, but in general the Government has been content to state early in the year what needs doing, and then to leave the public without further detailed guidance until the following year is well under way. [An example of Survey figures revised to meet tax changes subsequently announced is noted in *The Economist*, April 29, 1950, p. 956.] The whole approach to the interim period between *Surveys* implies a scepticism as to the influence of the *Survey's* plans on economic developments which may well be justified, but which is somewhat at variance with the declared philosophy of 'democratic' (as

concerting features of an attempt to understand the exact character and function of the Survey is the reader's discovery that he is coming to use quite interchangeably such terms as "estimate," "prediction," "forecast," "guess," "target," "need," "programme," etc. Hopes, expectations and admonitions are presented in confusing juxtaposition and, while extreme positions are clearly drawn, it is difficult for the reader to orient and reorient himself as he moves from section to section—or even from sentence to sentence.[48]

---

opposed to 'totalitarian') planning. Basing policy on someone's appreciation of what must be done, means taking care to keep him fully informed of what is happening and of what is expected of him in the near future."

With reference to several of the estimates in the 1949 *Survey*, the authors, in attempting a comparison with actual results during the year, were forced to say "Cannot be reconstructed."

48. The discussion of national income and the balance of the economy in the *Survey* for 1950, pp. 19–20, is illustrative:

"It is particularly difficult to assess the problem of maintaining internal stability in 1950. Much of the data necessary to form a considered view on the degree of disinflation achieved by the end of 1949, is still incomplete and provisional. As for 1950, the effects of devaluation on prices and the level of trade, the extent to which the special forces which have contributed to the rapid increase of productivity in recent years will continue, and the changes which may take place in habits of personal saving can only be guessed. The analysis which follows is based on a number of stated assumptions. The selection of these is very much a matter of judgment, and the most important depend on the sense of responsibility shown by the people as a whole to the needs of the situation. With different assumptions, the conclusions themselves would be different. As the year progresses and more data become available more certain analysis will be possible. Nevertheless, while too much weight should not be placed on the numerical estimates in the tables, they are sufficiently reliable to show the broad outline of the internal financial situation with which we must deal in 1950, and what is required of the nation if internal stability is to be maintained.

"As in previous years the basis of these forecasts is an estimate of the amount by which the national output is likely to increase during the current year. This year it has been possible to provide in Table 10 some detail of the growth of output which has been assumed in particular sectors of the economy. Since the industrial population is expected to be virtually constant between 1949 and 1950, the increase in

The *Survey,* as an annual report on the state of the economy, and as a statement of broad economic policy, is a useful document. As a prediction of things to come, it is interesting, but less reliable and useful. (The *Survey* for 1949 did not—naturally—forecast devaluation!) The setting of explicit targets is on the wane.[49] It is interesting to speculate on the standards of performance properly to be applied to the Survey. If targets are met, is it in point to praise the forecasting by government or the performance by, say, industry? Should it be said that the forecasting was accurate, that the government was firm in its requirements and direction, or that, in naming a target that could be met, the government was politically smart? If the target is not met, is the target (or prediction or guess) or the performance at fault; if it is greatly exceeded is the forecasting to be blamed or the performance to be praised? Or, in case of a discrepancy in *either* direction between estimate and performance, should it be said that "planning" has failed, since a disposition of resources has occurred which departs from the "plan"?[50] To repeat, the Survey as an annual report and a

the national output will depend upon how much productivity increases. It is very difficult to forecast the growth of productivity, and the figure which has been taken is more an assumption than a forecast. It has been assumed that productivity in the field of business enterprises as a whole will increase by about $2\frac{1}{2}$ per cent, compared with an increase of about 4 per cent in 1949. This corresponds to an increase in productivity in the industries covered by the Index of Production of $3\frac{1}{2}$ per cent in 1950 compared with about $5\frac{1}{2}$ per cent in 1949. With an increase in productivity of this magnitude, the output of business enterprises and the national product would increase in 1950 by over £300 million at constant prices. This assumption may, however, prove conservative, and the actual increase rather higher."

49. "Gone are the targets and estimates of earlier years, when the Government did at least try to set down what they thought ought to be done." *The Economist,* April 1, 1950, p. 689.

50. *The Economist* (April 1, 1950, p. 690) says, of the increase in productivity which occurred in 1949, "If one thing is certain, however, it is that this increase . . . was neither planned nor expected. Last year's Survey said that 'it is impossible to expect that 1949 will improve on 1948 as markedly as did 1948 on 1947' and that 'the period of rapid expansion in many parts of the economy is drawing to a close.' But

statement of policy is understandable and useful; beyond this, its nature and functions are less than clear.

In a very real sense, much that is true of the Survey is true of economic planning generally in Great Britain. British planning is tentative and hopeful—there is far more of prayer and prediction in its make-up than of project and precept.[51] The kind of economic planning undertaken by the British government has been severely criticized in its fundamentals by two groups—those who have seen in it a bureaucratic thrust for power, and those at the other extreme who have felt that it has never amounted to more than a wordy, wishful pretense—a cloak for planners too unimaginative and too timid really to plan. Without any reflection on those in the planning seat, it is fair to conclude that the truth is nearer to the assessment made by the second group than that made by the first—and that it is moving even nearer.[52]

---

this does not prevent the new Survey from basing its estimates on the assumption that the accidental—or at least adventitious—spurt in productivity in 1949 will be repeated in 1950."

Referring to the practice of ministers to attribute unforeseen difficulties to "events in the unregenerate outside world," *The Economist* (December 2, 1950, p. 933) observes: "No planner at home can guarantee an equally windless calm abroad; but it is not yet recognized by Ministers that this fact is a limitation on planning, not a moral defect in the foreign climate."

51. *The Economist* (April 1, 1950, p. 690), in an article appropriately entitled "Design for Drift," characterizes the *Survey* for 1950 as "a humble document, meek almost to the point of being meaningless. There is nothing here of the notions of 'democratic economic planning,' as proclaimed in earlier Surveys, which presented a working pattern for the year's economic effort and left all men of good will to work for it. Indeed, the perplexing thing about the *Survey* for 1950 is its lack of plan . . . [the Government] would have the nation believe that nothing much has to be done." The Chancellor of the Exchequer in his Budget speech referred to comments of this sort as "a peculiar complaint by those who profess to be opposed to planning." *The Times* (London), April 19, 1950.

52. " . . . most of the 'planning' that has been actually done or suggested has nothing specifically socialist about it unless we adopt a definition of socialism that is much too wide to be of any analytic

The world has long debated whether positive planning and control of economic activity in any considerable detail is compatible with the preservation of healthy, peacetime political democracy. It begins to appear that the test which many have thought was imminent in Great Britain is not, after all, to be made in the near future. The planning which the British are testing is certainly no threat to democracy; how much it contributes, or is capable of contributing, to the positive direction of the economy is still an open question.

use." J. A. Schumpeter, *Capitalism, Socialism, and Democracy*, 3d edition, Harper, New York, 1950, p. 410. Professor Schumpeter (p. 413) refers to rationing and detailed regulations of producer and consumer behavior as "a method for suppressing the effects of inflation" that "will disappear when they have served their purpose . . ."

CHAPTER 2

The Issue of Nationalization

THE SETTING

THE NATIONALIZATION PROGRAM of the Labor party
(and hence of the Labor government) is set forth in
its policy statements, *Let Us Face the Future* (1945), *Labour
Believes in Britain* (1949) and *Let Us Win Through Together* (1950). The first of these, prepared for the 1945 General Election that swept the party into power, proposed to
undertake the nationalization of coal, gas, electric power,
telecommunications, civil aviation, inland transport, the
Bank of England, and iron and steel.

By April 1949, these proposals, with the single exception
of iron and steel, had been carried out and the party declared its intention of adding water supply, all (suitable)
minerals not already owned by the public, meat wholesaling,
large-scale cold stores, beet sugar manufacturing and refining, cement, industrial insurance and, if warranted by further examination, certain sections of the chemical industry.
In addition, "the Government will, as the public interest
may require, use its powers to take land into public ownership and put it in charge of the Agricultural Land Commission for expert management";[1] and public enterprises to
compete with private firms will be started:

(a) If, after investigation by the Monopolies and Restrictive
Practices Commission, those operating the restrictions refuse to
mend their ways.

(b) If, despite adequate raw materials and labour supplies,
there is a persistent shortage of any product vital to national

1. *Labour Believes in Britain,* The Labor Party, London, 1949,
p. 14.

42

need; this would include products required for defence, export and European recovery, agriculture, housing, education and other necessary public services.

(c) If, to maintain a high level of employment, further industrial investment is needed in a Development or other area.

(d) If, under the auspices of a Development Council or otherwise, a demonstration plant or factory is needed to stimulate inefficient producers.

(e) If new products of social value are not being manufactured by private enterprise.[2]

The party's election manifesto for 1950 contained only one modification of the foregoing: industrial insurance was to be "mutualized" rather than "nationalized"—a concession to the Co-operative group.

Following the election of 1950 that returned the Labor government by the narrow margin of six seats over its combined political opposition, the government indicated its intention to give effect to the Parliamentary decision reached in the fall of 1949 to institute nationalization of the iron and steel industry on January 1, 1951, or shortly thereafter. Indeed, the first test of the strength of the government in the new House resulted in the defeat, by a vote of 310 to 296, of a motion by the Opposition pointed toward postponement of nationalization until after another election.

Arguments for Nationalization

The arguments advanced in Great Britain for nationalization have ranged from those based on broad ideological considerations to those urging the use of nationalization as an efficient tool for the achievement of immediate economic ends. In an assortment of recent party pronouncements, tracts and Parliamentary debates, it is argued that:

1. Nationalization will "democratize" the power—hitherto held without corresponding responsibility in the hands of a few—to control basic industries and, hence, the economy. "Steel determines the level of employment and sets

2. *Ibid.,* pp. 12–13.

the scale of the nation's production. In a democracy such power must belong to the people."[3] The point here is that this power belongs to the people and cannot properly be exercised by anyone other than the people's government, not necessarily that the people will use the power more equitably, efficiently or to better purpose.

2. It will increase productive efficiency by permitting the direct investment of public funds, by enlarging the scale of operations, by improving organization and effecting co-ordination, and by improving labor relations.

3. It will make available to the government an investment weapon that it can employ positively in the prosecution of its full employment policy.

4. It will constitute a protection against private monopoly because: (a) the monopoly may be nationalized; (b) a nationalized concern may be set up to compete with the private monopoly; (c) the *threat* of nationalization (in the form of either a or b) may induce the private monopoly more actively to serve the public interest.

5. It will stimulate efficiency in competing and related (or even unrelated) private firms, by serving as a model or as a threat.

6. It will lower costs and hence prices (and so redistribute wealth) through the substitution of low interest payments on "gilt-edged" public securities for exorbitant profits on private shares.

7. It will develop greater equality of opportunity through worker participation in management and promotions from the ranks.

8. It will increase efficiency and make for a fuller life for workers through the internal "democratization" of the industries.

9. It will increase efficiency by ending nepotism and "old school" favoritism in appointments and promotions.

10. It will prevent or mitigate local unemployment by facilitating the location of industrial units in depressed areas. Public industries can be located more easily and rap-

3. *Ibid.*, p. 9.

idly than private industries can be directed to locate, in order to serve overriding national social and economic interests.

11. It will prevent certain private industries from sabotaging nationalized industries by such practices as slowing up deliveries of equipment. (The remedy here would be to nationalize the offending private industry.)

12. It will, in certain cases (e.g., coal) forestall sheer physical breakdown.

13. It will substitute direct and positive public action for negative, costly and debilitating public regulation in the case of recognized "public utilities."

14. It will protect the public domain.

Since our present concern is to describe and explain the nationalization program in Great Britain rather than to argue its merits and faults, it is unnecessary to develop the opposing arguments at length. However, in answer to the claims of nationalization, the following arguments have appeared: The elaborate, overcentralized organization that inevitably characterizes nationalized industries will result in excessive cost, delay in decisions and action, discouragement of personal initiative and responsibility, obsession with grandiose schemes, and internal friction; political considerations will determine appointment, promotions and decisions; individual consumers will be helpless in the presence of gigantic public monopolies, and general elections are no substitute for the "market" as an agency of control; public competition with private firms is inherently unfair and the results are not indicative of relative efficiencies; and, finally, the record of private industry is such as to demonstrate that on sheer economic merit public ownership is not called for, and considerations of personal liberty *versus* the "police state" stand firmly arrayed against its institution.

The Background of Nationalization

The government's legislative record on nationalization since it assumed office in 1945 suggests either great accomplishment or excessive haste. The Bank of England Act, bringing the capital stock of the Bank of England under public ownership, came into force on March 1, 1946. The Gas Act, nationalizing gas supply, became law on July 30, 1948. Between these two dates, five other industries (coal, civil aviation, telecommunications, electricity and transport) were nationalized. The least that can be said is that the government lost no time in carrying out its campaign promises.

Individual members at the opposite extremes of the Labor party are bound to feel (and to express themselves) differently on whether or not all of the nation's industry should be nationalized. Official pronouncements, however, disavow any Labor intention to take over all industry, and state explicitly that nationalization is to be employed with discrimination, for specific purposes in particular instances.[4] The party's record since 1945 is entirely consistent with formal professions. With the exception of steel, the industries thus far taken over by the British government fall well within the recognized category of public utilities or have long been the subject of special government concern not only in Great Britain but throughout the civilized world.

Electricity, gas, transport, civil aviation and telecommunications are universally subject to government regulation in matters of price and service, if, indeed, they are not owned and operated by governments. Government regulation of banks differs from public utility regulation but is

4. See the summary of party positions in "Nationalization in Britain," *Labor and Industry in Britain,* British Information Services, December 1949, pp. 177–78. One major group within the Labor party urges caution. The report on the public control of industry proposed by the general council of the Trades Union Congress in August 1950 advocates improvement in operation of publicly owned industries before extending public ownership, and suggests consideration of selective and competitive public ownership and of public board control of private industries. See *The Economist,* August 26, 1950, p. 424.

The Labor manifesto for the 1951 election states simply that "we shall take over concerns which fail the nation, and start new public enterprises wherever this will serve the national interest." *The Times* (London), October 1, 1951.

no less detailed and intimate. Throughout the world, coal is regarded as a "sick industry" about which "something must be done" by government, and in England nationalization of the mines was preceded, under Conservative and Coalition governments, by cartelization under close government supervision and by nationalization of coal mine royalties.

Public ownership on a national scale is not new in Great Britain. The Post Office, including all telephone and domestic telegraph services, has long been operated as a government department. Through the Central Electricity Board (established in 1926) and the British Broadcasting Corporation (1927), the concentration and coordination of electricity supply by means of a national transmission grid, and the furnishing of broadcasting under conditions of national monopoly were undertaken as semigovernment projects.

Even the extension of nationalization to include an industry like iron and steel that elsewhere customarily operates without special government regulation or scrutiny, does not indicate that the issue in Great Britain is one of free private individual enterprise *versus* public ownership or state socialism. Cartelization and nationalization have proceeded so far and so deeply in Great Britain since 1930 that today "free private individual enterprise" is vestigial in major sectors of the British economy. Over a wide area, British industrialists look not to themselves or to the market, but to their trade association executives and committees for direction on prices, output and practices.

Much of the drive, initiative and freedom that are supposed to characterize free enterprise has passed from the English scene well in advance of any threatened nationalization. Government activities now being undertaken under the terms of the recently enacted monopolies legislation will hardly make the British economy much more competitive.[5] Cartelization, accepted and encouraged as the domi-

5. Monopolies and Restrictive Practices (Inquiry and Control) Act, 1948, 11 & 12 George 6, Ch. 66. See also *Monopolies and Restrictive*

nant form of business and industrial organization, sets the stage for, if indeed it does not invite, nationalization.

Assessment of Nationalization

The Labor government's program of nationalization is of such recent origin that any attempt at appraisal or evaluation can, at best, be no more than suggestive. None of the major projects is yet out of the transition stage and very little that has occurred, whether favorable or unfavorable, can be identified as peculiarly the product of nationalization per se. Operating results, good or bad, may just as reasonably be attributed to momentum or inertia carried over from private ownership, to temporary enthusiasm, to growing pains, to general conditions affecting all industries, to inexperience—even to the weather. But one thing can be said: nationalized industry in Great Britain is required to bare its soul—to expose its innermost workings and the results of its workings, whether pleasing or otherwise—to a highly critical and caustic audience of journalists, legislators and voters.

NONCONTROVERSIAL MEASURES

Four of the nationalization measures have aroused relatively little controversy and, to date, have involved little actual change. They are the nationalization of the Bank of England, of civil aviation, of cable and wireless communications and of gas.

Practices Act, 1948: Annual Report by the Board of Trade for the Period Ending 31st December 1949, H.M.S.O., March 1950; Monopolies and Restrictive Practices Commission, Report on the Supply of Dental Goods, H.M.S.O., 1950; and Report on the Supply of Cast Iron Rainwater Goods, H.M.S.O., 1951.

The Labor manifesto for 1951 promises a vigorous attack on monopolies and combines. The Conservative manifesto promises to strengthen the Monopolies Commission to enable Parliament to correct any operations in restraint of trade "including, of course, in the nationalised industries." The Times (London), September 29, 1951.

The Bank of England

The Bank of England Act[6] was introduced October 10, 1945, received the Royal assent on February 14, 1946 and came into force on March 1, 1946. Under its terms the capital shares of the Bank were taken over by the government and the stockholders were given 3% government stock calculated to bring them the same income they had enjoyed from their private holdings. The Court of Directors, formerly elected by stockholders and now appointed by the King, consists of a Governor, Deputy Governor and sixteen (reduced from twenty-four) members, not more than four of whom may be full-time directors. The Court is directly responsible for the management of the Bank, but subject to such directions as the Treasury, after consultation with the Governor of the Bank may think necessary in the public interest. The Bank has formal powers of guidance over the commercial banks of the country—powers it had, in fact, previously exercised for many years.

Aviation

The Civil Aviation Act[7] was introduced on April 2, 1946, and received the Royal assent and came into effect on the first of the following August. The British Overseas Airways Corporation had been created by Parliament in 1939 to operate air transport services formerly operated by Imperial Airways, Limited, and British Airways, Limited. Suitable compensation was paid at that time. Under the Act of 1946, three publicly owned and controlled corporations—the British Overseas Airways Corporation and two new corporations, British European Airways Corporation and the Brit-

6. Bank of England Act, 1946, 9 & 10 George 6, Ch. 27. See also *Bank of England Charter*, Cmd. 6752, H.M.S.O., 1946. A summary analysis of the statutory provisions governing the public corporations established to operate Britain's nationalized industries will be found in D. N. Chester, *The Nationalised Industries: A Statutory Analysis*, Institute of Public Administration, London, 1948.

7. Civil Aviation Act, 1946, 9 & 10 George 6, Ch. 70.

ish South American Airways Corporation—were established to provide civil air services in various parts of the world, and, in particular, in Europe (including the British Isles) and the routes between the United Kingdom and South America. The British South American Airways Corporation was later merged with the British Overseas Airways Corporation. The Board of each of the corporations consists of a chairman and eight other directors appointed by the Minister of Civil Aviation. The Minister has general powers of direction over each of the corporations, particularly in matters of reorganization and development.

An Air Transport Advisory Council (the chairman appointed by the Lord Chancellor and two to four members appointed by the Minister) is provided to consider representations from any person relative to service or rates, or any similar question referred to it by the Minister. The Council must make an annual report to the Minister who, in turn, is required to lay the report before Parliament together with a statement of any action of his own taken in response to any Council recommendation. In addition, each corporation is instructed to establish advisory or executive committees to have direction of matters of efficiency, particularly with regard to the circumstances and requirements of particular areas. Requirements laid down by the act relating to accounts, audits and annual reports and their disposition are similar to those established for all the nationalized industries.

Communications

The Cable and Wireless Act[8] (presentation on April 18, 1946, Royal assent on November 6, 1946, effective date January 1, 1947) brought under public ownership the share capital of Cable and Wireless, Limited, the private British company operating overseas telecommunication services. Government stock was issued as compensation to the holders of shares in Cable and Wireless, Limited, in the amount "which the operating company's undertaking might be ex-

8. Cable and Wireless Act, 1946, 9 & 10 George 6, Ch. 82.

pected to realise if sold in the open market on the appointed day as a going concern by a willing seller to a willing buyer on the basis of (a) the net maintainable revenue; and (b) the number of years' purchase to be applied thereto."[9] The directors of the company were superseded by a board appointed by the government. The Postmaster General was named as the responsible Minister.

Gas

The Gas Act[10] was introduced on January 21, 1948 and received Royal assent on the following July 30. The property of all gas companies was taken over on April 1, 1949 and compensation was paid on the basis of "stock exchange value."

A Gas Council (chairman, deputy chairman and twelve other *ex officio* members who are the chairmen of the twelve area boards) is provided for, but the function of the Council is largely consultative and advisory. Ownership of the gas undertakings is vested in the area boards (consisting of a chairman and from five to seven members, appointed by the Minister of Fuel and Power) and the boards alone have authority to manufacture and sell gas. It is the duty of the Council to advise the Minister on questions affecting the gas industry and matters relating thereto; and to promote and assist the efficient exercise and performance by area boards of their functions. The manufacturing and selling functions of the Council are confined to gas fittings and providing the plant required by the boards. In addition, the Council has certain research duties, some slight coordinating powers and certain powers of review on matters of finance. Area boards must provide the Council with returns, accounts and other information.

Consultative councils are established in each area to represent local authorities and consumers. Recommendations by the councils after consultation with area boards are made directly to the Minister. If, after investigation the

9. *Ibid.*, Sec. 2 (2).
10. Gas Act, 1948, 11 & 12 George 6, Ch. 67.

Minister finds complaints warranted, he directs the area board to effect remedies.

The Minister can also instruct the area boards or the Gas Council to carry out policies regarded as in the national interest, after consultation with the Gas Council and the area board concerned.

The act contains the usual provision as to aggregate revenue—each area board shall see that its revenues are sufficient to cover costs, taking one year with another. Each area board is here treated as a unit, whereas in the case of coal, electricity and transport, the injunction applies to the overall undertaking. Provisions respecting accounts are of the usual sort, as are those governing annual reports, except that the provisions are applicable both to the area boards and the Gas Council. The mandatory annual reports of the consultative councils to the area boards must be included in the annual reports the boards are required to make to the Gas Council. All reports are to be laid before Parliament by the Minister together with a report by the Minister as to the performance of his own functions under the act.[11]

11. The first reports of the area boards and the Council were announced in *The Times* (London), March 14, 1951. See *The Economist*, March 24, 1951, p. 697.

CHAPTER 3

Nationalization of Coal

COAL NATIONALIZATION came about as the natural, almost inevitable, consequence of a series of events and a piling up of forces that began with the recommendations of the Royal (Sankey) Commission in 1919. That commission, by the narrow margin of its chairman's vote, offered nationalization as the most feasible solution for the difficulties in which the industry, even then, had become mired. Twenty-four years later, speaking in the House of Lords, Lord Sankey restated his conviction:

Let me in my last words, and for the first and last time in this House repeat myself: "A great change in outlook has come over the workers in the coalfields, and it is becoming increasingly difficult to carry on the industry on the old accustomed lines. The relationship between the masters and the workers in most of the coalfields in the United Kingdom is unfortunately of such a character that it seems impossible to better it under the present system of ownership. Many of the workers think they are working for the capitalists and a strike becomes a contest between labour and capital. This is much less likely to apply with the State as owner, and there is fair reason to expect that the relationship between labour and the community will be an improvement upon the relationship between labour and capital in the coalfields.

"Half a century of education has produced in the workers in the coalfields far more than a desire for the material advantages of higher wages and shorter hours. They have now, in many cases and to an ever-increasing extent, a higher ambition of taking their due share and interest in the direction of the industry to the success of which they, too, are contributing."

Those words are taken from my report on the Coal Industry Commission. I stand by them today. I believe them to be true and that they will prevail.[1]

Prelude to Nationalization

In 1925 the government provided a temporary subsidy to support the existing level of wages in order to stay a threatened strike in the industry. A Royal (Samuel) Commission reported in March 1926, recommending against a continuance of the subsidy and against nationalization. The subsidy was withdrawn and a walkout that rapidly developed into a general strike began on the first of May. The general strike was soon over, but the miners remained out until November, when, badly beaten, they returned to work on the owners' terms. The condition of the workers grew worse, and the temporary improvement in the earnings position of the industry was soon swallowed up by the depression of 1930–1933.

Throughout the 1930's the industry was the subject of almost continuous examination by outsiders and by itself. A slight wage increase was granted in 1935 on a district basis, but the miners' demand for a national wage determination scheme was not accepted. A Joint Consultative Committee to provide for joint discussion between representatives of the national organizations of owners and miners was set up; and it was in this period that government-supervised cartelization of the industry was instituted, a development described at the time in the following terms:

In the British coal-mining industry today the total amount of coal that may be taken from British mines is determined by order of a central committee of colliery owners, acting under authority conferred by Parliament. The country is divided into seventeen districts and to each of these a specified percentage of permissible output is allocated. Within each district a local committee of mine-owners awards to each mine its permissible output, determined by recent past performance. Contributions

1. *Parliamentary Debates* (Hansard), House of Lords, Vol. 129, col. 419.

are paid into a central district pool in respect of excesses, and compensation is paid from the pool to cover shortages. Prices of coal are fixed for each district by the respective district commit-tees, and are coordinated in the markets by interdistrict con-sultation. Many weary (and fascinating) hours are spent work-ing out "cost" and "quality" rationalizations for prices dictated in fact by what the traffic will bear.

Since the first of August, 1936, a central selling scheme has been established in each district designed to meet conditions laid down by the government, namely (1) to cover all mine-owners in each district and to have a measure of permanency, (2) to prevent intercolliery competition effectively, and (3) to be so drawn that evasions cannot take place. Under this latest control mechanism the industry either has a single marketing agency for all the coal mined within each district or an arrangement by which the details of every contract made for the sale of coal by any owner are subject to review and revision by a district com-mittee. No mine-owner may sell to a buyer or at a price or terms disapproved by the committee. The industry, acting as a unit and with only a bare minimum of government "observation" can name the owner from whom any purchaser must obtain his supply, the price he must pay, and the amount of supply avail-able for the British market.

The present scheme has the hearty support of the mine-workers; indeed, it was the insistence of the workers during the wage controversy of 1935–36 that forced the industry and the government to formulate and put the new plan into operation. The mine-owners, notoriously individualistic, have accepted central selling willingly if not enthusiastically, as the last stop-gap to the nationalization of their mines. The government has, for several months, been conducting negotiations looking toward the nationalization of mine royalties, and legislation to provide for this program as well as for compulsory amalgama-tion of mine properties under the mandatory direction of a government board, has been promised.[2]

2. Ben W. Lewis, *Price and Production Control in British Industry*, University of Chicago Press, Chicago, 1937, p. 4. An account of the organization of the industry and its relation to the government from 1938 to 1945, and of the proposals for its postwar reorganization, will be found in *The British Fuel and Power Industries*, Political and Eco-nomic Planning, London, 1947, Part 3.

The movement for amalgamation had produced the Coal Mines Reorganisation Commission as early as 1930, but neither under its original, nor its subsequently augmented, powers was the commission able to carry out its modest program in the face of the stubborn opposition of independent owners bolstered by their "quotas." The Coal Mines Act[3] of 1938 took a step toward eventual nationalization of the mines by providing for government ownership of coal mine royalties—a program finally brought to a successful conclusion in 1945. By that time a global price of £64,559,- 559 had been divided among individual owners through an elaborate system of valuations and allocations.

The industry's self-government organization carried on under somewhat tighter government supervision through the early years of World War II. The Ministry of Fuel and Power was created, in June 1942, to take over from the Board of Trade the functions of the Mines and Petroleum Department, together with the control of gas and electricity. In July the government assumed full control over the operation of mines, and undertook to organize the industry on the basis of unified national service for the duration of the war and until the future of the industry was decided.

The authoritative report of the technical advisory (Reid) commission[4] that appeared in March 1945 dealt critically, constructively and convincingly with a wide range of technical problems besetting the coal mining industry. While the report did not elaborate on government-industry relations per se, it was critical of the attitude of the mineowners, who, while almost fanatically individualistic, were unwilling to accept competitive "survival of the fittest" as a principle. The report called attention to a number of significant facts and considerations that indicated the need for unified "area development," and stated flatly that the engineering and development changes required to put the industry on a

3. Coal Mines Act, 1938, 1 & 2 George 6, Ch. 52.
4. *Report of the Technical Advisory Committee Appointed by the Minister of Fuel and Power,* Cmd. 6610, H.M.S.O., 1945.

sound competitive basis "cannot be satisfactorily carried through by the Industry organized as it is today."[5]

Proposals for the reorganization of the industry were drawn up by interested persons and groups and presented for public consideration at this time—notably by the Tory Reform Committee (April 1944) and by R. W. Foot, newly appointed chairman of the Mining Association (January 1945), both of which sought to combine industry self-government and government supervision. In May 1945, the Coalition government advanced a plan that relied upon private ownership, but gave compulsory powers to a central authority to insure effectiveness in organization and efficiency in operation. The mine workers, through their Federation, and the Labor party had pressed for nationalization for years. Their case rested not only on emotionally charged considerations of "principle" reflecting the age-old conflict between "masters and men," but also on the contention that the industry under private ownership could not be organized and financed on the basis and scale dictated by technical requirements.

With Labor victorious in the 1945 General Election, it was a foregone conclusion that nationalization of the coal mines would be undertaken at once. The Opposition, although formally performing its role, did not resist strongly. In August *The Economist* reported that "Support for the principle of public ownership of the mines is now very wide, extending probably to two and a half of the three parties,"[6] and in November it went on to say: "In the coal industry, other methods have failed. The owners have been given every encouragement to put the industry on a rational basis; they have failed to do so. Moreover, a very large pro-

5. *Ibid.,* p. 137.
6. *The Economist,* August 18, 1945, p. 220. *The Economist* continued, however, "But that does not mean that the Bill will not be fought clause by clause in both Houses. Nor does it mean that public opinion will be content to accept any Bill that contains the magic word 'nationalisation.' . . . Coal will not only be the main business of this first session; it will be the making or the ruin of the new Government."

gramme of expenditure is required to re-equip and mecha-
nise the mines, and only the state can find the money. The
necessity for nationalisation is generally accepted."[7]

Coal Is Nationalized

The Coal Industry Nationalisation Act[8] was presented to
Parliament on December 19, 1945 and received the Royal
assent on July 12, 1946. Government stock and cash were
paid for the private shares in amounts designed to afford the
owners the earnings they would have received if the mines
had been left in private ownership. A Board was established,
consisting of a chairman, deputy chairman and seven other
full-time members, appointed by the Minister of Fuel and
Power for terms not to exceed five years. The Board is responsible for the daily operation of the industry and for the
development of policies. However, the act stipulates that

(1) The Minister may, after consultation with the Board, give
to the Board directions of a general character as to the exercise
and performance by the Board of their functions in relation to
matters appearing to the Minister to affect the national interest,
and the Board shall give effect to any such directions.

(2) In framing programmes of reorganisation or development involving substantial outlay on capital account, the Board
shall act on lines settled from time to time with the approval of
the Minister.[9]

The act provides for an Industrial Coal Consumers'
Council and a Domestic Coal Consumers' Council, composed of members to be appointed by the Minister. These
councils are directed to consider matters affecting supply
or sale and to report conclusions and recommendations to
the Minister.

The Board is directed to see, consistent with the proper
discharge of its duties, that revenue shall not be less than
sufficient to cover expenditures properly chargeable to revenue account (including interest and contributions to reserve

7. *The Economist,* November 17, 1945, p. 712.
8. Coal Industry Nationalisation Act, 1946, 9 & 10 George 6, Ch. 59.
9. *Ibid.,* Sec. 3.

fund) on an average of good and bad years. Accounts must
be kept as the Minister directs and in conformity with the
best commercial standards. Annual audits must be made by
auditors appointed by the Minister, and the audited statements of the Board laid before Parliament. In addition, an
annual report by the Board on its performance during the
preceding year and on its policies and programs is made to
the Minister and presented by him to Parliament. "The
report for any year shall set out any direction given by the
Minister to the Board during that year unless the Minister
has notified to the Board his opinion that it is against the
national interest so to do."[10] The consumers' councils, too,
report to the Minister and, through him, to Parliament.

The industry—comprising some 1,400 collieries with main
assets valued at £164,660,000, and employing 692,000 men,
together with many subsidiary properties—passed into the
hands of the government on January 1, 1947. In the preceding months the National Coal Board had been established, with nine members appointed on a functional basis,
as follows:

Lord Hyndley, Chairman
Sir Arthur Street, deputy chairman
Lord Citrine, manpower and welfare member
Mr. Ebby Edwards, labor relations member
Sir Charles Ellis, scientific member
Mr. J. C. Gridley, marketing member
Mr. L. L. H. Lowe, finance member
Sir Charles Reid, production member
Sir Eric Young, production member

Before the vesting date, the Board had settled the main
outlines of its organization. The coalfields were grouped
into eight divisions, each under a divisional board; and
under these the collieries were grouped into areas each one
of which was about the same size as the few larger undertakings under private ownership. Temporary arrangements

10. *Ibid.*, Sec. 54.

were necessary in a considerable measure at the outset, but from the very beginning the Board was acutely conscious of the problems of organization; any failure on its part to achieve ideal solutions (there has been much criticism!) can-not be attributed either to unawareness or indifference.

The First Year's Record

The Board faced extraordinary difficulties from the out-set. Output from the mines had been falling since 1940, and while the downward trend had been checked and reversed in the fall of 1946, the change came so late that, when the government took over, the country's stocks of coal had been reduced to eight and a half million tons—four million tons less than on January 1, 1946. Coal shortages were already interfering with the operation of a number of factories.

During January 1947, consumption of coal exceeded pro-duction by 300,000 tons. In this tight situation the weather turned suddenly worse, and for weeks Great Britain was in the grip of the severest winter it had known for decades. From January 23 until the middle of March, the produc-tion, transportation and delivery of coal were carried on under punishing conditions. This period was characterized by priorities and allocation, pools, prohibitions, curtail-ments of electric power and gas, widespread slowing down and stoppage of industry and the employment of all manner of devices to clear the snow and ice and enable miners to work and coal to move.[11]

Adjustments in wages and working arrangements also awaited the new Board. The five-day week had long been pressed by the miners, and it had been recommended on technical grounds by the Reid report. The probable effect of its adoption on output was uncertain: it might aid re-cruitment, improve spirits and increase production. It was urged that an official five-day week would yield more coal than a six-day week with irregular attendance on Mondays and Saturdays. To refuse the demand might lead to further

11. *Annual Report and Statement of Accounts for 1947*, National Coal Board, 1948, pp. 2–4.

unrest in the already agitated coal fields. "The stakes were high and the Board had to play."[12]

After extensive negotiations over details, the new arrangement became effective on May 5. The results were "disappointing."[13] Absenteeism was reduced, but even here the Board had to report that part of this improvement may have been due to the fact that, with a reduction in the number of working days there were fewer days on which a man *could* be an absentee. There was little increase in output that could be attributed to an acceptance of increased tasks, despite appeals both by the Board and the union. The only encouraging item in the record was that during the year, the net increase in the labor force was 26,000 men.

In October, at the instance of the government, negotiations were concluded providing for additional working time at overtime rates, the details varying in the different fields. The basic five-day week agreement was protected and the new agreement was to be effective until the end of April 1948 (later extended).

Substantial wage increases were granted to lower-paid workers and to others during the year. The Board was, of course, acutely conscious of the problems of worker-management relations. It gave much of its energy in attempts to improve not only the direct incidents of the employment contract, but also to establish arrangements under which grievances could be dealt with more satisfactorily and the men brought more generally and effectively into the spirit of cooperative endeavor. There were no official strikes, but despite the Board's efforts 1,635 unofficial strikes occurred during the year, with an established loss in output of 1,652,-000 tons, compared to corresponding figures in 1946 of 1,329 and 770,000. Nonetheless, the Board had some reason to feel that the year had brought improvement in the "human side" of the industry.

The Board concerned itself to some extent with long-term plans and a modest start was made on capital improvement,

12. *Ibid.,* p. 11.
13. *Ibid.,* pp. 13–14.

but, with a new and untried organization and a host of demanding problems, the Board was forced to concentrate during its first year on the immediate production of coal. Its record in this respect was good—even if not good enough: 197 million tons of coal—6 million tons above the output in 1946, but 3 million below the target set by the government. The coal was produced at an average cost per ton about 4s.3d. above the average cost in 1946 (an increase of 12.8 per cent) and despite increases in prices tardily introduced, the collieries as a whole incurred an operating deficit of £9.2 million. This loss, modified by ancillary profits and other income, was augmented by a loss on imported coal and other minor items and particularly by £15,120,279 "interest and interim income payable," bringing the net deficit for the year to £23,255,586. The Board commented:

This deficit is not a charge on the taxpayer. It has been met from the Board's resources and it must be overtaken in later years. It could have been covered out of price, but instead the Board incurred a deficit which will serve as an incentive to future economies. A joint stock company could have covered part of the deficit by not distributing any dividends. This expedient was not open to the Board.[14]

Earlier in the report the Board had pointed out that "If the Board had been free to close unprofitable collieries it would have been easy to improve the financial results, but for several reasons—not least the need to produce as much coal as possible—this could not be done."[15] Two comments on the record for 1947 are suggestive: *The Economist* characterized the Board's first year as "conditioned more by its inheritance than by its own efforts to change and improve it";[16] and the Board itself noted that "In 1947 the Board had to do many things at once."[17]

14. *Ibid.*, p. 125.
15. *Ibid.*, p. 124.
16. *The Economist*, July 17, 1948, p. 111.
17. *Annual Report and Statement of Accounts for 1947*, p. 126.

The Second Year

By the end of its second full year the National Coal Board had moved to the attack. The *Annual Report for 1948* is a more confident document than its immediate predecessor. The year 1948 was one of profit—£1,651,965 to be exact, in contrast with the deficit of over £23 million of the year before. Output rose by some 5.5 per cent over the 1947 figure (still short of the government target by one and a half million tons), the export target had been surpassed, and output per man-shift bettered the 1947 record by 3.2 per cent. Absenteeism dropped from 12.43 (1947) to 11.55 per cent, but was rising at the close of the year.

Unfortunately, however, the picture was still cloudy. On the debit side, the average cost of coal per ton in 1948 was 4s. 4d. above the average cost in 1947[18]—very largely attributable to increased wages instituted late in 1947, the full impact of which was not felt until 1948. Higher costs were slightly offset by the potentially significant fact that the *rate of increase* in costs had slackened in the later months of the year, and since then "costs have begun to fall." Commercial necessity forced the Board to raise prices both generally and on specified coals; the average increase in domestic prices was "more than" 5s. per ton, and "colliery proceeds were also increased by about another 1s. 6d. because regular exports of coal were resumed and they were sold at higher prices than coal sold at home."

The atmosphere in which the Board moved during its second year was much less charged with tension than that of 1947. To produce more coal, to improve its quality and to curb costs were the most pressing immediate objectives, but the Board was also able to give attention to basic problems and to the long-run reconstruction of the industry. There was some reorganization at the collieries, and the Board spent £25 million on capital account, most of which

18. *Annual Report and Statement of Accounts for 1948,* National Coal Board, 1949, p. 91. A summary review of operational and financial results for the year will be found in Chap. 12 of the report.

went into additions and improvements, largely plant and equipment. The expenditure was financed from the Board's own resources, so that "Advances by the Minister" remained at the £33 million borrowed in 1947.[19]

The report failed to disclose any significant improvement in the relations of the Board as employer with its workers. There were 1,528 work stoppages during the year, with an output loss of 1,062,300 tons. The principal causes of dispute were wages and methods of working and colliery organization. Machinery was available for the settlement of differences, but in many instances the men were unwilling to employ it or to abide by its results.[20] Those who went on strike in 1948 did so in defiance of their union, which had agreed to use the machinery and to accept the decisions made at any stage as final and binding. The problem was, therefore, partly one of union discipline.

Active work was begun on reshaping the price structure of the industry—an integral part of the Board's long-run program. The report carried a full discussion of the problems of classifying and evaluating the industry's 8,000 types of coal and of the considerations prompting the Board's decision to move gradually toward the reconstruction of the industry's price structure in relation to "zone-delivered" prices.[21]

Not the least of the Board's worries stemmed from the clear necessity that it faced of curbing costs:

The problem . . . is in part a long-term problem. In 1948, a number of old and inefficient collieries had to remain in operation in order to provide the output of coal which the nation needed. Some 80 collieries producing 4,000,000 tons of coal made losses of over £1 a ton each, and in total £5,500,000; as it takes up to ten years to reconstruct an old mine on modern lines or to construct a new one and get it into full production, it will be many years before all the old and inefficient workings can be replaced by new and up-to-date ones. . . . [During 1948] thirty-seven losing collieries were closed down. As and when reor-

19. *Ibid.,* p. 133.
20. *Ibid.,* p. 37.
21. *Ibid.,* pp. 71–73.

ganisation schemes are worked out involving the transfer of workers to more productive collieries, alternative employment will automatically be provided for many of the men displaced. . . . [For those for whom] . . . no alternative employment can be found in the industry . . . the Board and the National Union of Mineworkers agreed on a special scheme for making payments . . . for periods up to twenty-six weeks to give them time, wherever possible, to find fresh employment. . . . On a long view, the reshaping of the price structure will have a big effect on the economical working of the industry by influencing demand towards the kinds of coal that are cheapest to produce and deliver and away from those which are most costly.[22]

The Board was aware, as were its critics, of the imperative need for cost reductions if British coal and the products of British coal-using industries were to compete successfully in international markets.

The Board's consciousness of the problem of organization was sustained during the year by a good deal of critical comment from miners and its own membership as well as from interested persons on the outside. One of the Board's original members, Sir Charles Reid, resigned because of his disagreement with the Board's approach; and in May the Board appointed a committee under the chairmanship of one of its part-time members, Sir Robert Burrows, to investigate and make recommendations on the organization of the industry.

The recommendations of the Burrows committee, together with the Board's comments thereon, appear as an appendix to the 1948 report. The phases of the problem that have occasioned (and still occasion) most of the general controversy, relate to centralization *versus* decentralization and the part to be played by workers in management. From its beginning (and until the middle of 1951), the Board has been organized on a functional basis, with several of the members having departmental duties as well as general policy responsibilities, and the "line and staff" principle runs through the organization from Board, through division and area to colliery.

22. *Ibid.*, p. 99.

The 1948 report was received generally without enthusiasm but also without marked disfavor. Critics in the press and in Parliament viewed with alarm the increase in costs and prices (particularly in the light of rising competition in foreign markets), the failure of the Board to win the cooperation of the men in the pits, and the alleged tendency of the Board to be more interested in grandiose plans than in the daily job of producing coal. There was a good deal of shooting at the structure and superstructure of organization. More generous opinion, however, was impressed by the difficulties of the task and the signs of slight improvement in the situation, and, most of all, by the Board's insight and courage. *The Economist* concluded its sober view of the report with the comment, "The men who work it [i.e., the Board] are squaring up, as the report shows, to their task."[23]

The Report for 1949

A year later, the Board was able to report a profit of £9.5 million for the year 1949, after taxes and interest, together with a decision to use the profit to reduce the deficit of £21,800,000 with which it began the year.[24] Average selling price of coal increased by 9*d.* a ton during the year, but while production costs remained high, the cost of producing a ton of coal declined (by 6.3*d.*) for the first time in fifteen years despite the fact that miners' earnings rose by an average of 1*s.* 2*d.* a shift. For the first time, total output for the year reached the goal set by the government in its Economic Survey.[25]

Output per man-shift was about 23 cwts. This was above the figure for 1938, but output a man-year of 282 tons in

23. *The Economist*, June 25, 1949, pp. 1194 and 1197.
24. *Annual Report and Statement of Accounts for 1949*, pp. 8–9.
25. "It is estimated that total output in 1949 should be between 215 and 220 million tons, of which about 13 million tons will be opencast coal." *Economic Survey for 1949*, Cmd. 7647, H.M.S.O., p. 7. An output of 202,700,000 tons of deep-mined coal (5 million tons more than in 1948), was reached in 1949. *Annual Report and Statement of Accounts for 1949*, p. 4.

1949 compared unfavorably with 290 tons in 1938. The average number of faceworkers increased during the year, but absenteeism, which had begun to increase in the closing days of 1948, continued to rise (to 12.34 per cent) in 1949. There were over 1,600 strikes and "go slows" with a resulting loss in output of over 1.5 million tons. Wages and methods continued to be subjects of disagreement, and the problem of "concessionary coal" caused a major walk-out. The number of men in the industry declined by 17,400 during the year. Exports in 1949 increased by 3,112,000 tons over the 1948 figure of 16,133,000 tons. All of the Board's divisions, with the exception of Scotland, reduced costs and increased profits or reduced losses. Capital expenditure rose from £25 million in 1948 to £31 million in 1949; and at the end of the year authorized capital expenditure not yet incurred amounted to £63 million.

Editorial opinion, on the whole, took the report calmly. There was gratification at the increase in output and the improved financial showing; eyebrows were raised at the loss of employees and the growth of absenteeism; anxiety was expressed over the fact that the favorable profit returns were due largely to the higher prices charged in export coal and that, with the growth of productivity abroad, ability to charge differential (and highly remunerative) prices to foreigners would soon disappear. Any enthusiasm over the Board's performance was restrained: "There is certainly no great cause for congratulation in the fact that the best figures of before the war are only now just being surpassed."[26] On the other hand, criticism was sympathetic and, in general took the line that the Board was as aware as its critics of the difficulties ahead, and as alive to the possibilities of dealing with them.

Trouble in 1950–1951

The years 1950 and early 1951 were strenuous, and in the winter of 1950–1951 the Coal Board and the government

26. *The Times* (London), July 1, 1950. See also *The Economist*, July 8, 1950, p. 87.

were under heavy fire. On the surface, performance in 1950 was neither conspicuously good nor bad. Output rose slightly to 216 million tons (deep-mined 204 million, opencast 12 million), but it failed to reach the Economic Survey's goal of 218–223 million tons. Output per man-year increased to 293 tons, output per man-shift increased by 2.8 per cent to set a new record, and the number of shifts worked per man also increased. But another 20,500 men left the mines, absenteeism remained high (11.95 per cent), inland consumption of coal exceeded all expectations (6 million tons above 1949), and the net result was that with the coming of winter Great Britain did not have enough coal.

Wages were raised, Saturday working was begun again, the Prime Minister and others appealed to the miners, consumers were urged to economize, train service and electric power were curtailed, exports were reduced, coal was imported from the United States, and the price of coal was raised. It was still necessary for the government to cut the supply of coal to industries by 15 per cent in February 1951, in order to protect supplies for power stations. The Coal Board's year ended with a profit (reduced to £8.3 million by reason of cost increases and falling off in export revenues), and the government survived a motion of censure in the House of Commons in December 1950 and again the following February; but the country was short of coal.[27] As *The Economist* put it, "All that happened this autumn was that the drift of the workers from the mines, which has been going on steadily since early in 1949, got to the point at

27. See *The Times* (London), November 21, 1950, December 13, 1950, February 2, 1951 and February 15, 1951; *Annual Report and Statement of Accounts for 1950*, p. 1. For the first nine months of the year production performance held nearly to schedule, but on November 20, 1950 the Minister was forced to announce that stocks at the end of October were lower by 700,000 tons than had been hoped, that output of opencast coal would fall short of the estimate for the year by 750,000 tons and that output of deep-mined coal would barely reach the minimum estimate. *The Times* (London), November 21, 1950.

which it balanced the diminishing improvement in productivity."[28]

By the end of the first quarter in 1951 the picture had begun to brighten. The working force had increased by more than 10,000 men, and while part of this recovery was recognized as seasonal, there was reason to believe that the movement from the mines was tapering off. The government was working on a pension plan for miners, additional wage increases had been made, more houses for miners were in prospect, former miners were being allowed to return from the national service, and exemptions of miners from the national service were announced. The government was proposing extended opencast operations, and the use of foreign workers in the mines was contemplated. The chairman of the Coal Board warned that rearmament might so reduce the labor force that coal production would be forced even lower in 1951 than in 1950, but the *Economic Survey for 1951* stated that an output of between 219 million and 222 million tons "may be expected." In March *The Economist* noted that "In the last three months the coal industry has achieved a surprising spurt in activity, . . ." and that in the week preceding Easter "a labour force smaller by 5,400 men than that in the corresponding week of 1950, working more shifts per man than for years, mined . . . 300,000 tons more than last year."[29]

Cost prospects for the year were recognized as less favorable. It was estimated that wage increases granted since September 1950 would add £12 million annually to the Coal Board's costs and that a projected pension plan would add £2 million more for 1951. Increases in the prices of ma-

28. *The Economist,* December 16, 1950, pp. 1063–64.

29. *The Economist,* March 24, 1951, p. 701 (the note is entitled "Coal Cheer"). *The Times* (London), February 2, 1951, February 15, 1951, April 4, 1951. Within a few weeks, however, the cheer had turned once again to gloom. The number of workers (particularly face-workers) was declining, and in July enforced cuts in domestic consumption were announced. *The Economist,* July 7, 1951, p. 44; July 28, 1951, p. 234; September 15, 1951, p. 646.

terials to be purchased by the Board would cost still another
£13 million. Money would be lost on imports of coal, and
lessened exports would mean a sacrifice of the premium price
which the Board had been able to charge for British coal in
world markets. On the other hand, an increase of 4s. 2d. in
the pithead price of coal announced on February 1, 1951
was expected to increase the Board's revenue by more than
£40 million for the year.[30]

The Critics

   Public opinion in Great Britain has accepted nationalization of coal, but the National Coal Board has its critics.
Criticism of the Board revolves basically around the issue of
organization—centralization *versus* decentralization. It is
recognized by everyone that the immediate problem is one
of manpower (keeping more workers at work), but none of
the critics has been able to suggest measures likely to result
in early improvement. *The Economist* points out that nationalization was accepted with a minimum of opposition
and that while no one expected miracles, "Four years is a
reasonable trial period for most organizations, and at the
end of it we are importing coal." Admittedly, nationalization is not responsible for "the unwillingness of men to be
(and, especially, to remain) miners, and the unwillingness of

   30. *The Economist,* February 10, 1951, p. 338. The British Electricity Authority announced on February 12, 1951 that the increase in the
price of coal would add £7.5 million annually to its costs of generation
and that this would be passed on to consumers; *The Times* (London),
February 13, 1951. Steel prices were advanced almost immediately in
response to the rise in the prices of coal and coke; *The Economist,*
February 24, 1951, p. 450. The 1951 Labor manifesto makes the claim
that "the price of coal under nationalisation is less than in any other
country in Europe or in the United States." *The Times* (London),
October 1, 1951.
   At the end of May 1951 the Board introduced a "zone-delivered"
pricing scheme for household coal, designed so that "within each of
60 zones covering the country, coals of similar grades will cost the
same to the domestic consumer"; and so that he shall not have "to
pay for better coal than he receives." *The Economist,* June 2, 1951,
p. 1316.

miners to get coal," but, on the other hand, nationalization has not demonstrated any peculiar capacity to deal with this problem.[31] But no one has a prescription that promises early relief.

Both the Opposition in Parliament and others have dwelt on the Board's cumbersome administrative superstructure and its alleged unwillingness to decentralize its operations sufficiently to permit the development of local responsibility and initiative. The Board, it is said, is too far removed in spirit and in action, from the men in the mines.[32] The

31. *The Economist,* December 16, 1950, pp. 1063–64. See also *ibid.,* January 27, 1951, pp. 209–10 and February 3, 1951, pp. 278–80.

32. See R. A. Brady, *Crisis in Britain,* University of California Press, Berkeley, 1950, Chap. 3; D. Burn, "The National Coal Board," *Lloyds Bank Review,* January 1951, pp. 33–48; A. Beacham, "The Present Position of the Coal Industry in Great Britain," *The Economic Journal,* March 1950, p. 9; and Sir Charles Reid, "The Problem of Coal," *The Times* (London), November 21, 22, 23 and 24, 1948. The Conservative manifesto for 1951 promises "more decentralisation and stimulation of local initiative and loyalties." *The Times* (London), September 29, 1951.

The government has turned back two Parliamentary attacks on its operation of the coal industry since the General Election of 1950—on December 12, 1950 when the Opposition pressed for an independent inquiry into coal supplies (298–284), and on February 1, 1951 when the Opposition proposed a motion "deploring the contrast between Ministerial promises and present shortages" (300–289); *The Times* (London), December 13, 1950 and February 2, 1951. The Board was confronted with a difficult situation late in 1950 when Sir Eric Young, the production member of the Board, presented his resignation. Sir Charles Reid, who resigned in May 1948, and Young were the two original production members. There has been some disposition to interpret Young's resignation as the culmination of a disagreement with the Board over fundamental policies, but such information as has been made public suggests that the difficulties were mainly of a personal nature; *The Times* (London), December 5, 8, 11, 12 and 13, 1950.

Sir Eric's resignation was followed shortly by the death of the Board's deputy chairman, Sir Arthur Street. Lord Hyndley, chairman, and Mr. Lionel Lowe, also of the original Board, retired at the close of their terms of office, July 1951. Sir Hubert Houldsworth, the successful chairman of the East Midlands Division, was appointed as a new member and chairman of the Board; Mr. W. J. Drummond, chair-

Board, in turn, pleads its constant concern with the problem of organization and looks to the future.

Plan for Coal

As the Board sees the future, improvement is bound up fully as much with capital development and layout as with organization. With this in mind it has been at work for years formulating a national plan for the industry—"to find out which Areas should be expanded and which contracted, how much capital should be spent and how it should be shared out between the various claimants."[33] As early as 1949 the Board was able to announce in some detail the problems and considerations that were being taken into account, and the method by which it was seeking answers.[34] The 1948 report explained:

To begin with, an estimate is made of the probable demand for coal at that time [about 1960] both at home and abroad. A survey is also made of the outputs which could be achieved by the same date by the various coalfields at different levels of cost. These two sets of estimates are then compared and related one to the other, taking into account the cost of transporting coal to the different markets and the prices which consumers are likely to be prepared to pay. In outline, therefore, the plan is simple. It is an attempt to adjust the supply of coal to the demand at the lowest possible cost to the country. But though the outline is simple, the work is immensely complicated. There are four main factors to be considered—output, costs, demand, and price. None of these, however, can be estimated independently of the

man of the North West Division, and Sir Eric Coates were appointed as members of the Board, and designated as deputy chairmen. Sir Andrew Bryan, chief inspector of mines was also named to the Board. It was announced that the individual Board members would no longer have specialized or departmental responsibilities. *The Economist,* July 7, 1951, p. 44.

33. *Annual Report and Statement of Accounts for 1948,* p. 118.

34. *Ibid.,* Chap. 11. The Board emphasized that the plan must be flexible. "From time to time it must be revised. . . . Planning is not something that is done once and for all. It is a continuing process. It ensures that each unit of the organisation is at any time aware of its exact place within a slowly changing framework." *Ibid.,* p. 118.

others. . . . In addition to the four main factors there are many other points to be considered. . . . All these—and many other—inter-connections and complications cannot be taken into account all at once. This would put the task beyond human intelligence. To begin with, certain arbitrary assumptions must be made . . . [the demand for coal, future prices, future costs, future wage policy, and so on]. When the implications of these provisional estimates have been worked out, each of the assumptions in turn can then be examined more carefully, and the estimates altered. The work therefore begins with a simple comparison between an estimate of future output, and an estimate of future consumption. Gradually the other factors are brought in. The assumptions are changed in the light of further study, and slowly the plan begins to take shape.[35]

The Board's assumptions related both to factors outside its control (such as the general state of trade, the policies of governments and geological conditions) and policies within its power to determine. The Board expressed its awareness that the forecasts of home and overseas demands, despite the utmost care in calculation, "are fraught with difficulty and uncertainty." A detailed study was then under way of the possibilities offered by each coalfield in terms of cost and output, and in the light of geological conditions and past developments. The task of finding the right answers was overwhelming, but the Board was asking the right questions.

The completed plan was made public in November 1950, just as the Board was facing up to the immediate trials of the approaching winter.[36] The plan follows the principles

35. *Ibid.*, p. 119.

36. *Plan for Coal,* National Coal Board, 1950. The plan was to be discussed with the National Consultative Council for the Mining Industry, Domestic and Industrial Coal Consumers' Councils, the British Electricity Authority, the Railways Executive and others, before being presented (as modified) to the Minister of Fuel and Power for approval under Section 3(2) of the Coal Industry Nationlisation Act, 1946. Summaries of the plan will be found in *The Times* (London), November 15, 1950 and *The Economist,* November 18, 1950, pp. 824–26. The plan has now been submitted to the Minister. *Report and Statement of Accounts for 1950,* p. 13.

set out in its 1948 *Report.* The consumer is to be charged
the full production and transport cost of the particular type
and grade of coal that he buys. Expected demand at these
prices and expected costs in each coalfield determine the
relative distribution of total required production among
the coalfields, and this in turn indicates the appropriate allocation of capital investment.

Total demand, and hence total output, will reach 230 to
250 million tons by 1961–1965, 205 to 215 million tons for
domestic consumption and 25 to 35 million tons for export
and bunkers. The plan estimates that capital investment of
£635 million will be required. (£350 million to maintain
existing production to be obtained from depreciation allowances, and the remainder required to raise production
to be borrowed from the Treasury.) The projected investment is carefully phased, and specifically allocated as between fields and purposes. Investment of £520 million is
allowed for reconstruction of 250 of Britain's 950 collieries,
which are expected to provide 70 per cent of the total yield;
20 new collieries and some 50 drift mines will furnish another 10 per cent of the output; and the rest of the production will be provided by approximately 250 collieries which
will continue in their present state. About 90 other collieries will be absorbed in the course of reconstruction, and
the rest will gradually be closed. The increased output is to
come principally from Scotland, East Durham, Yorkshire,
East Midlands, North Staffordshire, South Wales and Kent.
Elsewhere output will decline.

Output is to increase by 18 to 20 per cent, but worker
productivity is to increase even more. It is estimated that
the production of 240 million tons of coal in 1965 will require 80,000 fewer workers than were employed in 1950,
and that there will be a saving in costs of about 7s. per ton
(mid-1949 prices). The saving is to be shared by consumers
and miners.

The plan was well received, considering the inauspicious
conditions under which it appeared. *The Economist,* although it raised questions and pointed to inadequacies in

analysis, congratulated the Board on "adopting an economically rational framework for the business decisions of a nationalised monopoly."[37] How well the plan will fare at the hands of the several consultative bodies remains to be seen.

37. *The Economist,* November 18, 1950, p. 824.

CHAPTER 4

Nationalization of Transport

THE HISTORY OF RAILROADS in Great Britain is the familiar story of speculative building, high finance, a confused network of lines, cutthroat competition, and amalgamations. The government moved actively into the situation at the close of World War I, and under the Railways Act of 1921 some 121 separate undertakings were combined into four main-line companies—the Southern; London and Northeastern; Great Western; and London, Midland and Scottish Railways. In the years that followed, additional steps toward integrated working arrangements were taken, but each of the four companies maintained separate financial and operating identities.

Highway transport, in the meantime, was making huge inroads into railway traffic and earnings. Motor haulage companies were free to set their charges at any level necessary to attract high value traffic; with low capital costs, flexibility of operation and freedom from the common carrier obligation to serve all comers, they prospered at the expense of their heavily burdened and somewhat lethargic rail competitors. The railroads took some advantage of the power given to them in the Railway Road Transport Act of 1928 to engage in road transport activities; but, in the main, they were more concerned to relieve themselves from competition than to operate road services.

At the outbreak of World War II, rails and roads were engaged in a competitive struggle that gave little promise of a stable solution, and the railroads were rapidly running down at the heel. During most of the war, the railroads were operated under the supervision of the Minister of War

Transport, acting through a Railway Executive Committee consisting of the chairman of the London Passenger Transport Board, four railway general managers and a government-appointed chairman. The structures of the companies were left intact, but operation was unified and revenues of the railways and the London Passenger Transport Board were paid to the government which, in turn, paid fixed annual sums to the companies.

The war left two transport legacies: a railroad system badly in need of rehabilitation, due to overwork and under-maintenance, and a general sentiment in favor of transport unification, coordination and integration. The *Financial Times* offered the conclusion that "the proper goal for British transport should be complete coordination,"[1] and *The Economist* said, "To regard transport as one whole appears so self-evident today that past resistance to this principle is the more surprising."[2]

Nationalization Achieved

Nationalization of transport was a main feature of Labor's program and in due course and on schedule the Transport Bill was introduced, debated and passed. The magic words were "unification," "coordination" and "integration." Everyone was in favor of the state of affairs suggested by these words, though they never spelled out the exact character and content of the concept, and even though the terms suggested different states of affairs to different people. The Labor position seems to be that unification was necessary, that it would come about by private agreement and practice if not by government action and, "as services move in this direction, they must be publicly owned and publicly run, with the whole of their accounts and the whole of their affairs subjected to Parliamentary and public examination."[3]

1. The *Financial Times,* September 2, 1946.
2. *The Economist,* October 5, 1946, p. 549.
3. The Minister of Transport, in *Parliamentary Debates* (Hansard), House of Commons, Vol. 431, col. 1637.

The government contended that only as a nationalized industry, with the resources of the country behind it, could rail transport secure the great sums of capital necessary for its rehabilitation and development. The Opposition—very restrained—focused on the bill rather than on nationalization. It argued that further inquiry (rather than immediate action) was called for; that the government had no plans or program, simply an urge for nationalization; that the setting up of separate executives for the several divisions of transport was inconsistent with unification; that the industry was too large to permit of efficient single control; that competition between road and rail for consumer favor should be encouraged; that the power of the Minister under the bill was inordinate; and that the proposed compensation to the private owners was inequitable. The debate in Commons was largely formal.[4]

The Transport Act was introduced November 27, 1946, received the Royal assent on August 6, 1947 and measures to put it into effect were begun at once.[5] The British Transport Commission, consisting of a chairman and four full-time members, was established, and on January 1, 1948, ownership of Britain's railways, including the London Passenger Transport Board, and of canals was vested in the Commission. The Commission is empowered to carry goods and passengers by rail, road and inland waterway. Railway (including the London Passenger Transport Board) and canal undertakings, together with their docks, harbor works and hotel appurtenances were transferred to the Commission; in due course all road haulage operations engaged in long-distance carriage for hire are also to be taken over.

The Commission is instructed to plan for the coordination of passenger transport in areas to be designated by the Minister of Transport, and for the provision of passenger

4. For the debate on the second reading, see *Parliamentary Debates* (Hansard), House of Commons, Vol. 431, cols. 1617–1722, 1785–1894 and 1973–2098; third reading, Vol. 437, cols. 36–172; on the Lords' amendments, Vol. 441, cols. 1160–1254.

5. Transport Act, 1947, 10 & 11 George 6, Ch. 49.

road services; the Commission is also to keep trade harbors under review with the possibility in mind of preparing area schemes. Compensation for railways, the London Passenger Transport Board and canals was based on the average stock market value of their securities on certain specified dates, for road haulage on the value of assets plus compensation for cessation of business and for privately owned railroad cars at original cost less depreciation.

Administration of the Act

The act places the actual management of the several transport agencies in the hands of five executive boards appointed by the Minister of Transport, consisting in each case of from four to eight members. These are the Railway, the Docks and Inland Waterways, the Road Transport, the London Transport, and Hotels executives. Provision is made for a Central Transport Consultative Committee and groups of consultative committees specialized by areas and functions.

The former Railway Rates Tribunal was reconstituted and re-empowered, and renamed the Transport Tribunal. The Tribunal is given reviewing powers over any charges or charges schemes imposed by the Commission. The general injunction as to charges is simply that,

All the business carried on by the Commission, whether or not arising from undertakings or parts of undertakings vested in them by or under any provision of this Act, shall form one undertaking, and the Commission shall so conduct that undertaking and, subject to the provisions of this Act, levy such fares, rates, tolls, dues and other charges, as to secure that the revenue of the Commission is not less than sufficient for making provision for the meeting of charges properly chargeable to revenue, taking one year with another.[6]

The general position of the Minister of Transport in relation to the Commission is similar to that of the Minister of Fuel and Power to the National Coal Board, but certain

6. *Ibid.*, Sec. 3 (4).

designated matters of policy call for his approval, or permit of his positive direction. Provisions for accounts, audits and reports to the Minister and to Parliament are much the same as those governing the Coal Board.

A month after the passage of the act the Minister of Transport made the following appointments of full-time members to the Transport Commission:

> Sir Cyril Hurcomb (Chairman); formerly Permanent Secretary, Ministry of Transport, and a past President of the Institute of Transport
>
> The Rt. Hon. Lord Ashfield; formerly Chairman, London Passenger Transport Board, and a past President of the Institute of Transport
>
> Mr. John Benstead; formerly General Secretary, National Union of Railwaymen
>
> The Rt. Hon. Lord Rusholme; formerly General Secretary, Co-operative Union Limited, and President of the International Co-operative Alliance
>
> Sir William Valentine Wood; formerly President of the Executive, London, Midland and Scottish Railway, and a past President of the Institute of Transport

In establishing its organization, the Commission proceeded

. . . upon the view that they are a policy-making and directing body which should act collectively and should not discharge executive functions, or be charged as individuals with functional responsibilities. This does not, of course, prevent advantage being taken of any specialized experience which individual Members may possess, nor does it exclude the establishment of common services for all Executives in certain strictly defined spheres of activity. But it does involve a far-reaching delegation of responsibility to the various Executives, so as to leave the daily operation and the conduct of the ordinary business of transport to be carried on by those Executives as the agents of the Commission.[7]

The Railway Executive membership was appointed November 21, 1947; the London Transport Executive on De-

7. *Report and Accounts for 1948*, British Transport Commission, 1949, p. 2.

cember 2, 1947; the Docks and Inland Waterways Executive
on December 23, 1947; the Road Transport Executive on
March 8, 1948; and the Hotels Executive on May 13, 1948.
In each case the Executive was made up almost without exception of persons possessing long experience in the industries over which they were given charge. The schemes of
delegation made clear that,

An Executive are thus free to maintain their contact with the
public and their workers and carry on all day-to-day business
without the Commission being brought in; but as between the
Commission and the Executive directions may be given by
the former by which the exercise of their delegated powers by
the Executives may be regulated. For instance, it is frequently
desirable that certain steps which may affect the policy of the
whole undertaking should not be taken without the Commission's prior approval.[8]

In fact, during the course of the first year the Commission
directed each Executive to submit for the Commission's
approval proposals for certain capital expenditures, proposed appointments, and proposed national agreements on
wages and conditions of work. On the other hand, while
the Commission worked closely with the Minister during
the year, he issued no formal directions to govern their decisions.

Problems of the First Year

The railways were taken over on January 1, 1948.[9] Even
before the formal vesting it was deemed necessary to set up

8. *Ibid.,* p. 6.
9. The properties acquired, and to be acquired, by the Commission
include all railways and facilities (approximately 52,000 miles of railway trackage, 13,500 stations, 20,000 locomotives, 45,000 passenger
cars and 1,235,000 freight cars), all canals (but only a few of the canal
barges and vessels), all London local transportation facilities, practically all intercity trucking properties, all dock and harbor facilities, all
hotel and restaurant properties owned by any of the above, and all
privately owned freight cars. The gross total book value of the main
capital assets of the Commission's consolidated undertakings on December 31, 1948, after deducting depreciation charges of £377,500,000,
stood at £1,288,900,000. *Ibid.,* p. 45.

a special Winter Transport Executive Committee. The strains on the railway system occasioned by the severe winter of 1946–1947, particularly in view of the sad condition of much of the railway operating equipment, led to a decision to anticipate emergency situations and to stimulate any necessary action. As a matter of fact, measures initiated by the committee proved almost too effective: the traffic diverted from rail to road in order to relieve congestion was not recaptured by the railroads for several months, probably contributing to the unsatisfactory earnings record of the railways during 1948.[10]

The other problems faced by the Commission were those that were to be expected during its first, transitional year, augmented perhaps by the gigantic size and diverse characteristics of the undertaking. The Commission's operating record and financial statement were dominated by the performance of the railways. A single-sentence summary of the record would be: general operating efficiency measured by physical performance improved somewhat during the year; operating costs rose because of higher bills for wages and supplies; the Commission showed a net loss for 1948. Prospects for 1949 were bad and for 1950 worse.

Unsatisfactory Financial Results

After meeting interest and other charges including certain special or nonrecurring charges such as preliminary organization expenses and the statutory provisions for redemption of capital, the *adverse* balance on the Transport Commission's consolidated net revenue account on December 31, 1948, stood at £4.7 million. The Commission's explanation for the presentation of its accounts on a consolidated basis is significant in the light of the charge frequently made that highway transport receipts are to be used to support the failing railways:

All businesses carried on by the Commission are to form one undertaking and the Commission have had carefully to consider the implications of this statutory direction upon the form of

10. *Ibid.,* pp. 11–12.

their accounts, upon their financial organisation and upon their policy. It is the operations of the Commission and the Executives as a whole which must be brought into balance, taking one year with another.

In any nation-wide transport undertaking covering the various forms of transport, different services and different methods of transport will show unequal degrees of profitability and will be unable to contribute at a uniform rate to overhead charges. Nor indeed is it possible in such an undertaking to avoid the provision of some services which are unremunerative even perhaps in the sense that they do not support their own direct costs of operation. There is nothing new in the acceptance of this principle. Within the main-line railway system itself there are areas of the country, and certain branch lines and perhaps certain traffics, which would not answer to the test of being self-supporting in either sense. Again, long before the policy of nationalisation or socialisation was adopted in regard to passenger transport in London, the private companies previously responsible had been forced to pray in aid the high earnings of surface transport to meet the cost of providing underground services necessary to deal with traffic which would not otherwise be handled. The degree to which one form of transport or one service can and should be called upon to support another will vary from time to time but, within reasonable limits, bold application of the principle may be essential to any adequate system of facilities for the country as a whole.[11]

The Commission made no attempt to hide its concern over its deficit. It pointed out that even though rates had been raised late in 1947,[12] and despite the fact that the Commission had paid no taxes in 1948, it still was unable to set aside anything for general reserve as it had hoped to do, or to make any contribution to a fund for enhanced replacement costs.[13] Further, the interest charges on British trans-

11. *Ibid.,* pp. 40–41.

12. As of October 1, 1947, passenger fares and rates on merchandise shipped by passenger trains were increased by 16⅔ per cent and other rail charges by 24 per cent. This amounted to a general increase of 55 per cent over prewar charges.

13. This latter item reflected the fact that although the Commission had begun charging annual depreciation on an "actual cost" as dis-

port stock represented a reduction of some £13 million from the normal distribution made to stockholders of the railway companies and the London Passenger Transport Board during the period of wartime control. Nor did the Commission, in its accounting, seek solace in the fact that 1948 was its "first year":

> It is true . . . that the Commission is still in the preliminary stages of a re-organisation of transport, that much of the equipment itself is only just beginning to recover from the dislocations of war, and that there is the eventual possibility of important economies, especially those to be expected from a concentration of each form of transport on the services for which it is most suited. But unfortunately the trends of traffic receipts and of expenditure in 1949 hold out no hope that the immediate future is likely to show better results, at any rate with the existing levels of fares, rates and charges. Since 1948, when prices were already rising, there have been further increases in costs, notably of wages, coal and steel. The net result is that a further marked deterioration of the working results is inevitable in 1949.[14]

Although, within the consolidated accounts, the railroads showed net receipts amounting to £26.2 million, they would have been charged with a substantial loss if the Commission's over-all capital charges had been assessed against them on the basis of relative gross income. Railroads were the center of the nationalization issue, and the prospects for railway profit in the years ahead are not bright.

---

tinct from a "replacement" basis, it seemed, nonetheless, to regard it as necessary to set aside amounts to compensate for any excess of replacement over actual costs. Attention should also be called to the fact that in addition to annual depreciation charges, the Commission is required each year to charge to revenue the sum necessary to redeem all its outstanding capital in a period of ninety years. This double charge means that British transport users are paying not only to keep the Commission's capital intact, but also to make a present of the capital to future users. *The Economist* (September 10, 1949, p. 570) commented, "Either the physical assets should be scrupulously maintained, or the Commission's debt should be redeemed; it is a task of supererogation to attempt both."

14. *Report and Accounts for 1948*, p. 42.

The Commission made a good deal of the fact that its direct costs were substantially above the levels obtaining in 1938. Railway workers (including London railway workers) were receiving average weekly earnings in 1948 about double their earnings in 1938, despite a shorter work week. Coal costs per ton were about 175 per cent of the 1938 figure and the coal was of poorer quality and inconveniently delivered. Other cost increases were even greater.

This paved the way for the Commission to ask itself a leading question: In view of the greatly increased costs offset only in part by the 1947 increases in rates "what factors were at work to enable the Commission to come so near to balancing their consolidated revenue account in 1948?" The answer was "efficiency" which the Commission discussed with some enthusiasm, dwelling on the greatly improved ratios between train or vehicle mileages and hours on the one hand, and ton-miles or passenger-miles carried, on the other. On the freight side, the factors responsible were identified as improvement in freight-car capacity and loading, decrease in empty cars hauled, longer hauls, bigger trains and decreased shunting, partially offset by a slight decrease in the rate of movement; and, on the passenger side, a reduction in unremunerative services and a much heavier loading of trains and vehicles (not to say "crowding"), offset in part by a slightly reduced rate of movement on certain services.[15]

The Losses Continue

The financial results of the Commission's second year were even less satisfactory than the results of 1948. "In spite of the improved efficiency in carrying operations and the savings achieved by reductions in staff and other measures . . . the year ended in a deficit (after charges for capital redemption and special items) of about £20.8 million."[16]

15. *Ibid.*, pp. 56, 61.
16. *Report and Accounts for 1949*, p. 33. The report did not appear until late in 1950, long after the public had been informed of the railways' continuing difficulties through evidence submitted by the

This brought the Commission's cumulative deficit at the
end of 1949 to £25.5 million, and no improvement other
than a possible increase in revenues through higher fares
and charges was in sight. "Price and wage levels continued
to rise throughout the year, while takings from passengers
and general merchandise tended to fall." Conditions grew
worse as the year advanced, and "by the close of the year
the estimated deficit was running at the rate of well over
half a million pounds a week."[17] Rail passenger receipts declined during the year by £8 million and rail freight receipts fell by £2 million.[18] Railway staff was reduced by
23,151, and other operating economies were effected, but
the amount saved by these operations (£6.5 million) was
more than offset by wage and other cost increases totaling
£7.6 million.[19]

The Commission completed some of the development
work begun by the railroads before the war, and laid plans
for further development when conditions might permit.
In other directions, however, it was "possible to do little
more than keep pace with current maintenance requirements and in certain directions to overtake to a very modest

---

Commission in support of applications to the Transport Tribunal for
increased charges.

The "working results" of the Commission's principal activities plus
earnings from other sources showed a surplus of £31.3 million before
charges amounting to £52.1 million for interest on British transport
stock, savings bank deposits, superannuation fund and other borrow-
ings, and annual installments for redemption of British transport
stock. *Ibid.*, p. 34. The report is summarized in *The Times* (London),
September 21, 1950, and in *The Economist*, September 23, 1950,
p. 523.

17. *Ibid.*, p. 33. The Commission commented that the general level
of wages and prices that it was paying was more than double the prewar level, while its charges on the average had risen by only 65 per
cent. *Ibid.*, p. 38.

18. *Ibid.*, pp. 40 and 42.

19. *Ibid.*, pp. 44, 45 and 61–62. Economy in the use of coal resulted
in a saving of £600,000 which was absorbed by the added cost of a
million pounds due to the rise in coal prices. *Ibid.*, p. 45.

extent some of the arrears of maintenance which have accumulated during and since the war."[20]

Rail Rates Start Upward

In the fall of 1949, the Commission asked for an increase of one sixth in its railway freight rates. The request, together with the supporting and opposing cases, was heard in public by the Transport Tribunal, and the Commission was thus required to disclose its affairs and policies to the world at large as well as to an "expert and independent tribunal." The essential facts, as reported in *The Economist*, were these:

Total traffic receipts of British Railways last year [1949] fell by more than £10 million, from £331.9 to £321.3 million. Estimates submitted to the Committee suggested that the Transport Commission's deficit for 1949 would be approximately £21 million, and for 1950 some £30 million. The gross yield from the sixteen and two-thirds per cent increase in freight rates which is sought would be £36 million on estimated freight receipts (before the increase) of £210 million; from this gross increase a deduction of almost £10 million has to be allowed for probable loss of traffic. Thus the benefit of the increase in freight charges, after discount for possible loss of traffic, might be put at £26 million—not enough to cover the estimated deficit in 1950, even if the increase had operated for the whole year, and still leaving the 1949 deficit to be carried forward. . . . The forecast presupposes some further net increase in railway operating costs of £2 million this year, and a loss of traffic of £5 million. Thus the marked deterioration of railway costs and revenues which dominated the Commission's economic position last year is, in

20. *Ibid.*, p. 17. The railways estimated their steel requirements for the year at slightly less than a million tons, but the government restricted their allocation to 810,000 tons. The Commission in 1949 estimated its investment program for 1950 at £100.2 million, for 1951 at £114.8 million, and for 1952 at £123 million, "but it was intimated to the Commission that approval could only be given to an investment not exceeding £95 million in 1950 and rising to not more than £100 million by 1952." *Ibid.*, p. 18. Following devaluation, the approved figure for 1950 was reduced to £92 million. *Ibid.*, p. 19.

the absence of any increase in charges, expected to continue. If charges were not increased, the Commission would, on its own showing, be faced with accumulated deficits ranging up to £100 million by 1952.[21]

Summing up the arguments, *The Economist* concluded:

The argument about railway productivity is thus concerned with the ability of railway management to reduce railway costs and improve efficiency to carry the reduced level of what must now be accepted as normal traffics. It is on this point that the evidence submitted on behalf of the Commission and the Railway Executive leaves room for misgiving. The general line of argument was that no spectacular economies were immediately in prospect; no suggestion of staff economies was admissable; the big economies would have to wait for integration, still some years off; and, as was stated by the Commission's witness with a touch of unguarded complacency, "we are getting very nicely along the road of economy." These attitudes suggest that there is nothing to prevent an annual application for higher charges, if the general level of costs continues to rise. If the Commission and the Executive value their standing with the public, they will take care to correct this impression. They will have to do better than to argue that higher costs are a matter entirely outside their control, that management can do little or nothing towards immediate economies, and that major economies will come in good time. The prospect of nationalised industries engaged in public debate about one another's costs [the coal, electric and gas industries were protestants at the hearing and the Commission countered with unflattering suggestions concerning the price and quality of coal] has been an engaging experience for the ordinary consumer who has had to suffer their higher prices without much opportunity for open complaint. But the debate has exposed the fallacy of supposing that all costs are given, and are not susceptible to change. The real problem, which will stretch far beyond the present application, is to secure those real economies in inland transport which were supposedly the justification for nationalising the transport industries. So far, only the first tentative steps have been taken towards merely beginning this task.[22]

21. *The Economist,* January 21, 1950, p. 151.
22. *Ibid.,* p. 152.

On February 6, 1950, the Tribunal advised the Minister of Transport that it saw no alternative to granting the Commission's request, and the recommendation was taken under extended consideration by the government.[23] In the meantime, on March 15, 1950, the Commission's affairs were the subject of debate in both houses of Parliament, during the course of which the activities and policies of the Commission came in for some very lively criticism.

It was argued that the nationalized transport industry was running at a loss of £500,000 a week or £50 a minute; that the British railways had priced themselves out of the passenger market; and that the fault was to be found largely in overcentralization, overstaffing and lack of a commercial outlook. The government reply was that unless rates were raised, the Commission would have an accumulated deficit in 1952 of £100 million, and that the Opposition had not offered a single businesslike suggestion for meeting the problem.[24] *The Times* observed:

The financial outlook for the Transport Commission is not too favourable even if the increases are granted. So far, this year is not developing any better than the commission expected. They expected 1950 railway traffics to yield £5 million less than in 1949 at present rates, principally as the net result of a fall of £7.2 million in passenger takings and a rise of £2.4 million in coal traffic; other changes were not expected to be great. So far, traffics this year have confirmed the commission's estimates. . . . On the expected net gain from an increase of one-sixth in rates, there would still be a deficiency of about £4 million a year (and probably a deficiency of £12 million this year). . . . The need for cutting costs will remain urgent in any case.[25]

On April 27, 1950, after nearly three months of hesitation, the government announced its decision to authorize

23. The Tribunal was satisfied that "a deficiency of approximately £30 million is to be expected in 1950" and "consider that in 1951 and 1952 the deficits at the present charges are not likely to be materially less than estimated for 1950." *The Times* (London), March 8, 1950.

24. *Parliamentary Debates* (Hansard), House of Lords, Vol. 166, cols. 242–95; House of Commons, Vol. 472, cols. 1091–1210.

25. *The Times* (London), March 18, 1950.

the Commission to increase railway freight charges in the amount requested by the Commission and recommended by the Tribunal.[26] The Opposition in the House of Commons moved (on May 10) to annul the regulations providing for the increase. The debate that followed was spirited, but produced nothing new in the way either of argument or conviction.[27] The new rates were approved and became effective on May 15, 1950.[28] Within six weeks British trans-

26. *The Times* (London), April 28, 1950. Speaking editorially, *The Times* was inclined to be philosophical: "It is not reasonable to criticize the Government for deciding to authorize increases in costs when such increases have become inevitable." Increases in charges were to be preferred to subsidies. On the other hand, *The Times* was not convinced that some part of the Commission's costs could not be reduced through improvement in organization, and called attention to the fact that it was the Commission that had applied for the increase although the real operating responsibility lies in the Railway Executive. *The Times* foresaw a substantial secondary effect of the increase upon the cost of living. *The Economist* (May 6, 1950, p. 1018) regarded it as "very dubious" whether "the efficiency of the Railway Executive and the Transport Commission is the highest that traders can reasonably expect."

27. *Parliamentary Debates* (Hansard), House of Commons, Vol. 475, cols. 397–534. In its comment on the debate, *The Economist* (May 13, 1950, pp. 1079–80) found a "real dilemma" in the fact that in weighing an application for increased charges, those who must make the decision (the Transport Tribunal, the government and Parliament) are forced to accept, almost without recourse, the professions of the applicant (the Transport Commission) as to its own efficiency. It is, indeed, a dilemma—a very familiar dilemma to Americans with decades of experience with commission regulation of railroad and public utility rates.

28. *Report and Accounts for 1950,* p. 26. In the public proceedings before the Tribunal it was estimated that if the increased charges were made effective the price of steel would have to rise by 10s. a ton, the average price of coal by 1s. 6d. a ton, and that the costs of the British Electricity Authority would be increased by £1,750,000 a year and the Gas Council by £2 million. On May 5, 1950 the Minister of Fuel and Power confirmed the estimated increase in the price of coal; on the same day the iron and steel industry announced its decision not to raise its prices as a result of the increase in freight charges. *The Times* (London), May 6, 1950.

port showed, for the first time since 1948, an increase in total receipts for the year to date.

In the meantime, as part of its policy of promoting integration through the formulation of uniform charges schemes, and also for the purpose of increasing revenues, the Commission on February 23, 1950 submitted a proposal to the Transport Tribunal for a widespread revision of rail and road passenger fares in the London area.[29] The proposed scheme was designed to eliminate age-old "inequitable anomalies" and to carry out the principle that all persons should pay the same fare for journeys of equal length and between common points by alternative routes, made at the same time of day. The scheme was expected, as well, to increase gross revenues by about £3.5 million. Extended hearings were held by the Tribunal in early summer, and on July 20 the Commission was requested to revise its proposal with a view to cutting the proposed increase in revenue by a million pounds. The Tribunal looked upon the London area scheme as an integral part of a country-wide passenger charges scheme yet to be formulated, and since it was too early to determine the exact contribution that London should make, "we consider that a present assessment possibly too low is more justifiable than one possibly too high."[30] The proposal as revised was approved by the Tribunal, and on September 15, 1950 the Transport Commission announced that the new passenger fares would be made effective on the first of October.[31]

Rail Labor Asserts Itself

The railway labor situation, uneasy since the beginning of nationalization, had deteriorated badly by mid-1950.

29. *The Times* (London), March 1, 1950; *Report and Accounts for 1950*, p. 25.

30. *The Times* (London), July 21, 1950; *The Economist*, July 29, 1950, p. 236.

31. *The Times* (London), August 29 and September 16, 1950; *Report and Accounts for 1950*, p. 25.

Service was interrupted frequently by slow-downs and flash walkouts. Demands for wage increases became more frequent, more general and more insistent. The position of the Railway Executive was clear—the railways could not afford to raise wages; the position of the employees was equally clear—railway labor was underpaid when the government took over the roads, and subsequent wage increases had failed to keep pace with the cost of living and with wage advances in other industries. In response to an arbitration award, the Executive increased the wages of the lowest paid employees by an amount totaling £2 million annually, effective in early September 1950, but on September 15 rejected a claim for a 7.5 per cent to 15 per cent increase made on behalf of practically the entire force of employees,[32] and said that because of the financial condition of the industry it could not make a new offer.

In November 1950, however, the Executive offered a general increase in wages, but negotiations broke down because the proposed increase was conditioned upon an acceptance by the workers of changes in working arrangements designed to improve efficiency and cut operating costs. At the request of the unions, a court of inquiry was set up by the Minister of Labor to determine and report the facts and the causes of the dispute. On February 13, 1951, the court recommended wage increases up to 5 per cent for 465,000 workers (a separate claim was pending for 149,000 railway shopmen), subject to acceptance by the unions of changes in working arrangements as proposed by the Railway Executive. The yearly cost of the proposed increases was estimated at about £7 million: "the maximum amount which it is within the capacity of British railways to pay without imposing intolerable financial burdens upon them."[33]

32. *The Times* (London), August 17 and September 16, 1950.
33. *Ibid.*, February 14, 1951. The recommendation of the court was similar to the November offer made by the Executive except that the court proposed larger increases in the higher grades—at an added annual cost of about £350,000. The proposed changes in working conditions included "the removal of rigid lines of demarca-

Affairs moved rapidly to a climax. The findings were accepted by the Executive as reasonable, but were rejected by the three unions involved. The unions held that the recommended increase was inadequate, and that changes in working arrangements should be considered as a separate issue and not as a condition for a deserved increase in wages. They insisted, further, that the government (in the person of the Minister of Labor) should be called into the proceedings along with the Railway Executive. Meetings continued, and new offers and counteroffers were made. The unions proposed to speed up negotiations on changes in working conditions if their wage requests were granted, and the Executive proposed added increases amounting to about £1.5 million yearly, conditioned as before. The negotiations broke down, only to be revived by the Ministry of Labor. Finally, on the evening of February 23, after five days of incessant meetings, the Executive gave way: increases up to 7½ per cent retroactive to January 1 were granted at an annual cost to the railways of £12 million. The unions "acknowledged the imperative need of the fullest cooperation with the Railway Executive in the elimination of the waste of manpower, in increasing efficiency and improving productivity" and undertook "to examine in that spirit any proposals which the Executive put forward . . . without delay."[34]

---

tion between the duties of associated grades or individual members of the staff; the abolition of calling-up of trainmen; . . . reducing the number of van guards in the London area . . . ; the extension of lodging turns . . . ; working of overtime within reasonable limits; . . . rostering of men up to nine hours; and the application of the five-day week where practicable."

34. *The Times* (London), February 24, 1951. As soon as the agreement was reached, the union leaders instructed their members throughout the country who had been engaging in "unofficial" strikes and slow-downs to resume normal working. Discussing the implications of the settlement, *The Economist* (March 3, 1951, pp. 465–66) commented, "No union in a nationalised industry will ever again accept as final either the 'no' of a public corporation as employer or the recommendations of an arbitration tribunal or industrial court. The union will always appeal over their heads to the Government." Two

Rising Costs and Rising Rates

By the close of 1950, the Commission had experienced another annual deficit, this time in the amount of £14.1 million, bringing its cumulative deficit to a total of £39.6 million. The railways were faced with an increased wage bill of £12 million in addition to the £2 million increase granted the previous September and the pending £2 million claim by the railway shopmen. Higher coal prices would add an additional £3 million a year, and the prices of all other materials and supplies were advancing. The only alternative to a subsidy was a further increase in rates and charges—and announcement of the increase came almost immediately. The Minister of Transport approved an emergency request made by the Transport Commission for a 10 per cent across-the-board increase in railway freight rates, effective April 16, 1951, estimated to yield £20 million yearly in additional revenue.[35] On April 13, the Transport Commission submitted to the Transport Tribunal a proposal to increase by 20 per cent the fares on main-line railway and London transport (road and rail) passenger service. The Tribunal's decision was not expected for several months.[36]

---

weeks earlier *The Economist* (February 17, 1951, p. 391) had said: "There seem to be only two possibilities: either a strike or wholesale surrender on the part of the Government. Either event would have disastrous repercussions on the industrial life of the country." Six months later *The Economist* (August 4, 1951, p. 304) was moved to say that "if any proof were needed that the unions can order affairs to their own wishes, the failure of the experiment to secure the better use of railway manpower is surely conclusive."

35. *The Times* (London), March 24 and 28, April 14, 1951. On April 23, 1950 the Opposition in the House of Commons moved to forestall the increase until an inquiry could be made into the possibilities of increased efficiency and economy. In the first test of Parliamentary strength following the resignation of Aneurin Bevan from the Cabinet, the government defeated the motion by a vote of 297–293.

36. *The Times* (London), April 14, 1951. The proposal, if approved, would add another £17 million to the Commission's annual revenue. Shortly after the request for increased rates was made, the three railway unions presented a joint claim for a wage increase at all levels

Road Haulage Is Nationalized

Part III of the Transport Act instructed the Transport Commission to acquire all road-haulage undertakings engaged predominantly in ordinary long-distance carriage for hire.[37] Under the British licensing system, "A" licenses are issued to public carriers, "B" licenses to those carrying for their own businesses but authorized to carry for outsiders, and "C" licenses to those carrying solely for themselves. The effect of the act was to place all "A" and "B" undertakings under threat of public ownership if the undertaking was carried on during any part of 1946, and if over half of its business was concerned with long-distance traffic (over a radius of more than 25 miles from its operating base or a distance of more than 40 miles within that radius). The Commission was given the sole right to carry on such long-distance haulage for hire after an "appointed day" to be fixed by the Minister. The Commission was free, however, to issue permits to old and new private undertakings to do long-distance hauling, and in the case of those who were engaged in long-distance hauling on November 28, 1946, the Commission was required to issue an "Original Permit" unless it was prepared to buy out the undertaking.[38] Every trader remains free under the act to carry his own goods over any distance in his own vehicles operated under "C" licenses. Before the Transport Act, there were a few very large haulage concerns in Great Britain and approximately 20,000 small haulers most of whom operated one or two trucks. This was the industry that the Commission in due

---

that would add about £19 million annually to railway costs. The unions rejected a counteroffer of selective wage raises involving about half of the sum requested, and their claim was passed on to the Railway Staff National Tribunal. *The Economist,* September 15, 1951, p. 646.

37. Transport Act, 1947, Secs. 39 and 41. "Ordinary long-distance carriage" does not include carriage of liquids in bulk, goods in specially constructed vehicles, furniture removals, meat, livestock, felled timber in special vehicles or carriage in vehicles specially constructed to carry abnormal indivisible loads.

38. *Ibid.,* Secs. 52, 53.

course was to take over and operate as a single system, integrated with the railways.

Early in 1948 the Commission began the acquisition by voluntary agreement of several major trucking concerns, giving to the Road Transport Executive a nucleus of strong, well-distributed operating units. Around this framework the Executive began to construct its organization—divisions, districts and operating groups with a very considerable measure of local authority and responsibility. In June 1948 it was announced that compulsory acquisition would begin on October 1, and that applications for acquisition by voluntary agreement would not be accepted after June 30, 1948. By the end of 1948, the Commission owned the share capital of 248 long-distance haulage undertakings, totaling 8,208 motor vehicles, 1,717 trailers and 1,867 horse vehicles.[39]

The Road Transport Executive established under the Commission's original organization was superseded in June 1949 by two newly created bodies—the Road Haulage Executive and the Road Passenger Executive. During the year the program of compulsory acquisition was carried on vigorously, and at the close of 1949 the Commission had become the owner of 1,880 undertakings and a total of 34,894 motor vehicles and 4,045 trailers. By the end of 1950 the totals had risen to 2,867 undertakings, 39,932 motor vehicles and 4,794 trailers.[40]

Late in the spring of 1949 the Minister of Transport set July 1 as the date within one month of which applications for "Original Permits" must be made; on October 31, 1949 the Minister, acting on the advice of the Commission, named February 1, 1950 as the "appointed day,"[41] after which it was necessary for practically all commercial long-distance haulers to have a permit issued by the Commission.

39. *Report and Accounts for 1948,* pp. 16–17.
40. *Report and Accounts for 1949,* p. 11; *Report and Accounts for 1950,* p. 11.
41. *Report and Accounts for 1949,* pp. 11–12.

The Commission processed over 17,000 applications for "Original Permits" and granted permits in nearly 11,000 cases.[42] The permits were revocable and the Commission announced in October 1950 that, as of February 1, 1951, 5,300 permits would be revoked (or not renewed), 3,800 would be continued and 2,700 would be modified.[43]

Road Policy Under Attack

The Commission's policy toward private haulers has been under attack. It is claimed that the Commission has harassed private operators and made it difficult for them to obtain licenses, and has evidenced a determination to drive them off the roads and strengthen its own grip on the industry. A motion offered by the Opposition in protest against the Commission's treatment of free road haulers barely failed of passage in May 1950.[44] A bill offered in the House of Lords and as a private-member bill in the House of Commons to increase the radius of free private haulage and to transfer to the licensing authorities the powers over permits now vested in the Commission, has had its third reading in the House of Lords and its second reading in the House of Commons.[45] In the debates the bill's proponents argued

42. Statement by the Minister of Transport (May 1, 1950), in *Parliamentary Debates* (Hansard), House of Commons, Vol. 474, cols. 1527-36.

Of the 17,246 applications, 10,974 had been granted as of May 1, 1950, 2,214 had been refused, 4,025 were invalid and 33 were waiting decision. A total of 167 undertakings had applied to be taken over under the act. *The Economist* (December 2, 1950, p. 961) gives the number of applications granted as "nearly 12,000."

43. *Report and Accounts for 1950*, p. 12. After further consideration, the number of permits revoked became approximately 5,200; the number continued in a modified form was increased to 3,300. *Ibid.*

44. The division on the motion resulted in a tie, 278-278. During the debate, the Minister of Transport pointed out that there were 4,426 new entrants into the industry in 1949; and that, as against a total of 801,761 private commercial vehicles, the Road Haulage Executive and the railways together owned only 49,390. *Parliamentary Debates* (Hansard), House of Commons, Vol. 474, cols. 1482-1540.

45. The bill moved rapidly from its first reading in the House of

that the Commission is engaging in unfair competition against private haulers; the government stood on the essential purpose and meaning of the Transport Act—that long-distance hauling should become nationalized.

Government supporters have claimed that many traders who might otherwise have used public haulage have for political reasons secured "C" licenses (granted without restriction) and are carrying their own goods. The number of "C" licenses increased from 383,700 in December 1946 to 708,-000 in September 1950. The answer given to the claim is that private haulage has increased as retail delivery service has been restored and trucks have become available for private owners, that most "C" licenses cover light loads carried for short distances, and that "the only answer to the competition of 'C' licensed vehicles is so to improve the efficiency of British Road Services as to make it uneconomical for the trader to use his own transport."[46]

Road Haulage in 1951

In a review of the industry on January 15, 1951, Lord Hurcomb, chairman of the Commission, stated that the organization of British Road Services (the Road Haulage Executive's operating agency) was virtually complete and that 1951 would be a year of consolidation. About 2,900 road haulage concerns have been merged into a national network of 40,000 vehicles, based upon 1,000 depots and subdepots, and employing 75,000 persons. The organization, now working smoothly, is decentralized on a territorial basis, with working units consisting of from 100 to 200 vehicles. In 1950 the total number of vehicles fell slightly

---

Lords, November 2, 1950, to its passage on second reading in the House of Commons, February 23, 1951. Whether the bill will emerge from committee for its necessary third reading is problematical. The favorable vote for the bill in the House of Commons (242–234) was not regarded as a defeat for the government, since it was a "private-member bill" and "the whips were not put on." *The Times* (London), November 3, 22, and December 13, 1950; February 14, 24, 1951.

46. *The Economist*, December 2, 1950, p. 961; January 13, 1951, pp. 96 and 99.

(.3 per cent), but the total of goods carried increased by 6 per cent to 3.7 million tons. Maintenance, repairs and over-hauling are being organized more systematically; experiments in persuading people to transfer suitable traffic to the railways are proceeding satisfactorily.[47]

It is too early to reach a judgment on the financial outcome of the road haulage project. In 1948 the Road Services earned £1,131,219 in net traffic receipts, and in 1949 net traffic receipts were £1,431,721, but the slightly larger net in 1949 was earned by nearly 35,000 vehicles as against approximately 8,000 vehicles operated in 1948. Undertakings were being acquired too rapidly to permit their immediate absorption into an efficient system, much poor stock was taken over, and costs of all kinds were rising.[48] The Road Haulage Executive announced in October 1950 that it had signed an agreement on wages and conditions that would mean an increase of about 7s. a week for the majority of nearly 50,000 workers.[49] Earlier in the year the Executive announced a rate adjustment to level out anomalies in the rates inherited from the private companies that it had acquired, and, in addition, a surcharge of 7½ per cent applicable to all general haulage and parcels charges after May 15. On January 20, 1951 another general increase of 10 per cent, effective January 29, was announced.[50]

Road Passenger Service

The Commission was given power under the Transport Act (Part IV) to prepare area schemes for the coordination

47. *The Times* (London), January 16, 1951.
48. *The Economist,* December 2, 1950, pp. 960–62. The Commission's costs for the capital used in road haulage are not certain; operations in 1949 may have involved a net revenue deficit. Another reason for higher costs is that the British Road Services finds it necessary to observe speed and "hours at the wheel" regulations more strictly than do private undertakings, with resulting longer hours, extra shifts and greater wage costs.
49. *The Times* (London), October 28, 1950.
50. *Ibid.,* May 5, 1950, January 25, 1951; *The Economist,* January 27, 1951, p. 222.

of passenger transport services (by road and rail) and for the provision of "adequate, suitable and efficient road transport services." It was expected that the schemes would vary with area conditions. The road passenger transport agency might be the Commission or any other designated authority, and it might acquire existing road passenger undertakings either privately or municipally owned. Much of the time of the Road Passenger Executive has been devoted to the preparation of these area schemes; and the Commission, through the Executive, has begun to acquire road passenger facilities.[51]

Integration and Charges Schemes

The Executives concerned have been so preoccupied with problems of acquisition, organization and operation that they have found it possible to do relatively little toward the actual achievement of integration of road and rail. Nonetheless, a measure of progress has been made. The Commission spoke hopefully at the outset, although in general terms, of the combination of the several parts into a single whole which is the task of integration—the integrated system to be efficient, adequate and economical and so contrived that users will have a maximum of choice between competing services.[52] It established a standing conference on coordination, and the several Executives and their officers throughout the country have been planning and experimenting with various measures for interchange of traffic and joint use of facilities. In December 1949 the Commission prepared, and issued to the trade unions concerned, a statement of the general lines along which coordination and integration might be expected to develop, and machinery for joint discussion was created.[53] On June 30, 1950, the Commission presented to its joint consultative council

51. The Commission began actively to acquire passenger road undertakings in 1950, and work on the area schemes was continued. *Report and Accounts for 1949*, pp. 13–16; *1950*, pp. 13–15.

52. *Report and Accounts for 1948*, p. 25.

53. *Report and Accounts for 1949*, pp. 21–22.

(the Commission, chairmen and representatives of its Executives, representatives of the three railway unions, the Transport and General Workers' Union, and the Confederation of Shipbuilding and Engineering Unions) a statement of policy "to serve as a directive from the Commission to the Railway and Road Haulage Executives as to the steps to be taken for the integration of their respective freight services."[54] Definitive steps in the application of the policy as outlined have yet to be taken.

The Commission has been continuously at work on the assignment given to it by the Transport Act, to prepare a charges scheme (or series of schemes) covering all the services provided by the Commission. This is, of course, the very heart of the problem of integration if free choice of services is to be allowed to users. Committees were organized and progress was made in the preparation of charges schemes for merchandise traffic and for passenger fares; but early in 1949 so much ground remained to be covered that the Commission asked and received permission from the Minister to extend by two years the terminal date (August 6, 1949) specified by the act for completion of the schemes. In December 1949 the Commission issued, for discussion, a draft outline of the principles it proposed to embody in a charges scheme for merchandise traffic.[55] The London Passenger

54. *Integration of Freight Services by Road and Rail,* British Transport Commission, 1950, p. 3. The statement stresses the complementary as distinct from the competitive character of road and rail; outlines the services for which, and the conditions under which, each is specially suitable and efficient; discusses the application of these considerations to collection and delivery services; and discusses the joint use of facilities, services and staff. See also *Report and Accounts for 1950,* pp. 20–23.

55. The proposal places more emphasis upon "loading capability" than on the "value factor" in the classification of goods, and gives special consideration to a "grouping" (zone) system in the calculation of distance. *Report and Accounts for 1949,* pp. 22–23. See also *Report and Accounts for 1950,* pp. 25–26. The date for completion of the schemes has been extended to the end of 1951. *The Economist,* August 4, 1951, p. 304.

Fare proposal[56] of February 1950 was the first concrete charges scheme to be presented for action.

So much for integration, coordination and the "look ahead." What these may actually amount to is still to be determined. In the meantime many skeptics are concerned lest these splendid words be employed principally to help bail out a declining rail industry by the use of funds drawn from excessive charges placed on road traffic.

Problems Ahead

In addition to the problems inherent in integration and coordination and the difficult day-to-day task of furnishing nation-wide transportation service, the nationalized transport industry faces many other troublesome issues in the years ahead: the proper relation of a state monopoly to Parliament and the government and to consumers; the proper relationship between nationalized transport and nationalized coal, electricity and gas;[57] wages and labor-management relations (including the participation of labor in management); the maintenance of "uneconomic" service because of public demand. These issues are basic, and the future of British nationalization depends largely on the skill with which they are resolved.

56. See p. 91.

57. The balance between the several interdependent nationalized industries, and between these industries and over-all government economic policy is not easy to maintain. For instance, the tax increase on gasoline provided in the 1950 Budget affected the costs and charges of road haulage (*The Times* [London], May 5, 1950); this in turn threw out of adjustment the relationship between road haulage and rail freight charges; if, as a result, rail rates were raised, the costs and prices of coal, electricity and gas—and, one step removed, of rail service itself—would be affected, with consequent effects on the charges for road haulage, and so on and on. It is entirely possible for the government to use its tax program to achieve diversion of traffic between road and rail in line with any transportation policy it may adopt. For instance, the Opposition was unkind enough to suggest that the increased taxes on gasoline and commercial vehicles in the 1950 Budget constituted an attempt to "featherbed" the railroads. *The Times* (London), April 4, 1950.

Nationalization of railways is a closed issue in Great Britain today; nationalization of road transport is still open. The Conservative party, in its 1951 manifesto, promises that "publicly-owned rail and road transport will be reorganised into regional groups of workable size," and that "private road haulers will be given the chance to return to business, and private lorries will no longer be crippled by the 25-mile limit." There is plenty of complaint over the operation and, particularly, over the financial results of the operation of the railways, but no voice is raised in favor of their return to private ownership. The degree to which rail nationalization is accepted in Great Britain is indicated by the fact that in the face of mounting deficits, the Federation of British Industries—the stronghold of private enterprise in Britain—proposes not that nationalization be abandoned, but that "part of the cost of maintaining Britain's railways should be charged to defence instead of being a charge upon rail users."[58] If rail losses continue to grow it is altogether possible that the present flat refusal of the government to consider either a subsidy or a scaling down of the interest charge on the Transport Commission stock may be gradually moderated.[59]

58. *The Times* (London), September 20, 1950. The Federation has charged the railways with excessive staffing, duplication of management, and retention of superfluous and uneconomic facilities. The chairman of the Railway Executive (John Elliot, who recently succeeded Sir Eustace Missenden, resigned) has offered a categorical denial. Specifically, on the last point, he stated that by the end of 1951 the total savings resulting from the closing of unremunerative lines and stations will be approximately £900,000 a year. *The Times* (London), April 14, 1951. The problem is discussed and statistics are given in *Report and Accounts for 1950*, pp. 23–24.

59. The government's position was stated strongly by the Minister of Transport in the debate aroused by the Commission's *Report and Accounts for 1949*. The Opposition's motion of criticism was defeated 296–284, but only after a spirited session. *Parliamentary Debates* (Hansard), House of Commons, Vol. 478, cols. 2053–2174.

In a later debate, July 31, 1951, the Minister stated that "at the moment" he did not consider any of the proposed solutions—subsidy, payment for strategic lines, cut in interest payments, drastic curtail-

ment of C-license transport—to be "correct." *The Economist*, August
4, 1951, p. 304. The Commission, in its *Report and Accounts for 1950,*
reviews the impressive list of cost increases that have occurred in the
past three years (pp. 37–39); notes the low price of transport relative
to its prewar level (p. 40); and names four factors that will determine
its financial future: (1) adequate financial and physical resources to
replace, re-equip and remodel its system; (2) a willingness on the
part of workers and users to accept changes in conditions and service;
(3) a speedier and more flexible scheme of public control over its
level of rates and charges; and (4) new rate bases which will recognize
that over a wide field the Commission's transport services are not a
monopoly (pp. 56–57).

CHAPTER 5

Nationalization
of Electric Power

THE MOVEMENT FROM small-scale to large-scale generation
and transmission of electric power first got under way in
Great Britain at the close of World War I, with the enactment of the Electricity (Supply) Act of 1919, and the establishment of the Electricity Commissioners for the purpose
of promoting, regulating and supervising the electricity
supply and of securing reorganization of the industry by
voluntary agreements.

Central Electricity Board

Further development was slow until the passage of the
Electricity (Supply) Act of 1926, and the setting up of the
Central Electricity Board (CEB) and its nation-wide system
of main transmission lines—the so-called "Grid." The Board
was authorized to concentrate the output of electricity for
public supply systems in a limited number of generating
stations selected for their efficiency and low operating costs;
to control the quantity, time and rate of output from these
stations (ownership of which was to remain unchanged); to
construct or acquire main transmission lines (the Grid); to
develop interconnections; and to purchase the output of the
selected stations and sell it to local undertakings, either
directly or indirectly.

The Central Electricity Board instituted a vigorous program of construction, purchase, sale, negotiation and promotion, with the result that by March 31, 1948, about two
fifths of Britain's electricity-distribution systems were being

supplied directly from the Grid, and most of the rest were connected to the Grid through the companies directly supplied. In 1926, when the Board took over, there were 491 authorized generating stations; by March 31, 1948, 143 selected stations were producing over 95 per cent of the country's electricity supply, and another 55 were under Grid control.[1]

In the meantime, formal and informal committee inquiries were taking place and recommendations were offered on the *distribution* of electricity supply. No legislation of general importance resulted, however, until after the close of World War II. In the mid-1940's many proposals for the reorganization of the electricity supply and distribution industry were made—all looking toward further concentration and wider use. Nationalization of the entire industry was an almost inevitable result of the Labor victory in 1945.

Provisions of Nationalization Law

The Electricity Act was sent to Parliament on December 20, 1946, received the Royal assent on August 13, 1947, and provided for the nationalization of the electric supply industry.[2] A British Electricity Authority (BEA) was established with a chairman and four full-time and seven part-time members. Under the Authority, fourteen area boards were set up, each with a chairman and from five to seven other members, all appointed by the Minister of Fuel and Power. Four chairmen of the area boards were to serve in

1. *First Report and Accounts, August, 1947—March, 1949,* British Electricity Authority, H.M.S.O., 1950, p. 7; *The British Fuel and Power Industries,* Political and Economic Planning, London, 1947, p. 158. For an account of the changing organization of electricity supply and distribution during this period, see *The British Fuel and Power Industries,* Part III, Chap. 3. See also M. E. Dimock, *British Public Utilities and National Development,* Allen and Unwin, London, 1933, Chaps. 6 and 7.

2. Electricity Act, 1947, 9 & 10 George 6, Ch. 54. See *Parliamentary Debates* (Hansard), House of Commons, Vol. 432, cols. 1404–1531, 1585–1702; Vol. 439, cols. 41–162, 215–400, 447–642, 968–1082; Vol. 441, cols. 1305–42.

rotation as members of the BEA, and the chairman of the North of Scotland board was to serve *ex officio*.

On April 1, 1948, the BEA and the area boards took over the ownership and operation of the industry (with minor exceptions) throughout Britain. Compensation to the owners followed the general stock-exchange-value plan employed in the nationalization of the transport industry. Local authorities were compensated by annual payments to cover the debt charges of their former undertakings. The project is spelled out in the BEA's first report in the following terms:

The British Electricity Authority exercise a general control of policy and are responsible for the generation of electricity and its supply to the Area Boards for the purposes of distribution. They have taken over the generating stations and associated main transmission lines which belonged to the former electricity undertakers and power station companies, together with the national network of main transmission lines (known as the Grid) which was owned and operated by the Central Electricity Board. As part of their administrative arrangements, they have established fourteen Generation Divisions, the areas of which correspond in general to those of the Area Boards.

The fourteen Area Electricity Boards have taken over the former local electricity undertakings, with the exception of the generating stations and associated main transmission lines. They distribute electricity to the consumers, and for this purpose buy from the Authority bulk supplies of electricity which are delivered to the distribution systems of the Boards either directly from the generating stations or from other points on the Grid.[3]

The structural relationship between the BEA and the area boards is fixed by statute. The Authority is empowered to give direction to the boards on coordination of distribution and in matters of policy (including financial policy) and development programs. The BEA fixes the tariff for bulk supply to the boards, and reviews the distribution tariffs set by the boards. It initiates all agreements respecting terms and conditions of employment for all persons em-

3. *First Report and Accounts, August, 1947–March, 1949*, p. 2.

ployed by itself and by the boards. The boards are required to send audited statements of their annual accounts, with the reports made by the auditors, to the BEA.

Under the act, the Minister appoints consultative councils (each composed of twenty to thirty members) for each area, to consider and make recommendations to the boards on tariffs and service. The council may carry its representations past the board to the BEA and beyond the Authority to the Minister. The Minister's relation to the BEA is much the same as his relationship to the National Coal Board. Any directions from the Minister to the boards are routed through the Authority. Provisions relating to accounts, audits and annual reports of the Authority are also similar to those enacted for the coal board.

Two recent comments on the law are worth noting:

The Electricity Bill completes the trio of the Government's major nationalisation schemes for the present session of Parliament. . . . After the revolutionary proposals of the Transport Bill, the mere proposal to take the electricity industry into public ownership looks almost tame. . . . there is a *prima facie* case for the unification of the electricity supply industry in this country, and the Bill does seem to be, on the whole, well designed to reap the benefits of unification without running too much of the risk that lies in complete monopoly. But, the terms of compensation are probably not fair, and certainly not fairly arrived at. And it is very difficult to believe that the advantages of nationalisation, which are mainly long-term, are large enough to justify such a high priority on the overcrowded agenda of the nation's business. . . . But, as a piece of industrial planning the Bill deserves praise.[4]

Political and Economic Planning makes the following observations:

It will not be possible to pass a final judgment on the nationalisation proposals until the Central Authority and the Area Boards have been in operation for some time. The real test will be whether the new organisation will encourage enterprise and development. The Bill is open to the objection as in

4. *The Economist,* January 18, 1947, p. 92.

the case of the nationalisation scheme for the coal mines, that the powers of the Minister of Fuel and Power are very wide. This may result in too much political interference with the operation of the Boards. On the other hand, if this danger is avoided, the proposed structure has the advantage of providing a large measure of competition between the various Area Boards; and, except in the matter of compensation, the Bill has received a more favourable reception than other measures of nationalisation.[5]

Nationalized Electricity Goes into Action

Three months before the Electricity Bill became law, the Minister of Fuel and Power appointed an organizing committee comprised of the following members, who subsequently became the nucleus of the British Electricity Authority: the Rt. Hon. Lord Citrine (Chairman), Sir Johnstone Wright, John Hacking, Lt. Col. E. H. E. Woodward, J. Eccles, E. W. Bussey, and Sir Henry Self. The function of the committee was to work on problems of organization and other matters that might require consideration before vesting day.

On April 1, 1948, the British Electricity Authority took over the national Grid of main transmission lines belonging to the Central Electricity Board and 297 generating stations, with associated transmission lines, owned by authorized undertakers and power station companies. The generating stations varied greatly in size; about a fourth of the stations produced about nine tenths of the national output of electricity. At the same time, the area boards assumed ownership of the distribution systems of some 540 electricity undertakings. The personnel of the vested industry, "including those employed in associated activities later to be undertaken by the Authority and the Boards," exceeded 145,000. The capital cost of the transferred assets was about £900 million.

The *First Report and Accounts* of the British Electricity Authority, covering the period from August 13, 1947 to

5. *The British Fuel and Power Industries,* p. 321.

March 31, 1949, appeared early in 1950, together with individual reports from the fourteen area boards. The report of the Authority was voluminous—in records, accounts and data, and in running discussion characterized by soul-baring, mild satisfaction and confidence for the future.

The financial results gave some reason for satisfaction. The industry as a whole earned a surplus of revenue over costs of £4,391,684 for its first year of operation under the new regime. The surplus, to be sure, did not accrue evenly from all parts of the industry; the Authority showed a deficit of £607,149 on its sales to area boards, but the boards, with two exceptions, earned offsetting profits. The Authority commented:

> This surplus, by no means large in relation to the combined revenues of £197.60 million, can be regarded on the whole as a satisfactory outcome of a year which has not been free from stresses and strains; a year in which the costs of labour and materials have continued to rise; in which load-shedding and other user restrictions have continued to fetter the expansion of sales and to limit revenues; in which additions to overhead expenses have been borne on relatively new and important ancillary services, such as labour relations, welfare, education and training; and in which it has not been possible to do more than set in motion the train of economies—in technical, operational and administrative processes alike—which should be the corollary to the creation of a fully-integrated organisation for electricity supply.[6]

The Authority's surplus was calculated after providing £30,610,000 for depreciation, writing off £700,000 in intangible assets of the dispossessed undertakings, and the spending (by area boards) of £341,836 on changes in systems of supply—considerably more than the predecessor companies had been able to devote to these purposes in 1947–1948.

During the first year, over 46,000 million kwh. of electricity were generated at BEA stations, the highest output in the industry's history, and an increase of 10.5 per cent over 1947–1948. At the end of the year, the area boards were

6. *First Report and Accounts, August, 1947–March, 1949*, p. 113.

supplying 12.2 million consumers—500,000 more than at vesting day. Farm customers increased by 8,727 during the year.

Plant Shortage Problem

The Authority recognized the "shortage of generating plant" as "the biggest problem of recent years and the cause of most difficulties in the supply industry—a direct result of the war and postwar economic conditions." The installed capacity at the end of March 1949 was 12,850,000 kw., but much of it was old, inadequate and costly to operate. The difference between the winter peak demand and the available generating capacity was 531,000 kw. and during the year "load-shedding" (restriction of supply) in one or more parts of the country was resorted to on seventy-nine occasions. "Greater demands for electricity could, of course, have been met at off-peak times." Plant with a capacity of 566,000 kw. was installed in 1948, compared with installations of 340,000 kw. and 307,000 kw. in the two preceding years.

Noting that present installed capacity was 12,850,000 kw. ("the largest [undertaking] of its kind in the world"), the Authority estimated that upwards of 30 million kw. of new plant would be needed within the next twenty years to care for replacement and new demand. A disturbing feature of the situation, however, was that "the capital cost of generating stations per kilowatt of installed capacity is now about three times as much as before the war, and the new stations and extensions of existing stations for 1950–1953 will cost on average about £50 per kilowatt."[7] Nonetheless, the Authority had thirty-eight new stations and forty-three extensions under construction or planned through 1953—"an expansion effort without precedent in this country." The extent to which manufacturing capacity, particularly for fabrication of pipes and boilers, could be expanded to meet the requirements of the construction program was recognized as an important limiting factor.

7. *Ibid.*, pp. 25, 145.

During the year, the Grid was extended by thirty-one miles to a total of 5,200 miles of main lines, and the reallocation of loads on a national basis led to substantial capital savings. Generating efficiency was improved—the thermal efficiency of steam stations increased progressively throughout the year.

Rates and Methods of Charging

The average revenue for each kwh. of electricity sold during the year was 1.176d.; 4 per cent higher than the average price in the previous year, and 12.6 per cent above the level of 1938–1939. The increase in price since 1938 was well below the corresponding increases in coal prices, wages and cost of living. Unless the industry had run at a loss, the 1948 increases would almost certainly have occurred even in the absence of nationalization. Many of the increases had been authorized before the BEA took over, and increases were made at once in some 150 districts where serious losses were expected. Domestic consumers paid, on the average, a lower price for electricity in the year 1948–1949 than before the war; the average revenue per unit, for lighting, heating and cooking alone was 9 per cent below that for 1938–1939.

The first year's report announced, further, that the Authority and the area boards were working actively toward the elimination of obsolete, eccentric and redundant methods of charges and a reduction in the number of types of tariff:

The new tariffs must be serviceable and equitable to all classes of consumers, and expressed in terms at once simple, understandable and precise. For the first time in the history of the supply industry, the whole field of tariff policy is under comprehensive and coordinated examination by the bodies having direct responsibility for supply.[8]

At the request of the Minister, the Authority reluctantly introduced into domestic tariffs a so-called "winter sur-

8. *Ibid.*, pp. 142–43, 150.

charge," for three months, to be followed by a "rebate" during the following nine months—in the hope of reducing peak demand. The scheme was not repeated in the winter of 1949–1950.[9]

Labor Adjustment and Administration

From the outset, the Authority gave active attention to the problem of working conditions and arrangements. National and local negotiating bodies were established to deal with terms and conditions of work, for all classes of employees. Progress was reported in the preparation of new national agreements; national and district joint advisory councils, on which all employee unions were represented, were established. Work stoppages occurred only in situations where the negotiating machinery was ignored. Safety and health received the attention of the BEA and the boards, and an enlarged general welfare program was begun. Programs of information, training and education were developed.

The Authority, as might have been expected, was preoccupied with problems of organization, and many pages of the first *Report* were given over to discussion of the considerations involved in achieving the correct balance of centralization and decentralization, and of ministerial responsibility and operating independence and efficiency. The Authority gave much thought and effort to organizing, arranging and encouraging the total operation so that the maximum of skilled services at the multiple points of production and distribution might be attained consistently with the working out of over-all policies of the Authority and the government. It is much too early to attempt an evaluation of results, but the BEA, like the Coal Board and the Transport Commission, is certainly conscious of the problem of organization.

9. *Ibid.*, pp. 68–70; *Second Report and Accounts, 1949–50,* pp. 46–47, 80.

Profitable Operation Continues

The Authority's second annual report, covering the year ended March 31, 1950,[10] was in the same confident vein that characterized its first report. This time, however, the note of impatience was stronger, amounting almost to irritation over conditions that, despite the Authority's best efforts, made it impossible to do the job it had set for itself.

The year was a success financially—the combined surplus of the Authority and the area boards was £7,163,236, bringing the combined two-year surplus to £11,554,920. The Authority incurred a "within-the-family" deficit of £1,993,-773 on its sales of power to the boards, but the policy of selling to the boards at less than cost enabled them to report a more than compensatory surplus.[11] Over 49,000 million kwh. of electricity were generated during the year—the highest figure in the history of the industry, and double the output of 1938–1939. At the end of the year 12,634,000 consumers were being supplied—an increase of 452,000 during the year and 2.5 million more than the number taking service in 1938–1939.[12]

10. *Second Report and Accounts, 1949–50,* British Electricity Authority, H.M.S.O., 1951.

11. *Ibid.,* p. 4. Combined revenues were £16.67 million greater than in 1948–1949, while net expenditures increased by £13.90 million. The Authority explained that its interim tariff of charges to its area boards, which was partially instituted during the first year of operation and which was determined before full information was available, was in the process of adjustment. Increases were made as of April 1, 1950; and on February 28, 1951 a further upward adjustment effective on April 1, 1951 was announced. This second increase took no account of the February 1951 increase in the price of coal which, it was estimated, would add some £7.5 million annually to the cost of electricity generation. *Ibid.,* pp. 9, 83–87. See also *The Times* (London), February 13 and March 1, 1951.

12. *Second Report and Accounts, 1949–50,* p. 3. Electricity sales in 1950–1951 were 12 per cent greater even than in 1949–1950, and more than 13 million customers were served. The increase in income was offset by increases in costs, leaving a surplus for 1950–1951 of £6.3 million—after paying £20.4 million for interest, and setting aside £36.1 million for depreciation and £3.5 million for tax reserve. *The Economist,* October 13, 1951, p. 878.

The average selling price to consumers per kwh. was 1.2*d*. This was 2.2 per cent above the 1948–1949 average, and 14.3 per cent above the average of 1938–1939. The increase reflected the full effect of consumer tariff adjustments made in 1948–1949; no general change in tariffs was made in 1949–1950. The Authority pointed out that the increase in the price of electricity since the war was much less than the increases in wage rates and in the general cost of living—"indeed, for electricity sold to 'domestic, commercial and small power' consumers, the average price of 1.515*d*. per unit [kwh.] was 5.1 per cent below the pre-war average."[13] New equipment and careful use and operation of existing equipment resulted in a further increase in the thermal efficiency of the Authority's steam stations during the year. Increased efficiency of generation combined with a drop in the average delivered price of coal resulted in a reduction of 2.7 per cent in fuel costs per kwh. Total fuel consumption was greater by 5.9 per cent than in 1948–1949, but the corresponding increase in electricity generated was 6.3 per cent.[14] In the meantime, however, the combined administrative and general expenditure of the Authority and its boards increased from £20,826,762 in 1948–1949 to £24,758,085 in 1949–1950.

The labor force employed by the Authority and the boards rose during the year from 156,100 to 170,500. The Authority continued work on the development of machinery, organization and agreements covering a wide range of employment and staff relations and problems. A national agreement covering wage adjustments for manual workers that had been under negotiation since prenationalization days was published in June 1949. Difficulties soon devel-

13. *Ibid.*, p. 3. Unit price in 1950–1951 declined to 1.181*d*. *The Economist*, October 13, 1951, p. 878.

14. *Ibid.*, p. 6. The reduction in the average delivered price of coal resulted from price adjustments in July 1948 and May 1949 which had the effect of reducing the pithead price of low-grade coal, of which the Authority is a large consumer, and increasing the prices of higher grades. *Ibid.*, pp. 6, 37–38.

oped, and during the subsequent negotiations unofficial walkouts occurred at a number of stations. The walkout at four London power stations in December 1949 caused considerable anxiety, disturbance and load-shedding, and men from the armed services were called in to maintain essential supplies. The strikers agreed to return after assurance that their grievance would be given immediate consideration, but an unfortunately worded notice posted by the Authority resulted in an extension of the stoppage for an additional day. Union leaders joined with the government and the Authority in efforts to end the walkout.[15]

The Problem of Capacity Again

On March 31, 1950 the Authority owned 293 power stations with a total installed capacity of 13,784,000 kw. (about 7 per cent above 1948–1949). New generating plant with an installed capacity of a million kw. was brought into service, and at the end of the year 43 new stations and 27 extensions were under construction or included in definite plans for early completion. The Grid system was increased by 121 route-miles of main transmission lines and cables during the year, bringing the total to 5,424 route-miles; and work was begun on an additional 292 route miles. Plans were actively in process both for additional generating capacity and for an extended super-Grid transmission system.[16]

Despite the increase in capacity, the Authority found it impossible to supply enough electric power to satisfy its growing list of consumers at periods of maximum demand. Load-spreading was accomplished through "the valued co-operation of industry and commerce and other consumers in reducing their requirements at peak periods," but it was still necessary to resort to load-shedding on 124 occasions.[17] This was the feature of past and prospective operation that gave the Authority its greatest concern. In its view, "the

15. *Ibid.*, pp. 53 ff.; *The Times* (London), December 13–17, 1949.
16. *Second Report and Accounts, 1949–50,* pp. 4–7; *The Times* (London), July 24, 1950.
17. *Second Report and Accounts, 1949–50,* pp. 12, 34.

ever-pressing problem of the shortage of generating plant and the emergency condition which it creates" can be effectively met only if the government finds itself able to allocate to the Authority's program a larger share of the total national capital investment. In 1950 the Authority and its boards (together with the North of Scotland Hydro-Electric Board) were granted £116 millon, "the largest single allocation apart from that for housing." Nonetheless, "the Authority have expressed the firm opinion that . . . the amounts allocated for 1950 are insufficient to meet the industry's needs and to maintain balanced development." The key position of electricity in the economy—its relation to productivity as well as social well-being—require the rapid expansion of electricity supply. The Authority's program is geared to this imperative national need; and from its viewpoint it is the duty of the government to appreciate this need and to direct a larger proportion of the nation's limited resources to its fulfillment.[18]

The Authority Under Attack

The Authority's reports suggest competence and confidence. They have drawn heavy fire, however, from sources outside the Parliamentary Opposition.[19] *The Economist* has taken up the attack with vigor and apparent relish. Comparing the first year's performance and promise with the vision conjured up by the Minister of Fuel and Power on the occasion of the Second Reading debates, *The Economist* professed complete disillusionment:

No one supposes that the Authority could have transformed the power supply facilities or worked any other miracle in this short time. But it is fair to look to it for a systematic approach to its task and a policy aimed at removing the faults for which the

18. *Ibid.,* pp. 11–16.
19. The Commons debate on the *First Report and Accounts* was mild, and the government motion that the House "take note" of the report was agreed to without division. *Parliamentary Debates* (Hansard), House of Commons, Vol. 478, cols. 247–313, 329–68. See also *The Economist,* July 29, 1950, p. 233.

old system was blamed. Neither this report, nor the Authority's known performance to date, contains anything to suggest that such an approach or such a policy exists.[20]

The Economist did not find fault with the results of the Authority's immediate trading, even though it did call attention to the record of rising costs. Its criticism was directed, rather, at the Authority's "dreamlike" attitude on capital expansion: in its preoccupation with grandiose plans for physical development, the Authority was over-looking the burdens involved in heavy capital expenditures, and the Authority was guilty, as well, of seeking to pre-empt more than its share of the nation's investment resources. *The Economist* continued:

First of all, the idea that new and more efficient power stations will make electricity cheaper needs to be exploded. . . . No foreseeable technical superiority of the new plants over the old is in the least likely to offset their increased initial cost in full; . . . To suppose that "expanding sales" in themselves offer a remedy is fallacious for the same reason. Unless the present load pattern is changed, sales can be expanded only by building more plant; for the existing plant is already stretched to capacity, and more, at peak load times. To the extent that demand increases and the Authority is able to install the new plant to meet it, electricity will cost not less, but more. If the plant could be more fully utilised, then sales could be expanded without extra investment, and costs might begin to come down. But this can be achieved only by spreading demand more evenly —over the year if possible, but at any rate over the day . . . the problem of peak loads is not merely an emergency; it is permanent, and inseparable from the search for an economic system of electricity supply. To blame the Authority for having failed to find a solution in its short life would be absurd; but is the essential question being tackled at all? There is no sign that it is. . . . Released, if only temporarily, from sordid financial impediments, the electricity supply industry has found itself bogged down not less firmly in unpleasant economic facts. This ought not to be blamed, as the report appears to blame it, on the cruel world—the consequences of the war, or the unaccountable

20. *The Economist,* January 21, 1950, pp. 147–51.

failure of a supplying industry to live up to extravagant promises which ought never to have been believed. If there is one service that should be required, above all others, from the board of a nationalised industry it is that this kind of happy-go-lucky expansionism—with all that it implies in resources pre-empted, immobilised, and going to waste—should be unthink-able.[21]

Once more *The Economist* returned to the attack, taking as a springboard the paper read by Sir Henry Self, the Authority's deputy chairman, before the Electrical Power Convention. Emphasis on more economical use of existing plant, by adjustments in charges and load, rather than concentrating so heavily on plant expansion, was again *The Economist's* theme.[22] And even more recently, in apprais-ing the Authority's second annual report, *The Economist* took the Authority to task for its "ambition of attaining the plant required to meet the hour or two of maximum demand in the hardest winter . . . when the last suburban housewife can switch on her last spare heater or toaster on the coldest morning in the year."[23] The fact that the price of electricity to the domestic consumer had been raised by the Authority only slightly ("the rise . . . has been scarcely perceptible") did not suggest to *The Economist* that any forceful attempt had been made to apply disincentives to the consumption of electricity at peak periods. The Authority

21. *Ibid.* Something of the Authority's attitude toward the need for expansion and the place of its claim in the hierarchy of industrial claims for investment capital and capital goods is indicated by the following excerpt from a speech made by Lord Citrine, chairman of the Authority, before the Electrical Development Association in April 1950: "From time to time I hear rumours—and I put them at no more than rumours—of the possibilities of cuts in our programme. I will say if that is even considered as a practical proposal it will come not merely as disappointing to the people in this industry who all these years have struggled so hard to improve its capacity, but it will be disastrous for British industry as a whole." *The Economist,* April 29, 1950, p. 957.

22. *The Economist,* July 1, 1950, p. 28.

23. *The Economist,* December 9, 1950, pp. 1014, 1016.

was seeking a solution to the problem of peak loads in a vast horizon of uneconomic capital investment.[24]

The Authority's Dilemma

An embarrassing dilemma confronts the Authority because of the rapid expansion of electric heating for houses that was well under way before the industry was nationalized. Domestic consumption for cooking and heating was encouraged by publicity and by a low rate per kwh., and this rate was profitable while the demand for such purposes as lighting was predominant, because it came largely at off-peak times. When, however, house heating by electricity became widespread, the situation changed, because this newer use gradually built up new hourly and seasonal peaks in many areas. The problem has been aggravated by coal shortages and cold weather, and the unrestricted sale of electric heaters. If the Authority discourages house heating by charging higher rates it will collide with the interests of those who have large investments in electrically heated

24. *The Times* (London), December 6, 1950, made much the same point both editorially and in its "City Notes." "It is tempting to speculate on what may be the effect on costs and prices if and when capacity catches up with peak demands." *The Times* was critical, too, of the increase in administrative costs.

The prospects for the winter of 1951–1952 are distressing. The demand for electricity is rising more rapidly than generating capacity, and power shortages are inevitable. During the summer of 1951, meetings were held and efforts made to publicize the peak-load problem and to develop extended programs for load spreading. *The Economist*, August 4, 1951, p. 303; August 18, 1951, p. 412. During 1950–1951, the Authority gave some attention to mechanical load-control devices. "Load limitation is the admission of failure in pricing policy," said *The Economist* (October 13, 1951, pp. 879, 881). "The B.E.A. still retains no purposive knowledge or control of the effects of its multiplicity of tariff systems."

The Trades Union Congress and the Federation of British Industries have recently been joined by the National Production Advisory Council in requesting closer coordination of national fuel supplies. *The Economist*, May 19, 1951, p. 1189. The Minister of Fuel and Power has named a committee to study the problem and make recommendations. *The Economist*, August 18, 1951, p. 413.

houses and house-heating equipment, as well as with popular preference. If it does not discourage electric house heating, it must reconcile itself to a policy of load-shedding
during cold spells or, as it is now disposed to do, it must
plan for, and use all its influence to secure, the construction
of a large amount of increasingly expensive plant that cannot be in full use except in cold periods.

The Authority's first years, with all the difficulties surrounding a "take-over" period, have been at least moderately successful from the viewpoint of output and earnings.
This is important. Its current emphasis on plant expansion
may be mistaken, but in the direction it has chosen it has
certainly proceeded with imagination and drive. Both capital expansion and more economical use of existing plant are
necessary if the Authority's long-run responsibility is to be
discharged. It is not in a position to dictate resource use to
the government or to the rest of the economy; it will not take
over more of the economy's capital and capital goods than
the government and the economy are willing to devote to
the production of electricity. It should continue to press for
more investment; it should, at the same time, work more
wholeheartedly and more effectively to level off (or level
up) the demand for its service.

CHAPTER 6

Nationalization of Iron and Steel

NATIONALIZATION OF THE STEEL industry in Great Britain—now an accomplished fact, although possibly to be undone tomorrow—is more important as a symbol than for the substantive effect it is likely to have on the development and performance of the industry in the years immediately ahead. For the first time the government's nationalization program has reached out to embrace an industry that is neither "in distress" nor a recognized "public calling." Steel is one of Britain's most prosperous industries and its output in recent years has broken all records and exceeded all targets; and, although it has operated for many years under both self-imposed controls and government supervision, it has been accepted in the public mind as a stronghold of private capitalistic enterprise.

The Issue

The legislation providing for steel nationalization was enacted during the flush days of Labor's first postwar government, when its huge majority in Parliament swept aside all opposition as inconsequential; but nationalization was actually undertaken as recently as late 1950 and early 1951, and only after Labor had narrowly beaten off three successive all-out attacks in the new Parliament. Nationalization was put into effect in the face of a defense situation that would have made it relatively easy for a government less determined (or less "possessed") to have withheld action in the interest of "national unity." On the other hand, the nationalization that has occurred appears at the moment to be a cardboard affair—little more than a formality. The British people (including iron and steel workers) are not greatly stirred up over steel nationalization, and such interest and concern as they have been encouraged to manifest relates very largely to the symbolic quality of the project.

The argument for the past five years, with the exception of the recent sallies on "timing," has been mostly doctrinaire and traditional. In favor of nationalization it has been argued that the industry is basic in the economy and that it is monopolistically controlled—and that such industries should as a matter of principle be owned by the public. Further, its output, price and investment programs are such an important part of the nation's total program for full employment that no direction other than that which the government can provide as an owner can possibly be satisfactory. There has been some inclination to recall the industry's unemployment record in the 1930's; and to argue that its recent excellent performance is to be attributed to the *threat* of nationalization. Little has been said about improving the industry's operating efficiency; at this point a defensive position has been taken—the government will act primarily as owner rather than manager, and the industry's operating policies and practices will not be disturbed.

The proponents of private ownership have stressed the advantages, in principle, of free enterprise (tending to overlook the cartel-like organization of the industry), and have pointed with pride to the industry's splendid performance during and since the war. They have accepted the government as consultant to, and supervisor of, the industry and have argued that in this position the government can protect and advance the public interest more completely and effectively than by stifling the industry under public ownership.

As nationalization came closer the arguments took on a new and more vigorous tone. The issue was one of tremendous importance, said the Opposition, and it was wrong to rush precipitously into nationalization before the electorate had given its clear and unmistakable consent. It was a "wanton act" to divide the country and disturb the industry at a time in the nation's history when unity was needed above all else. To this the government answered that the electorate had spoken favorably on two occasions, that the law was on the books, and that the threat of disunity and disruption came solely from the obstructionist tactics of the Opposition.[1]

Steel before 1951

Between the two world wars, and particularly in the period 1932–1939, the privately owned firms in the British iron and steel industry, with the encouragement of the government, wrapped and bound themselves tightly with layer upon layer of industrial "self-government." In 1937, the industry was characterized as "the most completely self-cartelized and controlled of any major British industry." The description continued:

Cooperating with and supported by the British Import Duties Advisory Committee at every step, the industry—completely disorganized at the turn of the decade—has built up behind a manipulated tariff wall a federated organization of some thirty-five price-fixing and quota associations together with probably forty more informal price and output groups, covering practically every iron and steel material and product produced in the British Isles. The British Iron and Steel Federation is headed by an independent chairman, approved by the government. In some of the associations the total industry output is limited by agreement of the members. In more, quotas are established fixing the allowable production of each member in terms of a percentage of the total industry output. . . .

In all the associations prices are set by the group acting as a unit, and on a level calculated to be satisfactory to the less effi-

1. The case for and against steel nationalization is set forth at length in the Parliamentary debates (see footnotes 8–11 in this chapter). The case against nationalization under the conditions prevailing in 1950 and 1951 is argued cogently and with force in *The Economist*, September 16, 1950, p. 470; September 23, 1950, p. 521; January 13, 1951, p. 92; February 10, 1951, p. 305; and February 17, 1951, p. 386.

cient members of the industry. By reason of an informal arrangement, price increases in the case of the more important products receive the approval of the Import Duties Advisory Committee before going into effect. Compliance with association rules is secured by various devices, of which the deposit of prepaid fines is the most common. As a further measure along this line, the Federation has secured the rather widespread adoption by the constituent associations of so-called "loyalty discounts," to be withdrawn from any recalcitrant member or any outsider—discounts so substantial that without their benefit any member of the industry not in good standing would be placed at a disastrous disadvantage.[2]

The organization thus developed was carried into and through the war, and in large measure continues even today under nationalization.[3]

During the war, the industry and the Ministry of Supply developed very close working arrangements (in which the Federation played a large part); in September 1946, the Minister of Supply appointed an Iron and Steel Board, with two members from management, two from the unions, one consumers' representative, one representative of the Treasury and a full-time chairman to carry out the following functions:

To review and supervise programmes of development needed for the modernisation of the iron and steel industry and to watch over the execution of approved schemes in such programmes.

To supervise as necessary the industry in current matters, including the provision of its raw material requirements, and

2. Ben W. Lewis, *Price and Production Control in British Industry*, University of Chicago Press, Chicago, 1937, pp. 14–15.

3. Details of the arrangements have changed from time to time and the industry operated during 1945–1951 under a more formal scheme of public supervision than the Import Duties Advisory Committee was able to provide. During this period the British Iron and Steel Federation issued statements discounting the restrictive activities of the associations and the Federation (since 1938 the industry has had difficulty producing *enough* steel), and extolling the competitive character of the industry and the value to the industry and to the British economy of the various services rendered by the Federation.

the administration, under power delegated by the Minister, of such continued direct control as may be required over the production, distribution and import of iron and steel products.

To advise on general price policy for the industry and on the fixing of prices for controlled products.[4]

The members served their two-year terms, but the chairman and four others declined to continue after October 1, 1948, in view of the government's public ownership program. Thereafter, until February 15, 1951, the staff of the Board, under the Minister of Supply, carried the task of public supervision. Throughout, the industry has been explicit in welcoming supervision (as distinct from ownership) by the public.[5] As a matter of fact, the industry has received much assistance from industry-government relationships and arrangements that have a strong flavor of subsidization.

Production in the industry has broken all records since the war. It has regularly exceeded the targets set in the government's annual Economic Surveys, and the industry has been carrying out with enthusiasm a long-overdue program of capital expansion and modernization.[6]

4. *Organisation in the Steel Industry,* British Iron and Steel Federation, London, 1948, p. 8.

5. *Ibid.,* p. 9. It is pointed out that (1) the industry has nothing to fear from supervision; (2) supervision will tend to allay suspicions that might be aroused by cooperative activity within the industry; (3) many industry questions, such as employment and location have social implications on which the managements may not be able to form an entirely comprehensive view; and (4) the function of Board supervision is not negative or restrictive, it is, rather, to watch over and stimulate the development of the industry in the national interest.

6. Steel production has risen 48 per cent in five years, and output per worker in steel smelting and rolling has gone up by 30 per cent. *The Times* (London), January 18, 1951. The industry's early postwar proposals for expansion will be found in *Iron and Steel Industry,* Cmd. 6811, H.M.S.O., May 1946.

The output of steel ingots and castings rose from 15,550,000 tons in 1949 to 16,290,000 tons in 1950, thus exceeding the forecast of 15,750,-000 to 16 million tons given in the *Economic Survey for 1950.* The *Economic Survey for 1951* states that capacity will increase in 1951, and that, if full supplies of raw materials were available, 16,750,000 tons could be produced during the year. It is expected, however, that

The Legislative Battle

Although the nationalization of steel was on the program that the Labor party took to the country in the election of 1945, it was not until the close of 1949 that the nationalization statute was enacted, and even this legislation carried provisos that the new Corporation might not be established before October 1, 1950 and that the property of the industry might not be vested in the Corporation before January 1, 1951.[7] The postponement was written into the act as the result of a compromise worked out with the House of Lords which, following the passage of the act by the House of Commons on its second reading in November 1948, had insisted upon certain amendments that the Commons, in turn, found unacceptable.[8] The House of Lords ultimately proved willing to concede much that it had found unpalat-

shortages of raw materials will keep capacity from being fully employed. *The Times* (London), April 4, 1951. The industry was confident in September that 16 million tons would be produced in 1951. *The Economist,* September 22, 1951, p. 700. The industry's expansion program is expected to provide capacity for an annual output of 18 million tons by 1953. *The Economist,* July 15, 1950, p. 138. The government announced in May 1950 that steel supplies were sufficient to withdraw steel distribution (with the exception of sheet and tin plate) from allocation and license. *The Times* (London), May 23, 1950. It seems probable, however, that controls will have to be reimposed because of raw materials shortages and the huge demands of defense production. *The Economist,* March 17, 1951, p. 635; August 25, 1951, p. 469.

7. Iron and Steel Act, 1949, 12 & 13 George 6, Ch. 72, Secs. 1 (3) and 11 (1).

8. The bill passed the House of Commons, November 17, 1948 on its second reading, 373–211. *Parliamentary Debates* (Hansard), House of Commons, Vol. 458, cols. 53–163, 215–326, 373–499. Amendments were considered and transmitted by the House of Lords on June 23, 28, 29, 30 and July 4, 1949; and again on July 18 and 20, 1949; the House of Commons returned those it did not approve on July 25 and 26, 1949. The House of Lords recorded its insistence on July 28, 1949. *Parliamentary Debates* (Hansard), House of Lords, Vol. 163, cols. 155–276, 353–479, 531–614, 637–744 and 747–828; Vol. 164, cols. 3–120 and 196–274; House of Commons, Vol. 467, cols. 1827–2215 and 2413–44; House of Lords, Vol. 164, cols. 625–64.

able in the bill provided only that a general election be allowed to intervene before the act was put into operation. The government agreed to the delay, the objections were withdrawn, and the Royal assent was finally given on November 24, 1949.[9]

The general election was held in February, 1950, and the Labor government escaped defeat by a narrow margin. The King's Speech which followed shortly made no mention of the government's plans relative to the steel industry, and the Opposition, in an effort to bring the issue once more to a head, moved an amendment to the speech, regretting the omission. The amendment was defeated by a vote of 310–296.[10]

On September 14, 1950, after months of apparent indecision, the government announced its intention to proceed on schedule with nationalization, and made public the names of those who had accepted appointment (effective October 2) as members of the Corporation. The Opposition immediately tabled a motion of censure, only to lose once more after a bitter debate—this time by a vote of 306–300.[11]

The appointments were formally made,[12] and the vesting date was set as February 15, 1951. As the appointed day drew near, the Opposition made a final attempt to prevent or

9. *Parliamentary Debates* (Hansard), House of Commons, Vol. 469, cols. 2039–87; House of Lords, Vol. 165, cols. 957–68.

10. *Parliamentary Debates* (Hansard), House of Commons, Vol. 472, cols. 474–594. In the debate, apart from the substantive merits of nationalization, the government took the position that since the Iron and Steel Act was on the statute books there was no occasion to refer to it in the address—the government naturally expected to carry out the law when the time came.

11. *The Times* (London), September 15, 1950. *Parliamentary Debates* (Hansard), House of Commons, Vol. 478, cols. 1252–56, 1719–1842. Winston Churchill, for the Opposition, proposed as a compromise that the late Iron and Steel Board be revived and its powers of control extended, and that nationalization be indefinitely postponed.

12. R. A. Maclean, who had accepted appointment as a part-time member, withdrew two days after the announcement because he felt that in the highly charged political atmosphere he could not "usefully or happily serve." His place was filled in time for the official appointment. *The Times* (London), September 19, 1950.

postpone the action. The Conservative party moved to censure the government for seeking to "give immediate effect
to the nationalization of this industry," in view of "the
record production attained by the . . . industry and the
urgent needs of the rearmament programme . . ." and
the motion was given formal support by the Liberal members of the House. The motion failed, 308–298; at midnight,
February 14, 1951, the iron and steel industry came under
government ownership.[13]

Steel Under Nationalization

The Iron and Steel Corporation of Great Britain is now
the owner of the capital shares of 80 of Great Britain's principal iron and steel corporations. Its capital commitment
is well over £200 million and it has become responsible for
the production of the major share of the country's output
of iron ore, pig iron, ingots and iron products. (See Table 3.)
Compensation to the former holders of the securities was
made in government-guaranteed British Iron and Steel
stock, bearing a return of 3½% and redeemable in 1979–
1981. The exchange of stock was made on the basis of the
average of the market prices of the steel companies' stock
on a group of dates in 1945 and 1948. Negotiations for compensation were carried on with each of the acquired companies.[14]

Despite the transfer of ownership, the morning of February 15 saw little change in the operation of Britain's iron
and steel industry. Nationalized iron and steel is organized
quite differently from any other state-owned industry in
Great Britain. The Corporation, consisting of seven members who operate as a board rather than functionally, is
empowered to appoint directors and special executives in
the constituent companies, and to review their major devel-

13. *The Times* (London), February 7, 8 and 14, 1951. The Liberal
members added an amendment to the original amendment to the
effect that "a privately owned monopoly, such as the iron and steel
industry has been, should be controlled in the public interest." *Ibid.,*
February 7, 1951.
14. *The Economist,* February 17, 1951, p. 386.

TABLE 3

STEEL INDUSTRY UNDER PUBLIC OWNERSHIP

Divisions of the Industry	Total (1949) Production	Publicly Owned Companies[a]
Scheduled activities	(In Thousands of Tons)	Per Cent
Production of:		
Iron ore	13,394.0	97.8
Pig iron	9,498.5	97.0
Carbon steel ingots	14,433.5	99.6
Alloy steel ingots	690.8	92.6
Hot rolled products:		
Plate	2,038.7	97.5
Sheet	1,430.3	92.6
Tin plate base	750.7	88.3
Other hot rolled products	6,732.6	90.3
Total hot rolled products	10,952.3	91.8
Other activities		
Production of:		
Cold rolled strip	273.3	73.4
Bright steel bars	307.8	16.7
Steel castings	236.1	24.1
Tires, wheels and axles	243.1	95.2
Steel forgings	163.0	48.0
Steel drop forgings	311.1	11.7
Hot finished tubes, pipes, fittings	989.8	70.1
Steel wire	783.1	44.0

Source: The Economist, February 17, 1951.

a. Ninety-two corporations were taken over, but 12 were subsidiaries.

Note: The companies acquired are named in the Third Schedule of the Iron and Steel Act; others, whose average annual output during 1946 and 1947 was less than the specified minimum, remain in private ownership subject to license by the Minister. Iron and Steel Act, 1949, Sec. 11; Second Schedule and Third Schedule, Sec. 29; The Times (London), January 16, 1951. Many of the publicly owned steel companies carry on activities other than the production or processing of steel.

opment projects and operating policies. The individual companies retain their individual identities, however, and they are continuing with their former boards of directors and their former policies. It is expected that, as in the past, they will compete with each other and with the privately owned companies outside the fold. It has been emphasized from the outset that the hand of the Corporation is to rest lightly on the day-to-day activities of the companies. Indeed, the Corporation is required by law "to secure the largest degree of decentralization consistent with the proper discharge" of its duties under the act.[15] In theory, the new organization is to blend the best of free, competitive individual initiative with the best of coordinated responsible behavior in the public interest.

The Corporation may form new companies, conduct and promote research, provide common services for its companies and assist in their financing. Its duty is to promote the efficient and economical supply of industry products, in the right types, qualities and sizes and at reasonable prices, and without undue preference or unfair discrimination.[16] The Corporation is required "to secure that the combined revenues of the Corporation and all the publicly owned companies taken together are not less than sufficient to meet their combined outgoings . . . taking one year with another."[17]

15. Iron and Steel Act, Sec. 3 (1,c). Following an expression of "desire" by the Corporation, five directors of Thomas Firth and John Brown, Ltd., resigned in July 1951. *The Economist,* August 4, 1951, p. 304.

16. The Iron and Steel Act, Secs. 2 and 3. Room is left for individual companies to exercise business discretion in price and supply matters; the Corporation's duty to prevent undue preference or unfair discrimination is "without prejudice to such variations in the terms and conditions . . . as may arise from ordinary commercial considerations or from the public interest." *Ibid.,* Sec. 3 (1,b). The Corporation may borrow short-term money or issue stock with the consent of the Minister and the Treasury, and its constituent companies may borrow temporarily with the consent of the Corporation. *Ibid.,* Sec. 32.

17. *Ibid.,* Sec. 31. The Minister of Supply approved an increase in steel prices in August 1951. *The Economist,* August 18, 1951, p. 413.

The Corporation is subject to direction by the Minister of Supply "in relation to matters which appear to him to affect the national interest," and specifically in carrying out programs of reorganization and development, and programs of research and employee-training. The Minister may direct the Corporation to discontinue or restrict any of its activities and to dispose of any of its assets, or to secure such action on the part of any of its companies.[18] He is required to set up an Iron and Steel Consumers' Council consisting of a chairman and from 15 to 30 other persons representing consumers of the industry's products to advise him and the Corporation on matters affecting consumer interests.[19]

The shift from private to public ownership was completely uneventful. The chairman of the Corporation called upon the industry to cooperate—"to forget politics, to accept the change . . . to come into the team, and give their help."[20] The private companies came only formally "into the team." They offered no obstruction, but neither did they offer cooperation. They gave no help in filling the roster of the Corporation, with the result that no prominent member of the industry is a member of the Corporation.[21] The British Iron and Steel Federation continues to function, with the express approval of the government, as the principal centralizing agency in the industry during the period of transition. The Minister of Supply proposed in the Commons debate of February 7, 1951, that an interim period of three

18. *Ibid.*, Sec. 4. Annual reports to be laid before Parliament, as well as special reports at the request of the Minister, are required of the Corporation. *Ibid.*, Sec. 4 (5,6,7).

19. The Council may act on its own motion, or at the request of the Minister, the Corporation, a consumer or any applicant for a producer's license. *Ibid.*, Sec. 6.

20. *The Times* (London), February 14, 1951.

21. Only two of the Corporation's seven members were drawn directly from the industry. The Minister of Supply and the Iron and Steel Federation differed, in public statements, as to whether the Federation had attempted to dissuade important men in the industry from serving on the Corporation or had taken the position only of advising any prospective appointee who consulted the Federation that he would be unwise to accept. *The Times* (London), September 22, 1950; *The Economist*, September 30, 1950, p. 548.

months following the vesting date be recognized, during which representatives of the Corporation would sit with and participate in the activities of the Federation's committees.[22] The Corporation announced on February 16, 1951, however, that it had been unable to reach agreement with the Federation on the necessary arrangements.[23]

Nationalization has occurred as a matter of law, but it seems clear that the industry will not consider itself as really nationalized, and will delay all government steps toward reorganization until and unless another general election returns the Labor government to power with a strong working majority. If the Conservative party should be voted into power, the steel industry would, of course, be denationalized as soon as possible.[24] In the meantime, the Corporation and the Federation will make the motions that have to be made; but the Federation will do its best to keep the industry in readiness for a return to private ownership, and the Corporation will be restrained in its assertion of authority.

ISSUES AHEAD

It is much too early to attempt a definitive appraisal of nationalization in Great Britain. Experience to date has been brief, and the record is equivocal both for the period itself and in what it suggests for the future. Nationalization has not brought the millennium to Britain, and it has not brought economic ruin; neither millennium nor economic ruin is in sight.

Events thus far, however, have given substance to many problems and issues that until recently had been considered and debated largely in the abstract. In addition, actual experience has brought to life issues hitherto dormant or con-

22. *The Times* (London), February 8, 1951.
23. *Ibid.*, February 17, 1951.
24. The Conservative manifesto for the 1951 election states flatly that the Iron and Steel Act "will be repealed," and promises to revive, "with added powers if necessary," the former Iron and Steel Board. *The Times* (London), September 29, 1951. It may well be that the problems of reselling the industry back into private hands would be more difficult than many have anticipated.

cealed. In surveying British nationalization at this stage it will probably be more useful to set out certain of these issues than to attempt broad generalizations respecting the success or failure of the program to date. When considering these, it will be useful to keep in mind that these issues are not academic or remote in Great Britain today; they are "hot" and immediate.

1. The nationalized industry as an "insulated" monopoly. The consumer may protect himself from abuse, inefficiency and indifference only by withholding his custom or by appeals to his representative in Parliament. His vote in a General Election serves little purpose in this connection, because he expresses himself at the ballot box on a bundle of issues, not on the partial conduct of a single industry. For instance, was the outcome of the 1950 General Election a mandate to go forward with nationalization, or a command by the electorate to slow down? If Parliament intervenes in behalf of the consumer it opens itself to the charge of political interference in the conduct of a business enterprise. If it keeps hands off, the consumer is at the mercy of an irresponsible monopoly. Can the consumer consultative-council device really be effective? Should nationalized industries be brought within the purview of government antimonopoly action?

2. The relation of the nationalized industry to the government of the day. To what extent should the government, in seeking to effectuate over-all policy (e.g., full-employment policy), dictate to the board of a nationalized industry on a matter which, in the absence of government policy considerations, would be handled differently as a matter of individual business judgment?

3. Price and service policy. Should prices be set on a strict business, cost-revenue basis, or should consumers be subsidized at the expense of taxpayers in the "public interest"? To what extent should some consumers be carried below cost at the expense of other consumers in the same industry? How should price conflicts between two or more nationalized industries be handled? Can the industry, with political

immunity, withdraw from rendering uneconomic services? What are the possibilities of price tribunals?

4. Centralization *versus* decentralization. A host of organization problems common to all large-scale enterprises, but aggravated by their setting in a nationalized industry where operations are carried on under blinding spotlights. Should board members be representatives of interest groups? Functional boards *versus* policy boards? The most effective combination of "line and staff" throughout the organization? Are stagnation and featherbedding inherent in nationalized industries?

5. The position of labor in a nationalized industry. What is the full effect of the loss of labor leadership by reason of the appointment of top union officials to better paying government positions? Does the "loyalty" of labor to its "own government" require it to relax demands for wage increases in the face of evidence that the nationalized industry cannot afford them; or in the face of a Labor government plea to stabilize wages in the public interest? To what extent can appeals and exhortations be substituted for straight economic incentives in attempts to improve performance? Must a Labor government—in order to remain in office—require its nationalized industries to accede to the demands of labor and further the long-run cause of labor?[25]

25. The *Political Quarterly* (London) devotes its April–June 1950 issue to the nationalized industries, raising a series of pertinent issues relating to organization and operation. The material appearing in this issue of the *Political Quarterly* has been expanded and brought up to date in book form, under the editorship of W. A. Robson, with the title *Problems of Nationalized Industry*, Allen & Unwin, London, 1951. See also A. H. Hanson, "Parliamentary Questions on the Nationalised Industries," *Public Administration*, Spring 1951, pp. 51–66; M. F. Scott, "Investment Policy in a Nationalized Industry," *Review of Economic Studies*, 1949–1950, pp. 179–88; A. Beacham, "Nationalization in Theory and Practice," *Quarterly Journal of Economics*, November 1950, pp. 550–58; *The Economist*, November 4, 1950, pp. 680–81; December 30, 1950, p. 1190; R. L. Heilbroner, "The Socialist Devils of England," *Harper's Magazine*, October 1951, p. 34.

CHAPTER 7

Town and Country Planning

DURING THE DECADES when the Industrial Revolution was transforming the economic character and molding the physical development of Great Britain, almost no restriction was applied on either the type or location of industrial, commercial or residential building. The land area of Great Britain is smaller than that of several of the states of the United States; its population is equal to a third of the entire population of all of the states. With fifty million people crowded into a limited space, the uses to which land is put is a matter of great public concern. Nonetheless, free enterprise and free individual choice in land use long had their way in Britain. Factory owners and builders put up what they pleased, where they pleased. Amenities were not preserved, and communities made no provision for sanitary housing, easy transport or proper educational and recreational facilities. Coordinated, long-term planning was entirely absent, and the result was uneconomic, unhealthy and inconvenient congestion in certain areas, "suburban sprawl," loss of agricultural land and defacing of the countryside.

Early Legislation

Early legislation, beginning with the House and Town Planning etc., Act of 1909, dealt with these matters. In 1932, however, the first complete code of planning law was enacted in the Town and Country Planning Act, and the structure and processes of land planning were established —on paper. According to this law, individual plots of land were considered not as isolated units which were of concern solely to their owners, but as parts of a larger whole in which the neighborhood and community and, indeed, the entire nation had a legitimate interest. Local authorities were authorized to prepare planning schemes for their areas; and, after notice was given that a plan was under preparation, any individual development undertaken without permission (granted or withheld by reference to what the plan was likely to be) was subject to later removal without compensation if it proved to be inconsistent with the plan finally established.

Planning on a regional basis was made possible by bringing the county councils into the picture. The act of 1932 extended the scope of planning to include both built-up areas and areas not scheduled for development, and sharpened the powers of the local authorities. The proportion of the increase in value which might be claimed by public authority under the betterment provisions[1] was raised from 50 to 75 per cent, but the postponement of public claims until gains were actually realized, was formalized. Powers of land acquisition were also strengthened.

Despite the formal legislation, however, town and country planning at the outbreak of World War II was still not an active force. In the words of the Scott report, "The story of the 1932 Act is one of high hopes and subsequent disappointment."[2]

The Problem of Compensation

Most of the land in Great Britain is held in private ownership. While private owners are subject, of course, to the regulations commonly imposed upon landowners by modern governments, the common law of England provides that owners "cannot be forced to give up their land or to use it in such a way as would be tantamount to an expropriation of property right or interest without being paid at a fair market price for loss of actual or potential develop-

1. See pp. 138, 146 ff.
2. *Report of the Committee on Land Utilisation in Rural Areas* [*Scott Report*], Cmd. 6378, H.M.S.O., 1942, p. 40. On this subject generally, see *ibid.*, pp. 39–44.

ment value."[3] Effective control of land development would, thus, have required the state to pay compensation to private owners.

Public control of land does not, it is contended, decrease the value of all the land; if it reduces the value of some land by forbidding development on it, the value of other tracts would be correspondingly increased, since the total demand for development is not affected by public regulation and its annual average rate is not changed. "If all the land of the country were in the ownership of a single person or body," wrote the Uthwatt committee, "the mere shifting of values from one piece of land to another would not call for any financial adjustments and the need for paying compensation . . . would disappear."[4] Since land, however, is owned by different persons, it would, theoretically at least, be possible to balance the compensation necessary to pay those who were injured by land control with the betterment charges assessed against those who were benefited by it.[5]

In practice, however, while landowners pressed claims against the public for compensation with alacrity and imagination, local authorities found it almost impossible to assess betterment charges with any accuracy or to make a convincing case for requiring the payment of charges in specific instances. The prices of *developed* land were high,

3. *Town and Country Planning in Britain*, British Information Services, May 1949, p. 9. See also *Report of the Royal Commission on the Distribution of the Industrial Population [Barlow Report]*, Cmd. 6153, H.M.S.O., 1940, pp. 112 ff.

4. *Report of the Expert Committee on Compensation and Betterment [Uthwatt Report]*, Cmd. 6386, H.M.S.O., 1942, pp. 15–16.

5. For a critical attack upon the concept of "shifting value," see Sir Arnold Plant, "Land Planning and the Economic Functions of Ownership," *Journal of the Chartered Auctioneers' and Estate Agents' Institute*, May 1949, p. 9: "the value of a piece of land depends, first, on its individual economic potentiality and secondly on the opportunities and willingness of risk-bearers to develop it, and exploit that potentiality. If development is prohibited on a piece of land which enjoys both a special potentiality and the favourable interest of a risk-bearer, it cannot be assumed that an equivalent result will erupt automatically elsewhere. There is no economic law of the conservation of value. . . ."

and the compensation or purchase price legally had to be calculated on the basis of the most profitable use to which the land might be put. Land already occupied by buildings was, of course, almost prohibitive for any public use such as road widening, open spaces, rebuilding of slum areas, industrial facilities, etc. Compensation for, or purchase of, *undeveloped* land involved fantastic calculations of *potential* development value.

If future development somewhere in the area seemed likely to occur, each landowner might reasonably claim that it was bound to occur on his land; and thus multiple claims over a wide area could arise out of a potential development that could possibly take place only on a single plot. In other words, "potential building value is necessarily a 'floating value' and it is practically impossible to predict where it will settle."[6] On the other hand, in ascertaining the betterment charge, "there immediately arises the difficulty of establishing the amount by which a particular parcel of land has increased in value as the direct consequence of the restriction imposed on the other land and not from other causes."[7]

Further, betterment was recoverable only on realization within a maximum period of fourteen years, and subject to the governing provisions of the Town and Country Planning Act of 1932, which was still the basic legislation in effect when the Labor government assumed office. The result was that when public planning of land use was put into operation through restriction or purchase, either compensation or purchase price had to be paid by the public, whereas the betterment charge could rarely be collected. The *net* result was that public authorities could not afford to put land planning into general operation:

. . . planning has so far been governed almost entirely by short-term financial considerations. Because local authorities have not been able to afford to pay heavy compensation for loss of

6. *Report on the Preservation of the Countryside,* Minister of Health's Town and Country Planning and Advisory Committee, as reported in *Town and Country Planning in Britain,* p. 10.

7. *Uthwatt Report,* p. 16.

development values, they have had to allow building to take place in too haphazard a manner. Suburbs have spread in a mass of houses unbroken by open spaces. Where some open space has been left it has been far too little because the planning authority have striven to keep the shift of values within their own area. When local authorities buy land they have had to pay prices swollen by "floating value." As a result there has been a tendency to site schools, clinics, libraries wherever land was cheapest, often at great inconvenience to the people who use them.[8]

Negative Approach to Land Planning

Another major impediment to public planning of land use throughout the interwar period lay in the structure of, and the approach reflected by, the planning system. Planning was made the business of local authorities, and although sometimes the authorities formed themselves into joint bodies for regional action, national considerations received only secondary and sporadic attention. Many local authorities were entirely inactive, and joint committees (whose make-up coincided only fortuitously with "natural" regional requirements) were frequently subjected to the pressure of local interest. Private interests were left to undertake land development and, in the absence of a central driving and coordinating force, public planning was concerned more with what should not be done than with what should. It could forbid abuses and within limits it could prevent bad development, but it was powerless to require good development. In a large measure it acquiesced in plans drawn up by private developers. Planning procedures fixed by statute were characterized by long-drawn-out consultations and negotiations; the entire process suggested leisurely futility.

The Barlow Commission

In the years of the war definite progress occurred—first, in the appearance of three successive ground-breaking re-

8. *Town and Country Planning Bill, 1947: Explanatory Memorandum,* Ministry of Town and Country Planning, Cmd. 7006, H.M.S.O., 1947, p. 8.

ports and second, in the governmental action that immediately followed.

The Barlow commission was appointed in 1937

. . . to inquire into the causes which have influenced the present geographical distribution of the industrial population of Great Britain and the probable direction of any change in that distribution in the future; to consider what social, economic or strategical disadvantages arise from the concentration of industries or of the industrial population in large towns or in particular areas of the country; and to report what remedial measures if any should be taken in the national interest.[9]

After two years of investigation and study, the commission found that "the disadvantages in many, if not in most of the great industrial concentrations, alike on the strategical, the social, and the economic side, do constitute serious handicaps and even in some respects dangers to the nation's life and development," and that definite remedial action should be taken by the government.[10] The problems, it went on to emphasize, "are national in character," and their solution "must be sought along the lines of national inquiry and national guidance."[11]

The members of the commission were not of one mind on all points, but they were unanimous in their conclusions that "national action is necessary," that "a Central Authority, national in character, is required," and that the activities of the authority "should be distinct from and should extend beyond those within the powers of any existing Government Department." They agreed, also, that the objectives of national action should be redevelopment of congested urban areas; decentralization or dispersal both of industries and industrial population from such areas; and encouragement of a reasonable balance of industrial development throughout the various regions of Great Britain, with appropriate diversification within each region.[12]

9. *Barlow Report*, p. 1.
10. *Ibid.*, p. 195.
11. *Ibid.*, p. 201.
12. *Ibid.*, pp. 201–02.

The majority of the commission recommended that the national authority take the form of a national industrial board, under the Board of Trade, with functions to include the collection and coordination of information relative to location of industry, research and collection of information bearing on such resources as land, agriculture and amenities that may be affected by industrial location, and advice to any interested party on the problems of industrial location. The board was to report on the nature and extent of such further powers as it might require to give effect to the objectives outlined by the commission, and was to exercise licensing powers over the establishment of any new industrial undertakings proposed in the area of London and the surrounding counties.[13]

The Scott Committee

The Committee on Land Utilisation in Rural Areas (Scott Committee) was appointed by the Minister of Works and Buildings, in October 1941, "to consider the conditions which should govern building and other constructional development in country areas consistently with the maintenance of agriculture" together with the relation of the location of industry to such matters as "part-time and seasonal employment, the well-being of rural communities and the preservation of rural amenities."[14] Its report, rendered in August 1942, while concerned primarily with the protection of agricultural land and the preservation of natural amenities, was in essential agreement with the conclusion of the Barlow commission that the organization of the planning function demanded a centralized national authority.[15]

13. *Ibid.*, pp. 204–07. The members of the commission who submitted supplementary and dissenting reports were generally in favor of more positive and far-reaching governmental activity than the majority was prepared to recommend. *Ibid.*, pp. 208–43.

14. *Scott Report*, p. iv.

15. *Ibid.*, pp. 80–82. The committee's recommendations bearing on the substantive issues involved in the future of rural areas are set forth, in summary, on pages 91–99 of the report.

The Uthwatt Committee

The Barlow commission had considered the vexing questions of compensation and betterment; but, after analyzing the problems and outlining proposals that were brought to its attention, it had concluded with the unanimous recommendation that the government should appoint a body of experts to examine the questions of compensation, betterment and development generally.[16] This suggestion was acted on promptly, and in January 1941, the Minister of Works and Buildings named an Expert Committee on Compensation and Betterment (Uthwatt Committee) to analyze the subject of "the payment of compensation and recovery of betterment in respect of public control of the use of land" and "to advise, as a matter of urgency, what steps should be taken now or before the end of the war to prevent the work of reconstruction thereafter being prejudiced."[17]

The Uthwatt report was presented to Parliament in September 1942, and the general course it proposed was adopted as the government's approach to the problem on which, hitherto, all positive efforts at planning had foundered. Planning on a national basis and as a positive force was, once more, the keynote of the report; its principal recommendation advocated acquisition by the state, on payment of fair compensation, of development rights in private holdings of land, and prohibition of private development without state consent.[18] The committee's proposals on this score have been summarized as follows:

(a) that the State should acquire development rights of all land outside built-up areas, with fair compensation on a "global

16. *Barlow Report,* pp. 117, 203.
17. *Uthwatt Report,* p. 1.
18. "We wish to make it clear . . . that the system we regard as necessary for an effective reconstruction, and which we have therefore assumed, is one of national planning with a high degree of initiation and control by the Central Planning Authority, which will have national as well as local considerations in mind, will base its action on organised research into the social and economic aspects of the use and

basis in ratio to market values at March 31, 1939." Such land
should be compulsorily acquired at the residual agricultural
value if and when needed for development, and be granted to
the developer on leasehold only; . . .

(b) that all land should be deemed from a fixed date to be
covered by a Planning Resolution; . . .

(f) that the betterment problem should be dealt with by a
periodic levy (of, say 75 per cent) on the increase on annual site
values of all developed land, whatever the reason for such increase of values, the values to be assessed quinquennially by the
machinery in being for rating purposes.[19]

Britain's wartime Coalition government responded vigorously and with imagination to the flow of official recommendations. The Ministry of Town and Country Planning
was established in 1943 to take over central planning powers
from the Ministry of Works and Planning, and to insure
"consistency and continuity in the framing and execution
of a national policy with respect to the use of the land." Top
level administration of land planning on a national basis
was at last formally accepted. The Town and Country Planning (Interim Development) Act of 1943, supplemented by
the Town and Country Planning (General Interim Development) Order of 1945, placed all land not yet covered by
a planning scheme under a "planning resolution"; gave
local authorities additional powers (of refusal, revocation
and direct action) over interim development; and gave the
minister further powers (both mandatory and of review)
over local authorities.[20]

development of land, and will have the backing of national financial
resources where necessary for a proper execution of its policy.

"It is apparent, therefore, that the Central Planning Authority we
have assumed is an organisation which does not yet exist, and that
'planning' has a meaning not attached to it in any legislation nor,
until recently, in the minds of the public." *Ibid.*, p. 12.

19. *Town and Country Planning in Britain*, pp. 16–17. (The recommendations are summarized in detail in the *Uthwatt Report*, Chap.
12.)

20. *Ibid.*, pp. 17–18.

The White Paper and Legislation of 1944

In June 1944, the Coalition government published its views on land planning in a White Paper—a statement that indicated the distance all parties had come in their thinking since 1932.[21] The aims of planning policy were catalogued with great fullness; it was suggested that powers of public purchase of land be facilitated and that the exercise of development rights in the hands of private owners be subject to the control of planning authorities; and a government position on compensation and betterment was announced —for public discussion.

The White Paper modified (because of "practical" considerations) the Uthwatt proposals to provide for (1) public control, mainly through licenses to develop, of all land use; (2) payment by landowners of a betterment charge of 80 per cent of the added value of their land arising through permission to develop it; (3) payment to owners of fair compensation, upon refusal of permission, for any loss of value that existed on March 31, 1939—the compensation to include nothing for "floating" or potential value (although the *individual right* to compensation should be determined at an early date and the level of payment should be decided at the end of five years); and (4) the assessment and payment of compensation, and assessment and collection of betterment to be centered in a national land commission, leaving local authorities free to plan, without financial responsibility.[22]

Legislative action followed at once—although it did not embrace the full program that had been suggested. The Town and Country Planning Act of 1944 was designed to make it possible and easier for local authorities, with the consent of the Minister, to purchase land under a wide variety of conditions and for a wide range of purposes, e.g., war-damaged areas, areas characterized by obsolete development and bad layout, and land required for relocation of

21. *Control of Land Use*, Cmd. 6537, H.M.S.O., 1944.
22. *Town and Country Planning in Britain*, pp. 18–19.

population and industry or to secure balanced development. Compulsory public purchase was provided for, and
a new device—the declaratory order—was contrived to enable land to be scheduled effectively for compulsory public
purchase in advance of immediate and pressing need.

Other provisions in the act were pointed toward increased collaboration between local authorities in planning
matters, particularly with reference to the problems of
congestion and relocation of population. Emphasis was to
be placed on private development through the leasing of
lands appropriated by local authorities—thus combining
public direction and control with private assumption of
risk. Local authorities were required by the act to clear
their plans with the Minister before final steps were taken,
and other provisions of the act strengthened even more the
supervisory and reviewing powers of the Minister.

Still other clauses covered such matters as government
financial assistance in planning programs, and protection of
open spaces and common land and buildings of special
architectural or historical interest. The controversy on
compensation and betterment, however, had not sufficiently
crystallized to permit definitive action at this time, and
the act was silent on this most annoying of all planning
problems.

The Labor Government Revises the Law

It remained for the Labor government, in the Town and
Country Planning Act of 1947,[23] to deal head-on with compensation and betterment, and to introduce what appeared
to be a larger measure of centralization, positiveness and
flexibility into the nation's planning machinery. The act
introduced "a new planning system whereby such projects
as the reconstruction and redevelopment of entire towns,
the preservation of green belts, the provision of open spaces
in overcrowded areas, and the allocation of land for new
houses, factories and community buildings in the right

23. Town and Country Planning Act, 1947, 10 & 11 George 6,
Ch. 51.

place became practical possibilities which can and will be put into effect."[24] It was bold in its sweep and in the intimacy of its contact. But it was not so bold as many had hoped; it did not provide for nationalization of the land, and the compromise devices which it established in lieu of nationalization were so intricately contrived as to jeopardize the working of the act.

To achieve its objectives, against the background of floundering and frustration, the act repealed or consolidated existing planning legislation (except the act of 1943, the New Towns Act of 1946[25] and those parts of the act of 1944 concerned with redevelopment of specified areas); established a Central Land Board under the Minister; named councils of counties and county boroughs as the local planning authorities, and set up an elaborate schedule for the allocation of functions among authorities, councils, boards and committees; imposed upon authorities the *duty* of conducting a survey and preparing a development plan for their respective areas; provided expressly that, with a few exceptions, no development (inclusively defined as "the carrying out of building, engineering, mining, or other operations in, on, over or under land, or the making of any material change in the use of any buildings or other land") might proceed without permission; provided a comprehensive system for controlling outdoor advertisements; and added to the already well-stocked armory of powers and procedures for compulsory public (minister, board, authorities, councils, etc.) purchase of land.

The distinctive contribution of the 1947 act, however, consisted in the thirty-five clauses dealing with "Payments out of Central Funds in Respect of Depreciation of Land Values," "Development Charges" and "Application to Special Cases."[26] Briefly, the act provided that (with minor exceptions) any change in the use of land, whether by a

24. *Town and Country Planning in Britain,* p. 3.
25. See pp. 154 ff.
26. Parts VI (Clauses 58–68), VII (Clauses 69–74), and VIII (Clauses 75–92), respectively.

present owner or a prospective purchaser, be subject to permission from the local planning authorities, and that permission for all future development become finally effective only upon payment of a development charge assessed by, and payable to, the Central Land Board. The amount of the development charge was to equal the difference between the "restricted" (or "use") value of the land in its existing use and its value in the new use or "development." Development rights as private property were cut off, and land, thenceforth, was supposed to be transferred from owner to new owner at the value for the use to which it was actually being put at the time of the sale.

Existing owners were thus deprived of any benefit from increased value of their land arising from development, but the act, while specifically denying any *right* to compensation, nonetheless provided a fund of £300 million from which compensation was to be paid by the Board to existing owners who could establish claims, in order that hardships might be alleviated. It was realized that many land owners had paid prices for their land based on its increased value for development purposes. Since the act required owners to pay a development charge to the Board in the event of permitted development, failure to compensate owners would have subjected them to a double payment. Instead of postponing determination and payment in each case until such time as planning permission might be requested and either denied (thus restricting development rights) or granted (thus subjecting the owner to a development charge), it was decided to establish a global sum for compensation and open the door for the presentation and determination of all claims on an over-all scale—thus settling the entire matter at one time, for always.

Claims were submitted, under the act, prior to June 30, 1949, by all landowners who considered that their land had development value as of the "appointed day." It then became the duty of the Central Land Board to divide the global sum between England and Wales on one hand and Scotland on the other, and to prepare a scheme (subject to review by Parliament) for payment of the individual claims, as approved, from the global sum. Payments, in the form of government stock, are to be made not later than June 30, 1953.[27]

Method of Estimating Global Compensation

The atmosphere surrounding the framing and passage of the 1947 act is suggested by the way in which the government estimated £300 million as the amount of the global compensation fund. The Barlow report had mentioned the conclusion of one expert that the cost of compensation "might be in the region of £400 million" and had characterized this figure as an "intelligent guess." The Uthwatt committee had suggested a calculation which involved "taking the rate of development of undeveloped land outside towns at 45,000 acres per annum—the average rate of development in the immediate pre-war years—and the average development value at £200 per acre," arriving at a resultant annual figure of £9 million, and then capitalizing this figure at an appropriate (unnamed) rate. The government followed through on this calculation—employing a figure of "15 to 16 years' purchase"—and reached a "rounded-up" capital sum of £150 million. The sum was

27. The government considered the possibility of determining compensation piecemeal, that is, building up the global sum by adding together individual claims as made and allowed, but decided that this would not produce a fair sum—"that is, a fair sum to the community . . . In the Uthwatt view, by reason of floating value, between two and three times too much would be paid if piecemeal valuation formed the basis of compensation." Emphasizing the exaggerated nature of floating value, the Minister of Town and Country Planning pointed out that the amount of land zoned for housing in England and Wales under draft schemes in 1937, when less than half the country was covered by such schemes was sufficient to provide accommodation for nearly 350 million people—many times the number who would ever actually use the land for housing. Land zoned for housing presumably has "development value," but it is clear that only a small portion of the zoned land would ever, in fact, come to have a real development value equal to the amount projected. *Parliamentary Debates* (Hansard), House of Commons, Vol. 432, cols. 977–78.

then doubled, to cover, as well, "the development and re-development value of land in built-up areas," and the result was £300 million "which is exactly the amount of the global sum."

The government took notice of many factors indicating that this amount was excessive, but, since future trends could not be calculated with certainty, preferred to err, if at all, on the side of generosity. The crowning touch in the government's presentation of the calculation was the Minister's remark to Parliament: "Such figures as I have given, I have mentioned merely to indicate that the £300 million was not arbitrarily decided upon . . . and that, taking account of all the circumstances, and making the best calculations possible [this figure] can be accepted as a reasonable one."[28]

When land is acquired under compulsory purchase the price paid by the public will be equal to the restricted or existing use value calculated on current prices, and under ordinary circumstances the landowner has no claim to compensation if his request for permission to develop is refused. Thus, as one study puts it:

The combined effect of these provisions . . . is to "peg" the value of the land to its use on the "appointed day" plus such development charges as have been paid. . . . in the future the market value of land will be the same as if the land were sold subject to a perpetual restriction limiting its use to that on the appointed day, a restriction which can be lifted from time to time only by paying a development charge to the Central Land Board (after planning permission has been obtained) equal to the increased value of the land for the use for which permission

28. *Parliamentary Debates* (Hansard), House of Commons, Vol. 432, cols. 979–82. The Minister was answering the contention that the act should provide for an expert committee to determine an appropriate figure, rather than to name an arbitrary amount out of hand. See also, in col. 1226, the statement by the Chancellor of the Exchequer: "There is no logical method of calculating this thing. Therefore, we had to make a guess at what would be reasonable. My right hon. Friend has made his guess, I think it is as good as anyone else's guess."

has been granted. Thereafter, the market value of the land is held to be its use or restricted value for the use now permitted, and a change of use must be accompanied by new planning permission and payment of a new development charge.[29]

How "Positive Planning" Is Done

In administering the new "positive planning" features of the 1947 act, the Minister, while given extensive authority and responsibility, is still not free from potential entanglements with other ministers or with contrary-minded or lethargic local planning authorities. The Central Land Board, appointed by and responsible to the Minister, is

29. D. Monson and A. Monson, "The Development and Practice of Compensation and Betterment in Present English Planning Law," *Land Economics,* May 1949, p. 179. The following advice by the Central Land Board to prospective purchasers of land is instructive: "(1) . . . building value now belongs to the State and not to the seller. (2) *Always* ask first (and before the price is settled) whether the development charge is going to be paid to the Central Land Board by you or by the seller. (3) Do not buy as part of the purchase price of the land the seller's claim on the £300 million fund. The right to a payment from the fund is not yet established and its amount cannot yet be known. The amount will in any case be related to the circumstances of the owner of the land on 1st July, 1948, and not to those of any new buyer. A buyer of such a claim is therefore buying a risk at a 'certainty' price. (4) If the *seller* agrees to pay the development charge, ask him the amount which he has agreed with the Central Land Board. You can then safely pay building value for the land in the knowledge that you yourself will not be liable for any development charge, when the seller has paid it. (5) If *you* are to pay the development charge (and, unless the seller is willing to pay it, you will have to do so) you should never pay building value for the land. If you do, you will be charged the building value over again in your development charge. You should pay what is known as existing use value and no more. A rough guide to existing use value of land is its value to use it as it is actually being used (as, for example, agricultural, allotment, or garden land) with a prohibition against erecting any building on it except for agriculture." *Advice on Buying and Selling a Site for Building a House,* Central Land Board, 1948. Analogous advice is given to sellers, and the statement concludes: "If sellers will sell, and purchasers will only buy, as advised in this pamphlet, land can be sold at a price which will not hinder or prevent houses being built."

concerned almost exclusively with adjudication of claims on the compensation fund, and ascertainment of development charges. The local planning authorities, on whom rests the burden of initiating development plans, are the councils of counties and county boroughs. This means that, while the planning units are larger and fewer than under earlier legislation, they are still bodies whose principal duties are in areas other than planning and whose make-up is not determined by the Minister.[30]

The core of the new system for positive planning lies in the development plans. Each local planning authority is required to carry out a survey and to prepare a development plan for its area. The act specifies:

The survey will involve a physical, economic and sociological analysis of the potentialities and future requirements of the area, dealing, for example, with natural resources, distribution of industry, communications, housing requirements, the community structure. It will provide the evidence on which the proposals in the plan are based.

The plan, which will consist of a series of maps and documents, must be submitted to the Minister within three years of the appointed day (although the period may be extended in particular cases). As initially submitted it will usually be in the nature of an "outline" plan, and will show, for example, major road improvements, the land to be reserved for agriculture, the part of a town destined for comprehensive redevelopment and the direction in which a town may expand. It will also show broadly the stages by which development is to be carried out, and it may designate as subject to compulsory acquisition the land needed in the first stages. . . . The local planning authority can at any time submit proposals for alterations or additions

30. The local planning authority may delegate its functions to a committee with a minority of nonauthority members (and the committee may delegate its functions to subcommittees); provision is made for consultation with county district councils, and the district councils are given substantial responsibility for putting development plans into effect. The Minister may enlarge a planning unit by establishing a joint board consisting of two or more local authorities. The number of local planning authorities was reduced by the act from more than a thousand to less than two hundred.

to the plan, so that it can be brought up to date whenever necessary, or so that details can be filled in over a part of the area when development is about to take place. Every five years the authority are required to carry out a fresh survey and review the plan.[31]

The Minister has extensive power over the activities of local planning authorities, both in the making and in the administration of plans—power to initiate action, to amend and, on appeal, to modify or revoke. On paper, the planning reins are firmly in his grasp, and the whip is close to his hand. Nonetheless, as one critic has pointed out, "whatever concerted planning is to be carried out depends, initially at least, solely upon the local authorities. . . . under all circumstances [the Minister] must operate through them. Hence, the degree and quality of the national physical planning that might be brought about must arise mainly as a result of a hoped-for congruence among these local plans and confluence of them. Although they may be modified by the general guidance and tutelary coercions of the Minister, the initiative lies in local hands."[32] This, however, is not only the weakness but the strength of democratic planning.

Too Early to Appraise Results

It is much too early to attempt a definitive appraisal of Britain's planning machinery in operation. Much criticism has developed—a good deal more, in fact, than was apparent when the act was on its way through Parliament. Most of the criticism, however, is directed at results that are feared rather than results that have been experienced.

A large number of surveys and plans have been made,

31. *Town and Country Planning Bill, 1947: Explanatory Memorandum, Part I—General Notes*, pp. 6–7. See also Part II of the act, and the discussion by the Minister of Town and Country Planning, in *Parliamentary Debates* (Hansard), House of Commons, Vol. 432, cols. 961–63.

32. Robert A. Brady, *Crisis in Britain*, University of California Press, Berkeley, 1950, pp. 426–27.

but the shortage of materials and labor in relation to the great and varied demand for their use, has served to hold actual development (planned and unplanned) within narrow limits. However, the structure of local government in Britain, together with the democratic character of its political institutions, is likely to prevent for many decades (if not forever) anything approaching a full fruition of the planning dream.

Surveys and plans have already gone far enough in connection with the great metropolitan regions—London, Birmingham and others—to demonstrate that cities and regions can be thoroughly planned only on a national basis and as part of a national plan. It is equally plain that in Great Britain the drawing and execution of plans affecting the physical layout of localities is going to be carried out mainly by local authorities. The structure of planning laid down in the 1947 legislation, with the local planning authorities still held responsible for the work, was not the ideal of planning experts—but neither was it accidental. Conciliation and coordination of local interests will occur and national interests will make themselves felt, but the systematic yielding of localities to anything but the most flexible of national plans is simply not in the cards. There is little evidence that the issue will be pressed.[33] And in so far as the difficulty is aggravated by the outmoded structure of local government, any changes that may be made are not likely to be designed primarily for the purpose of facilitating planning.

The New Towns

The opportunity for the full exercise of positive planning powers would seem to have been created by the passage of the New Towns Act of 1946,[34] following the submission by the New Towns Committee of two interim

33. *Ibid.*, pp. 426–41. The difficulty is inherent in the British political character—it is not peculiarly a "defect" either of planning legislation or of planning administration.

34. New Towns Act, 1946, 9 & 10 George 6, Ch. 68.

reports and a final report. The act empowered the Minister of Town and Country Planning, after consultation with the local authorities concerned, to designate any area (including the area of an existing town) as the site of a new town, and to establish corporations for the development of new towns on such sites. Plans are to be developed by the corporation and if approved by the Minister will serve to set the pattern for all development permission. Each corporation may acquire, hold, manage and dispose of land, and, subject to the Minister's approval, may employ compulsory acquisition; may take over the supplying of public utility and other services and may provide housing accommodations. Annual reports by the corporations are to be laid before Parliament, and when the purposes of the corporation have been gained, it is to be dissolved and its properties are to be transferred to the local authority covering the area. Capital cost, to be repaid, is to be advanced to the corporation from a consolidated fund.

Both new and extension towns are contemplated and variety and experimentation rather than uniformity will be sought. Populations of from 30,000 to 50,000 are regarded as optimum for the new towns, but with a related district may be somewhat larger.

A balanced social and economic composition is desired; layout, facilities and services are to reflect the best in modern planning. By the end of March 1949, nine development corporations had been established; the master plan of one corporation had been approved, another had been submitted, and the plans of three corporations were nearing completion. Considerable land had been acquired, and building construction and the provision of services were under way.[35]

35. See *Reports of the Ayecliffe, Crawley, Harlow, Hatfield, Hemel Hempstead, Peterlee, Stevenage and Welwyn Garden City Development Corporations for the period ending 31st March, 1949,* H.M.S.O., July 1949. The Crawley corporation appended a list of "consultations and approvals required for the execution of plans," and of "authorities whose plans and projects have to be co-ordinated with those of the corporation." *Ibid.,* p. 58.

New town sites "have been chosen with very careful consideration of such matters as the size of the area, the accessibility of water, gas and electricity, situation in the light of future industrial development, and the claims of agriculture. Nearly all will be extensions of existing small towns. . . ."[36]

It is by no means certain that events will justify the early optimism. *The Economist* comments that the report of the new towns corporations for the year ended March 31, 1950, "provides fresh evidence that the Government does not understand how to build a town." Particular reference was made in the report to the "tangled thicket of controls," and *The Economist* decried Whitehall's "passion for perfection and uniformity. . . . over four years after the passing of the New Towns Act, the programme is still hanging fire."[37]

Despite the apparent opportunity to build from scratch, the new town project presents in somewhat different form many of the problems and uncertainties that characterize planning generally in Britain. Professor Brady points out that "decentralization dominated the thinking behind the New Towns Act," and that it is becoming "impossible to tell where new-towns development began and replanning of old towns left off." Difficulties arising from jurisdictional overlaps and jealousies will reappear when the new towns are turned over to their respective local authorities. Thus, a national plan into which the new towns will fit, and under which the development of the new towns will dovetail

36. *Town and Country Planning in Britain*, p. 31.

37. *The Economist*, December 9, 1950, p. 990. For particular reference to "cumbrous controls" and the "profusion of officials," see *The Times* (London), December 5, 1950. For a defense of the new-towns agencies, see the statement of the chairman of the Crawley Development Corporation as reported in *The Economist*, October 6, 1951, p. 788. By March 31, 1951, 933 houses and 150,000 square feet of factory space had been built and occupied; 3,082 houses and 490,000 square feet of factory space were under construction. *Town and Country Planning, 1943–1951*, Cmd. 8204, H.M.S.O., 1951, p. iii (*The Economist* characterized the results as "paltry," in its issue of May 12, 1951, pp. 1085–86.) For the story of the new towns from the viewpoint of the Ministry concerned, see *ibid.*, Chap. 9.

with the development plans for the "city regions" of which
they are satellites, is a clear necessity. It is crucial, then,
whether or not the careful consideration in selecting sites
for new towns is to be taken as indicating the existence
(formally or *de facto*) of such a plan.[38]

Has Development Been Retarded?

Such concern over the Town and Country Planning Act
of 1947 as was expressed in the Commons debate on the
second reading was leveled largely at the failure of the government to go all out for nationalization (from members
generally favorable), and at the alleged inadequacy of the
compensation provisions (from those on the opposite side of
the floor).[39] In the months that have followed, however, the
provisions governing development permission and development charges have proved to be the principal target. The
attack has called into question both the theory and admin-

38. See R. A. Brady, *op. cit.*, pp. 441–45.
39. Note particularly the jibes by the leader of the Liberal party, in
Parliamentary Debates (Hansard), House of Commons, Vol. 432, col.
1004, and the defense offered by the Labor party (col. 1009) that "We
did not have it [nationalisation] in our election programme in 1945."
See also the statement by the Chancellor of the Exchequer (Mr. Dalton), later to become Minister of Town and Country Planning, "We
are moving toward the nationalisation of the land, and not by slow
steps," *ibid.*, col. 1230. The amendment offered by the Opposition to
the motion for second reading stressed the inordinate haste with
which the bill was being pushed, the arbitrary treatment of compensation, the looseness of the development charge provisions, the use of an
outdated and inadequate standard of values in the case of compulsory
acquisition of land, and the uncertainty created by the fact that
matters which should have been carefully defined in the legislation
were left for decision by subsequent orders. *Ibid.*, col. 1129. "The
inadequate standard of values in the case of compulsory acquisition"
related to the 1939 standard embodied in the original bill. As the act
finally emerged, this was changed to use value "calculated on current
prices."
In the main, however, the Opposition was singularly indifferent
throughout the entire debate: on the evening of the second day, it
was pointed out that "their biggest attendance so far today in this
Debate has been 15. At one point their numbers sank to three, and
now they are getting up to 15 again." *Ibid.*, col. 1168.

istration of the development charge and the procedure and practice involved in seeking permission to develop. The Ministry and the Central Land Board have issued many instructions and comments, and a stream of critical literature has appeared and continues to flow.

The burden of the charges is that delay, confusion and inequities have resulted and that much-needed development has been slowed almost to a standstill. It is argued that permission is required for changes in structure and use of the most inconsequential sort and that the processes of decision-making at this point and later in fixing the amount of the development charge are irritating to the point of exasperation. The standard practice is to assess development charges in amounts equal to the full difference between existing use value and value in the permitted contemplated use, and this, it is alleged, removes almost completely any desire on the part of the owner either to develop or to sell his property. Examples are cited at length of individual inequities that have resulted and of absurdities that have occurred in specific cases—always with "and so he decided not to go ahead with the improvement" or "and so he withdrew the property from the market" as the clinching conclusion.[40]

The answers of the government's defenders are, first, to deny the allegations of delay—decisions on development

40. Among the best-considered critical statements are two articles by Sir Arnold Plant: "Land Planning and the Functions of Ownership," *Westminster Bank Review,* May 1948, pp. 1–8; and "Land Planning and the Economic Functions of Ownership," *Journal of the Chartered Auctioneers' and Estate Agents' Institute,* May 1949, pp. 1–17. Professor Plant argues that any expropriation of development rights should be confined to undeveloped (including agricultural) land; that the attempt to apply detailed control over every material change in use of developed land seriously hinders and endangers the prompt and effective redeployment of Britain's resources at a critical stage; that the task of assessing development charges for every material change in the use of developed land constitutes an impossible burden; and that, apart from objections to principles, the sheer burden of administering the act in its present application is greater than the country can afford at this time.

charges are given in ordinary cases within a month of application—and, second, to attribute any retarded development and movement of property to shortage of resources and labor and the newness of the procedures rather than to any inherent defects of the scheme. Planning has probably taken much of the blame which should properly have been directed to the building licensing authorities and to the general policy that has favored public over private housing.

Many critics who are friendly to planning are now urging that the development charges be assessed at something less than the full difference between existing use value and value in the permitted use, both as a measure of fairness to owners who, it is feared, will be inadequately reimbursed from the compensation fund, and to serve as an incentive for development. It is pointed out that this was contemplated in the Uthwatt report and also, at the outset, by the government itself.[41]

There is, as well, concern over the fact that the development charge, at best, can never be determined with scientific correctness, and that the process has come, upon occasion, to resemble a "deal" between the applicant and the Board. Those who feel this concern sometimes overlook that under typical market conditions the determination of the price of a piece of land by the "higgling" between buyer and seller is not itself an exact process. The Central Land Board has from the outset encouraged discussions and negotiations between applicants and official valuers. "The process is not so much one of bargaining," it says, "but rather of investigating merits in the light of all available information."[42]

In the opinion of the Board, sales of land for develop-

41. Thus, in the Commons debate the Minister reminded the "hon. members that the Board will be working under the Minister's general directions, and that no Minister, and no Board, would ever fix the charges so high that development would be prevented." *Parliamentary Debates* (Hansard), House of Commons, Vol. 432, col. 984. See also, *ibid.*, col. 983.

42. *Report of the Central Land Board for the financial year 1949–50,* H.M.S.O., 1950, p. 6.

ment at prices equal to or near existing use value "are more the exception than the rule." Building licenses are difficult to obtain, and the developer who has one is often willing to pay an inflated price for land even though he is liable, in addition, for payment of a development charge. He "is still paying less in the total cost of his house than he would have to pay for an existing house with vacant possession."[43]

Although the act conveys large powers (with a full array of standards and procedures) of compulsory public acquisition of land, which may be employed in cases of refusal by owners to sell at "existing value," no one in a responsible position seems to advocate or even to contemplate any considerable use of these powers either as a program or as a threat. Up to April 1, 1950, about 1,200 applications for such action had been made to the Central Land Board, but only 15 compulsory purchase orders had been issued, of which ten had been confirmed by the Minister.[44]

Recommendations for Change

Possibly the most useful list of responsible and reasonably objective recommendations for change is that contained in a statement issued early in 1950 by the Town and Country Planning Association, which urged consideration of the following measures:

1. Amendment of the Development Charge Regulations . . . to reduce the percentage of charge so that a reasonable incentive to dispose of land is restored.

2. Liberalization of the practice in levying development charges, especially in cases of extensions of existing uses within sites approved for such uses. This does not imply that the requirement to obtain planning permission should be waived.

3. The powers of guiding the location of industry to be op-

43. *Ibid.*, p. 10. "The Board's policy throughout has been to discourage people from buying and selling land for development at inflated prices." The tendency for land sales to take place at prices above existing use value continued through the following year. See the *Report of the Central Land Board for 1950–51*, as reported in *The Economist*, August 25, 1951, p. 441.

44. *Report of the Central Land Board, 1949–50*, pp. 11–12.

erated so as to check as far as practicable new establishments and extensions in congested areas and actively to promote them in new towns and suitable country towns. Additional powers may be necessary to prevent the reoccupation of vacated factories for industry, subject to fair compensation.

4. Closer coordination between Government Departments responsible for various aspects of development in their claims for land use, including location of industry, agriculture, housing, service requirements, mineral workings and transport. As the Ministry of Town and Country Planning is the only Ministry that has the function of judging claims for land use in the light of all the factors, its position should be strengthened, and the Minister should be of senior status. Any major departmental issue concerning land use should be dealt with by a Cabinet Committee of which the Minister of Town and Country Planning should be chairman.[45]

The Economist takes the position that

the basic defect of the . . . Act is that it sacrifices all other considerations to that of making public planning powers effec-

45. "The Working of the Town and Country Planning Act, 1947," *Town and Country Planning*, February 1950, pp. 5–6. See also the comments by F. J. Osborn in "Planning and Its Critics," *Town and Country Planning*, May 1950, pp. 172–76. The *Journal of the Town Planning Institute* for September–October 1949, contains a symposium (pp. 225–37) under the title, "The 1947 Act: The First Year." For another symposium, see "The Working of the Town and Country Planning Act," *Journal of the Royal Institute of British Architects*, July 1950, pp. 335–41. In May 1950, the Royal Institution of Chartered Surveyors went on record in favor of payment in full of compensation for loss of development value in each individual case (rather than awarding a share in the limited fund), the payment to be made only when land is actually developed or when its development is definitively prohibited by public authority; together with the substitution of a variable development charge for the 100 per cent charge now imposed. *The Economist*, June 3, 1950, p. 1208. These proposals were endorsed later in the year by the Federation of British Industries. *The Economist*, November 18, 1950, p. 797. The Association of the British Chambers of Commerce went a step further in recommending that the £300 million compensation fund be canceled, that development rights be restored to landowners and that all who have paid development charges be reimbursed. *The Times* (London), November 15, 1950.

162   BRITISH PLANNING AND NATIONALIZATION

tive. In pursuit of this aim it has instituted a thoroughly bad
form of taxation which would never be tolerated on its own
merits. As a planning Act it is mainly good, as a taxing Act it is
wholly bad. To amend or repeal its offending sections in the
ways suggested [see footnote 45] would probably reduce somewhat its effectiveness as a planning measure; but this would be
at least a lesser evil than the stranglehold on development
which the Act now threatens to impose.[46]

In a more recent critique,[47] *The Economist* contends
that "in less than five short years the town planners' dream
has faded." There is a plenitude of plans matched by a
multiplication of controls, "but of concrete results, in the
shape of an improvement in the living and working conditions of the people, there is little—pathetically little—to
show. . . . The strategy of the planning authorities," it
continues, "has been such as to produce the minimum of
results for the maximum of friction." The arrangements
for compensation claims and development charges "were
conceived by the Labour legislators as wholly secondary to
the aim of establishing effective planning control of private
development. Rarely have the means chosen been so utterly
disproportionate to the end in view." Aroused by these
comments, however, one of planning's staunch supporters,
in a letter to *The Economist,* urges understanding and patience: "the official plans could not appear for three years,
and . . . in the meantime a new administration has had
to make interim decisions while the public is in the dark
about the relation of restrictions to aims. . . . Thus, while
it is most desirable to consider whether the financial clauses
of the 1947 Act can be amended, we cannot scrap the principle underlying them without either gross hardship to
owners or abandoning the social purposes of planning."[48]

46. *The Economist,* November 18, 1950, p. 797.
47. "The Town Planners' Dream," *The Economist,* March 3, 1951,
pp. 470–71. See also "Town Planners' Apology," *The Economist,* May
12, 1951, pp. 1085–86.
48. F. J. Osborn, in *The Economist,* March 24, 1951, p. 680. In a
letter to *The Times* (London), December 22, 1950, L. Dudley Stamp,
generally sympathetic, refers to the "veritable jungle of controls which

The view that change is required is probably shared by a considerable sector of British opinion: the positive planning provisions of the act that in any event are not likely to be too effective are accepted; the compensation provisions are questioned for their liberality and contrariwise for their inadequacy; development charges, it is felt, should be reduced from the 100 per cent standard.

The call for a more important position in the government for the Minister of Town and Country Planning[49] was answered in the Cabinet shake-up of 1950 which placed Hugh Dalton in the Ministry, and elevated the Ministry to the Cabinet. The demand for closer integration of related functions was met in January 1951, by changing the name of the Ministry to the Ministry of Local Government and Planning and bringing housing within its jurisdiction.[50]

The act and its administration were the subject of extended debate both in the House of Lords and the House of Commons in the spring of 1950.[51] The Minister announced in May 1950 that for virtually all building work on farms, most ordinary additions to houses, and some small extensions to factories, planning permission would no longer be required. Simplified procedures for obtaining

---

effectively restrain the gnats but allow the camels to escape." And the Parliamentary Secretary of the Ministry of Town and Country Planning is reported as saying that planning would succeed only "if we stop being pernickety and fussy about things that don't matter very much." *The Times* (London), September 7, 1950.

49. Pointing out that a thoroughgoing, active program requires the utmost cooperation between the Ministry of Town and Country Planning and the Ministries of Health (housing), Agriculture (farm land), Transport (roads and transportation), Works (building licenses), the Defense Departments (taking and releasing lands), the Board of Trade (location of industry) and the Treasury (finance), it has been argued that the Minister of Town and Country Planning should be the leader in planning strategy and should occupy a high cabinet position. See F. J. Osborn, *op. cit.*

50. *The Times* (London), January 18, 1951.

51. *Parliamentary Debates* (Hansard), House of Lords, Vol. 166, cols. 383–444; *ibid.,* House of Commons, Vol. 476, cols. 106–63.

permission were also announced. This "experiment in freedom" was expected to reduce the total number of applications for planning permission by at least 40 per cent.[52] In
the Commons debate the Minister promised to give consideration to further changes, but on one point he remained
adamant: the development charge would not be varied—
in his judgment, under existing full employment, the
charge had not been shown to have a deterrent effect on
development. The only amendments to the 1947 act now in
prospect involve merely the correction of what the Ministry
refers to as "errors in drafting."[53]

In the meantime, administration of the 1947 legislation
goes on. The Central Land Board has received more than
935,000 claims for compensation for loss of development
rights, all of which must be processed in time for the issu-
ance of compensation stock before July 1, 1953.[54] For the
period July 1, 1948 to March 31, 1950, the Board received
190,497 applications for the determination of development
charges, and was able to dispose of 167,803.[55] Revenue from
development charges received by the Board during this
period amounted to £2,663,651, and another £2,473,307 in
development charges was allowed to be set off against claims
for compensation in special cases of land use.[56]

52. *The Times* (London), May 11, 1950. See also *Town and Country
Planning, 1943–1951*, pp. 14–15.

53. The proposed amendments had their second reading on January 23, 1951. The Opposition professed disappointment at the
"mouse" introduced by the government, and urged "radical" changes
that would unfreeze the land. *The Times* (London), January 24, 1951.

54. *Report of the Central Land Board, 1949–50*, p. 4. Over half of
the claims were presented during the final week of the twelve-month
period allowed for the purpose. The Board reported in 1951 that it
had been able thus far to settle less than a quarter of the (minor)
claims. *The Economist*, August 25, 1951, p. 441.

55. *Report of the Central Land Board, 1949–50*, Appendix A. In
1950–1951, the applications for determination of development charges
fell by 25 per cent. The Board disposed of 78,000 applications, imposing charges totaling £4,455,000 in 20,000 cases. *The Economist*,
August 25, 1951, p. 441.

56. *Report of the Central Land Board, 1949–50*, Appendix C. Under

The present working and the over-all effects of the 1947 legislation—in terms of administrative costs, inequities, direction of planning, private development initiative and official morale—are certainly enveloped in confusion. Much that is attributed to the act is at least partially due to other causes. Any complicated change in existing commercial and legal patterns involves time for its full achievement. The act grew from reports and earlier legislation sponsored by, and participated in by members of the Conservative as well as of the Labor party. Despite these considerations, however, it is difficult to believe that the present structure of town and country planning in Great Britain will remain long without modification.[57]

announcement by the Board, a private owner of a building plot suitable for a single house, provided he lodged a claim before July 1949 and starts to build for his own occupation by January 1, 1953 (or if he sells his plot, assumes liability for the development charge, and if the purchaser starts building by January 1, 1953) may receive full compensation for loss of development value on his plot, and the right to set off the development charge against his claim. Similarly, under particular circumstances, building firms are entitled to set off development charges against claims. *Ibid.*, pp. 9–10.

57. "The whole system of town planning and development charges needs drastic overhaul," declares the Conservative manifesto for 1951. *The Times* (London), September 29, 1951. For a critical review of the situation by an American observer, together with a reply from England, see P. F. Wendt, "Administrative Problems Under the British Town and Country Planning Act of 1947," *Land Economics*, November 1949, p. 427; and P. F. Wendt, "A Reply from England on the Effects of the British Town and Country Planning Act, 1947," *Land Economics*, November 1950, p. 397. The attitude of the newly constituted Ministry on all the controversial issues discussed in this chapter will be found in *Town and Country Planning, 1943–1951*.

CHAPTER 8

The Distribution of Industry

THE ESSENTIAL LEGISLATION governing the distribution of industry—passed by the Coalition government in 1945, and stemming from earlier acts and reports for which Conservative and Coalition governments were responsible—is broad enough to sanction imaginative and elaborate plans for the direction of industrial location.[1] No industry may locate its buildings without government permission, and the government may hold out attractive inducements for industries to build in locations it deems desirable. The government may promote such important interests as industrial efficiency, enhancement of amenities, balance of population and national defense.

Here—on paper—is planning with a vengeance. Concern, however, over the plight of Britain's so-called special ("depressed" or "development") areas was the dominant force in motivating the legislation, and the resulting program has taken form primarily in the light of that concern.

1. Most of the legislation is contained in the Distribution of Industry Act, 1945, 8 & 9 George 6, Ch. 36. Technically, the act was passed by the Conservative government. The bill was introduced and defended on its second reading by the Coalition government, but by the time of final passage and approval Labor had left the government, although the membership of the House of Commons had not changed. The very important provision giving power to the Board of Trade to prohibit building in unapproved areas by refusing necessary certification was added, under the Labor government, in Section 14 of the Town and Country Planning Act, 1947, 10 and 11 George 6, Ch. 51. The Distribution of Industry Act, 1950, 14 George 6, Ch. 8, clarifies and adds slightly to the government's powers to provide industrial facilities.

166

The Depressed Areas in the 1930's

Early in the 1930's Britain became acutely aware that the unemployment afflicting the greater part of the economy had struck with particularly devastating force in certain geographic areas. Percentages of unemployment in these regions ran consistently at levels about twice as high as the figures (themselves formidable) for the rest of the country. (See Table 4.) In certain of the special regions, and in cer-

TABLE 4

PREWAR UNEMPLOYMENT, JULY 1932–JULY 1939[a]

Year	Age of Worker	Development Areas[b]		Rest of Great Britain	
		Number	Percentage	Number	Percentage
July 1932	16–64	820,000	38	2,019,000	19
July 1937	14–64	410,000	18	925,000	8
July 1939	14–64	323,000	13	906,000	7

Source: Distribution of Industry, Cmd. 7540, H.M.S.O., October 1948, p. 6.

a. Excluding persons insured under the agricultural scheme.

b. The "Development Areas" include, but are somewhat larger than, the "Special Areas" involved in the "Special Areas" legislation of 1934.

tain towns within the regions, unemployment was even more stark in its incidence and effects. The areas where unemployment was most severe—and which at the outset were singled out for public attention—were Durham and Tyneside, West Cumberland, South Wales and Monmouthshire, and southwest Scotland. In the town of Jarrow, in the first of these areas, and in Merthyr Tydfil in South Wales, early unemployment totaled between 70 and 80 per cent of the insured workers.

The depressed areas were dependent upon coal mining and the iron and steel, tin plate, shipbuilding and engineering industries. During the years between World War I and World War II, an average of more than half of the insured labor force of the areas was tied to these exporting, raw material and capital goods industries; and it was precisely here that the shrinkage in foreign markets and the general cyclical decline took their greatest toll.[2] There was no appreciable expansion in other industries in the area to absorb those thrown out of work in the principal industries, and the reduced purchasing power of those immediately affected was reflected in reduced incomes and unemployment in all trades throughout the regions. *Under*employment was piled upon *un*employment; and women and children who sought to augment the dwindling incomes of their families found scant response to their search for work.

No part of Great Britain was free from the blight, but the Midlands and London were sustained by the development of new, light industries; the concentration of industry and population that later proved so distressing was given substantial impetus by the rush to Birmingham and London. Many workers migrated from Wales and the north to the Midlands and the south, but while the overcrowding of the expanding centers was aggravated,[3] the depressed areas experienced little noticeable alleviation.

The Special Areas Act of 1934

Government investigation into the plight of the depressed areas[4] was followed by passage of the Special Areas (Devel-

2. Thirty per cent of the industrial population of South Wales was employed in coal mining alone. *Report on the Location of Industry*, Political and Economic Planning, London, 1939, p. 38.

3. "Between 1921 and 1937 half a million people migrated to the London area alone. The consequent duplication there of housing and services already provided elsewhere was clearly a waste of resources and the congestion in the London and Birmingham areas was increased. Moreover, when war came, these areas suffered from serious labour shortages and vulnerability to war attack." *Distribution of Industry*, p. 8.

4. See *Reports of Investigations into the Industrial Conditions in Certain Depressed Areas of I—West Cumberland and Haltwhistle, II —Durham and Tyneside, III—South Wales and Monmouthshire, IV —Scotland*, Ministry of Labor, Cmd. 4728, H.M.S.O., 1934. The Board of Trade had engaged the services of five universities in 1931 to make "industrial surveys" of depressed areas. The resulting reports over-

opment and Improvement) Act of 1934. The six areas indicated above were designated officially as "Special Areas" (not "Depressed Areas" as they were called in the original bill), and two commissioners were appointed (one for England and Wales, and one for Scotland) to undertake "the initiation, organisation, prosecution and assistance of measures designed to facilitate the economic development and social improvement" of the areas.

The commissioners were to act in cooperation with government departments, local authorities and voluntary organizations, but it was expected that they would display a large measure of independence and initiative. Passages from the Parliamentary debate indicate that they were to "cut across lines" and "get on with their jobs." They were, however, to act under ministerial control. The commissioner for England and Wales was required to seek the sanction of the Minister of Labor on all lines of policy, and he was "as much subject to orthodox financial control as any Government Department." At the end of his first six months in office, the commissioner remarked that "Whilst [these limitations] may not actually hamper the freedom and initiative of the Commissioner so far as making proposals is concerned, they do result in restricting his powers to carry these proposals into effect."[5]

The task of the commissioners was not the immediate mitigation of unemployment, but economic development designed to enhance employment prospects in the long run. They sought principally to attract into the Special Areas some of the expanding industries that were springing up in the Midlands and the south. Unfortunately, the commissioners were precluded by the act from giving direct financial assistance toward the establishment of new industries

lapped the Ministry of Labor's report in three areas. See *Industrial Survey of the Lancashire Area (Excluding Merseyside)*, Board of Trade, H.M.S.O., 1932; *of Merseyside*, 1932; *of the North East Coast Area*, 1932; *of South Wales*, 1932; and *of the South West of Scotland*, 1932.

5. *First Report of the Commissioner for the Special Areas (England and Wales)*, Cmd. 4957, H.M.S.O., 1935, p. 6.

operating for profit, and their powers to provide funds through local authorities for general improvements and facilities in the areas were closely limited. At the outset, then, persuasion and exhortation were practically the only means at their disposal, and these, needless to say, were not conspicuously effective for the purpose.

Inducements to Locate in Special Areas

To attract industry, the government resorted at first to establishment of trading estates operated by private non-profit companies, and, subsequently, under new legislation, to indirect Treasury assistance to small enterprises. Trading-estate companies were set up in northeast England and in South Wales in 1936, in Cumberland in 1937 and in Scotland in 1937 and 1938.[6] In each instance, businessmen and public-spirited citizens of the area were encouraged by the commissioner to form a nonprofit company to select, purchase, develop and lease sites, buildings and facilities for industrial development. Buildings and facilities were available for tenants on a lease basis. The commissioners supplied the necessary financial support free of interest for an initial period; thereafter interest was payable at 4 per cent. Directors of each company were chosen by its members, with one named by the Treasury.[7]

In 1936, the Special Areas Reconstruction Association was formed (under the provisions of the Special Areas

6. *Distribution of Industry*, p. 8.

7. See D. F. Heatherington, "Location of Industry," *Foreign Commerce Weekly*, May 4, 1946, pp. 3, 51–53. The estates were located with a view to labor supply and markets, land was subdivided, and both standard factories and factories built to specification were erected. Tenants were responsible for repairs, taxes, insurance and utility charges. Trading estates, both those operated on commercial lines by private corporations, and those established in connection with town planning schemes (and there are many varieties of these types) have had a long and substantial history in Great Britain. See *Report on the Location of Industry;* and S. R. Dennison, *The Location of Industry and the Depressed Areas,* Oxford University Press, Oxford, 1939.

Reconstruction [Agreement] Act, 1936) "to give financial assistance to firms which had reasonable prospects of succeeding, and . . . the Treasury guaranteed roughly one quarter of any losses the Association might suffer."[8] Also in 1936, the Nuffield Trust was established with a fund of £2 million to assist business enterprises in the Special Areas. As a private agency, it was able to assist more directly than the government, even to the extent of purchasing shares in the individual operating companies. The Special Areas (Amendment) Act of 1937 provided the sum of £2 million and granted the Treasury additional power to lend assistance to business firms in the Areas, and authorized the commissioners to make limited contributions toward rent and tax costs of industrial firms, and to provide factories for rental. During its life the Reconstruction Association loaned about £750,000; the Nuffield Trust extended financial assistance amounting to about £2.2 million. Loans made under the 1937 legislation totaled about £1.16 million; contributions of some £55,000 were made toward rent and taxes; and about £5.5 million was spent for factory sites and buildings. In addition, the government had appropriated, by April 1939, £16 million to aid local authorities to improve basic services in the Areas.

Assessment of Results

It is not possible to identify precisely and hence to evaluate the results of the government's Special Areas program up to the outbreak of World War II. Some 12,000 men were employed in factories leased by the commissioners, most of them on the three main estates—Team Valley, Treforest and Hillington. Unemployment figures for the Areas showed marked improvement by the spring of 1939, but much of the gain must, of course, be attributed to the general rearmament. And it was still true that unemployment percentages in the Areas were twice as high as those for the country as a whole. This first program for the Areas was tentative and

8. *Distribution of Industry*, p. 8. The capital of the Association— a million pounds—was privately subscribed.

probing in character, and inconclusive in its outcome. It uncovered the difficulties of the problem; but it moved only cautiously toward a cure.

In his third report, the commissioner for England and Wales dealt at length with the relationship between the industrial rehabilitation of the Special Areas and the distribution of industry throughout Britain.[9] The drift to London was gaining in volume—while 213 new factories were established in London in 1935, only two new factories and six extensions were recorded in the whole of the Special Areas—and the commissioner proposed a bold new program of open government financial assistance to industries willing to expand in the Special Areas, plus a modified embargo on the expansion of industry in Greater London.[10] The second part of his proposal touched off a debate in Parliament, the result of which was the appointment in 1937 of the Royal Commission on the Distribution of the Industrial Population (Barlow Commission) whose report, completed in 1939, was referred to in Chapter 7.[11]

The Barlow commission was enjoined to inquire into the causes of the existing geographical distribution of industry, and the social, economic or strategic disadvantages arising from concentration of industries in certain areas, and to propose remedial measures. The resulting report is a landmark document on the general subject of industrial location, and it has played an important part in all subsequent government activity relating to the distribution of industry.

The commission found a serious and increasing concentration of industries in London and the Midlands,[12] and

9. *Third Report of the Commissioner for the Special Areas (England and Wales)*, Cmd. 5303, H.M.S.O., 1936, p. 8.

10. *Ibid.*, pp. 5–11 and 162–63. The commissioner was careful to distinguish between *compulsory* location of industry, to which he was opposed, and *restriction* of location (telling industry "where it should *not* go, unless good cause can be shown for so doing"). *Ibid.*, p. 8.

11. See Chap. 7, pp. 140–42.

12. The population increase between 1921 and 1937 for Britain as a whole was 7.5 per cent, but for Greater London it was 18 per cent. "Although London and the Home Counties and the Mid-

concluded that serious handicaps and even dangers to the nation's life and development were resulting from the trend.[13] The commission unanimously agreed that national action, through a newly constituted central authority, was necessary in order to achieve redevelopment and decentralization of industries and population from congested urban areas, together with a reasonable balance of industry throughout Britain and appropriate diversification within each division or region. A majority went on to recommend that the proposed board should be vested from the outset with powers to regulate (i.e., power to refuse consent to) the establishment of additional industrial undertakings in London and the surrounding counties.[14]

White Paper on Employment Policy

Consideration of the recommendations of the Barlow report was precluded by the war, but the Special Areas problem and the problem of strategic decentralization combined to produce a wartime order assigning to the Special Areas one fourth of the total war-factory space, even though the Areas contained only one eleventh of Britain's population.[15] The problem of the Special Areas continued to rest heavily on the mind of the Coalition government, however, and in its now famous White Paper on employment policy, issued

land group of counties contain between them only about 35 per cent of the total population of Great Britain, they contain nearly 70 per cent of the population added during the period." The number of persons in Great Britain insured against unemployment increased by 22.3 per cent between 1923 and 1937; the corresponding figure was 42.7 per cent for Greater London. *Report of the Royal Commission on the Distribution of the Industrial Population* [*Barlow Report*], Cmd. 6153, H.M.S.O., 1940, pp. 36–37.

13. *Ibid.*, p. 195.

14. *Ibid.*, pp. 201–03 and 206. Other members of the commission were in favor of extending government powers of regulating industry location to all sections of the country, and of employing positive powers of development. *Ibid.*, pp. 208–43.

15. Joseph Sykes, "Postwar Distribution of Industry in Great Britain," *Journal of Business*, July 1949, p. 188.

a year before it went out of office, the Areas came in for particular consideration.

The government's policy set forth on this occasion served as the basis of the Distribution of Industry Bill introduced into Parliament in the winter of 1945.[16] The White Paper was directed in the main to long-term policy for maintaining total expenditure, but it recognized that "patches of longer-term unemployment develop in particular industries and areas when the demand for their products is insufficient to provide work for the whole of their labour force. This is due to a temporary or permanent decline in an industry or group of industries caused by technical change, the trend of fashion, or the growth of foreign competition."[17]

The problem was identified with the Areas which had been the special concern of the government throughout the decade preceding the outbreak of war, and the government here proposed to meet it not only through its general program for maintaining expenditure throughout the economy as a whole, and by promoting as fully as possible the prosperity of the Areas' basic industries—coal, steel, engineering and shipbuilding—but also by measures tailored to the peculiar dimensions of the Areas. Specifically the government undertook to "attack the problems of local unemployment" in three ways:

(a) By so influencing the location of new enterprises as to diversify the industrial composition of areas which are particularly vulnerable to unemployment.

(b) By removing obstacles to the transfer of workers from one area to another. . . .

(c) By providing training facilities to fit workers from declining industries for jobs in expanding industries.[18]

16. *Employment Policy*, Cmd. 6527, H.M.S.O., May 1944. (See also Chap. 1, pp. 5, 6.) The President of the Board of Trade (Hugh Dalton) opened the debate on the second reading of the bill, March 21, 1945, with the statement: "This Bill is based upon the Government's White Paper on Employment Policy—paragraphs 20 to 30 of Chapter III of the White Paper." *Parliamentary Debates* (Hansard), House of Commons, Vol. 409, col. 837.

17. *Employment Policy*, p. 10.

18. *Ibid.*, p. 11

By way of elaboration, the Paper stated that the government would assume the power to prohibit the location of new factories in districts "where serious disadvantage would arise from further industrial development," and would use its influence to steer new factories into areas calling for industrial diversification. Account would be taken of strategic as well as industrial and social considerations. On the positive side, the government would provide an array of inducements—licenses for building, government-constructed factories, government contracts, financing (loans and share capital), and basic services—to lure industrialists into the Areas. The Areas, henceforth, were to be termed "Development Areas," and the list would be constituted, through additions and deletions, in the light of changing economic conditions. A number of departments would be involved in the program and the government as a whole was to be responsible for policy, but it was proposed that "the channel for the expression of Government policy in this matter" should be the Board of Trade.[19]

Distribution of Industry Bill

The program moved a step nearer to action with the introduction by the Coalition government of the Distribution of Industry Bill embodying the proposals of the White Paper. The Parliamentary debate on the second reading was moderate and, as might be expected, ran the full range from opposition to the measure as "bureaucracy and Socialism carried to the last limit" to grudging support because "it falls far short of what I want."[20] The bill was put forward "to abolish distressed areas, and also to make a beginning with the carrying out of the principles of the Barlow Report."[21] *The Times* characterized the measure as "a triumph

19. *Ibid.*, pp. 12–13. It was noted that in a few cases, where industrial conditions had changed permanently or where wasting assets had become exhausted, a redistribution of population rather than direction of industry was the appropriate remedy.
20. *Parliamentary Debates* (Hansard), House of Commons, Vol. 409, cols. 859, 898.
21. *Ibid.*, col. 837.

for the principles of the Barlow Report," and in a letter to that paper, Sir Montague Barlow gave hearty approval to the bill, without apparent reservation.[22]

Opponents in the House of Commons commented, however, that the main thrust of the legislation was toward relief for the Development Areas and that planned distribution of industry for the country as a whole was not the major goal. "I cannot quite agree," said one member, "that this Bill follows the Barlow Report. If it does follow it, it is a long way behind."[23] Another member asked, "Should we not be thinking on a larger scale about the industrial development of this country as a whole, rather than one section?"[24] To still another the bill appeared "about as relevant to our industrial situation as a sticking plaster on a wooden leg. From the point of view of the country as a whole there is nothing in this Bill."[25] Members called attention at several points to the fact that no *plan* was provided, either for industrial location or for the organization and processes by which a plan might be evolved. The proposition that too much was being left to the discretion of ministers was heard both from those who feared planning as an institution and from those who deplored the absence of a plan and the apparent lack of awareness that a plan was called for.

In short, the bill was offered as a coalition measure by a Coalition government,[26] and when, after the committee

22. *The Times* (London), February 23 and March 8, 1945. *The Times* raised a few cautious questions, but in the main was very favorable in its attitude.

23. *Parliamentary Debates* (Hansard), House of Commons, Vol. 409, col. 912. "It is wrong to call this Bill the Distribution of Industry Bill," he continued, "because it is nothing of the kind. It is a Special Areas Bill."

24. *Ibid.,* col. 900.

25. *Ibid.,* col. 879. And, "To members of the Labour Party I would say: 'For God's sake get out of the habit of claiming that since half a loaf is better than no bread, it is therefore better than a whole loaf'—a mentality which is becoming indigenous in the Labour movement." It might be added that the debate brought out the usual volume and types of claims and arguments relative to the special interests of the constituencies represented by the speakers.

26. As the Liberal leader, Clement Davies, put it: "It is one of the

stage, it finally emerged as the Distribution of Industry Act, it had even been stripped of the one provision that had given it significance as an instrument for the *control* of industrial location. Clause 9 of the bill, which gave the Board of Trade power to prohibit new factory building in certain areas of the country was eliminated before the third reading. It remained for the Town and Country Planning Act of 1947 to give the government such power as it possesses today to direct (but only by negative order) the location of industry.[27]

Provisions of Distribution of Industry Act of 1945

The first eight sections of the act deal with the Development Areas. The earlier Special Areas acts were repealed; the old Special Areas were enlarged and renamed "Development Areas"; and the government was given power to assist the establishment of new industries in the Areas.

The Board of Trade may build factories in the Areas and purchase land—if necessary by compulsory purchase order—for that purpose. With the consent of the Treasury, the Board may make loans to industrial estate companies to provide industrial premises in the areas. (The trading estates have generally been known as industrial estates since the war.) Provision is also made for improving the basic services of the Areas. These services include facilities for transport, power, lighting, housing, health and other services on which the industrial development of the Area depends. The Act also provides for the reclamation of derelict land in the Areas for industrial use or to improve amenities. Lastly, the Treasury may give financial assistance

---

worst instances of the work which is being done by the Coalition Government . . . I wish that the country could make up its mind what it wants." *Ibid.,* col. 928. See p. 166, footnote 1.

27. Town and Country Planning Act, 1947, Sec. 14, discussed below. Wartime control of building licenses enabled the government temporarily to exercise *de facto* control over location. See *Notes for the Guidance of Applicants for Building Licenses* (3d edition), Ministry of Works, 1948; and *Industrial Building: Notes for the Guidance of Industrialists who wish to carry out Building Work,* The Treasury, Economic Information Unit, 1949.

[through limited loans or grants] to undertakings already established or proposed in the Areas.[28]

The reconstituted Development Areas were listed, and it was provided that the Board of Trade might add to the list, and that three years after passage of the act the Board should take under consideration the need for additions to, or removal of, any Area on the list.

Distribution of industry in the wider, national sense was covered in a single, emasculated provision to the effect that sixty days' notice must be given to the Board of Trade before contracting for, or beginning the erection of, any industrial building with a floor space in excess of 10,000 square feet.[29] The waiting period was provided to give the Board an opportunity to talk over the proposed erection with the interested parties and to use its influence to guide the location of the building in the light of the general public interest.

When the act was passed the government could, under its war powers, prohibit the erection of any building, whether for considerations of location or for any other reason (or, indeed, for no reason at all!) by the simple process of refusing to grant permission for the use of the requisite labor and materials. These powers of prohibition, however, were temporary and exceptional, and their indefinite employment for the purpose of directing industrial location could not be justified.

Defect Remedied by Labor Government

The Labor government finally met the problem head on, and in the Town and Country Planning Act of 1947 inserted the provision that local planning authorities might not consider any application for the erection of any industrial building with a floor space in excess of 5,000 square feet "unless it is certified by the Board [of Trade] that the development in question can be carried out consistently with the proper distribution of industry."[30]

28. *Distribution of Industry*, p. 11.
29. Distribution of Industry Act, 1945, Secs. 9 and 10.
30. See p. 166, footnote 1 and p. 177, footnote 27.

The government today cannot compel industries to build in locations that are not to their liking, but it has resources which it can offer to induce entry into areas of its choice, and it has effective power to bar any construction in locations of which it does not approve. The 1947 legislation accomplished not only a stiffening of the power to control location; it effected as well a desirable tie-in between location of industry and town and country planning. Industries may locate only in areas that are suitable from the broad, national viewpoint; within the areas their sites will be governed by considerations reflected in the development plans prepared by the local authorities.

How the Laws Are Administered

Administration of the Distribution of Industry Act of 1945 has centered in the Board of Trade, and the Board has maintained a close working relationship with other interested ministries—Town and Country Planning, Treasury, Labor, Works, and those concerned with the affairs of particular industries, private and nationalized. In 1943, the Ministry of Production established a Location of Industry Planning Room to further and facilitate the proper location of wartime factory construction. In January 1945, the Board of Trade took over responsibility for the planning room, and in subsequent years it has become the physical center of the industrial location operation. The room is fitted with maps and records with pertinent details relating to every British factory employing more than 100 workers and every industrial area. The records are kept up to the minute and the information is available to—indeed, is forced upon—all persons concerned with industrial location. Here, with a minimum of effort, an industrialist interested in establishing a new factory can obtain for any site "information on the potential labor supply, proximity to transportation, availability of public utility services, factory space, and similar factors."[31]

31. D. F. Heatherington, "Location of Industry," *Foreign Commerce Weekly*, May 11, 1946, pp. 12, 33. See also "Part Played by the

Information on file at the London headquarters of the Board of Trade is supplemented by even more detailed information available in the Board's regional offices. The regional boards for industry, formed during the war and consisting of representatives of employers, workers and regional officers of the ministries are expected, as part of their larger advisory role, to cooperate and advise with the regional offices of the Board of Trade and with interested industrialists, on problems of location.

It is the avowed purpose of the Board of Trade to "steer" new factory construction in the direction pointed by its plans (or its "hunches") for the distribution of industry. Its procedures are entirely informal. A "case" starts with an inquiry by an industrialist, and the processes thereafter consist of pressure, inducement and negotiation. The Board has no mandatory authority over location, and it is keenly aware that, while it may refuse permission to build in overbuilt areas, its success in controlling the location of industry depends almost entirely upon its ability to persuade. In many instances, industrialists have been convinced simply by information the Board has furnished that their own interests would be better served by changing from their original plans. In other cases, the Board has supported its position successfully with firm oral persuasion, and in still others with financial inducements. Upon occasion the Board has yielded, and upon others the Board and the applicant have proved equally adamant and have achieved only a stalemate and a withdrawal or postponement of the construction project.

The Board's Distribution of Industry staff is not large and, to the visitor, its operations do not suggest feverish activity. Nonetheless, it is probably responsible for little of the delay that afflicts the beginning of industrial construction projects in Britain. At least, any delay at this point overlaps with other delays stemming from shortages of materials and labor, and reflects a studied policy of requiring

Location of Industry Planning Room," *Board of Trade Journal*, H.M.S.O., June 18, 1949, p. 1280.

careful consideration by all parties of the location of the undertaking, rather than bureaucratic red tape or the lethargy of officialdom.

The Board of Trade may, on its own initiative and responsibility, offer inducements in the form of physical facilities, but the consent of the Treasury is required for Board aid in the form of loans or grants. To assist in the discharge of this reviewing function as well as to advise in the matter of financial aid to be extended by the Treasury on its own initiative, the Development Areas Treasury Advisory Committee has been set up. The committee members are drawn from banking, labor, management and public administration, and their task is primarily to examine and pass upon applications for financial assistance. Board of Trade approval is required in all cases, and, in addition, there must be a showing that the project will, in due course, be able to stand on its own feet as a successful business venture.

What the Government Has Done

The government has carried on a varied program under the act—dovetailing with, continuing and expanding the policies and activities of its predecessors. It has provided finance and factories for the Development Areas, has cleared sites, improved public services and converted some of its munitions factories as well as nonindustrial buildings. It has worked both directly and through local authorities to provide houses for key workers in the Areas. And, of course, through provision of information and by restricting expansion in congested regions it has steered private industrial construction and enterprise into locations indicated by government policy.

Concretely, this has meant that over half of the factories sited in Great Britain since the war have gone into the Development Areas. By August 1950, 1,122 new factories and extensions had been built in the Areas, at a cost of over £48 million; and 249 others were then under construction at a cost in excess of those already completed. Government factories, built at a cost of £22.5 million, accounted for 530 of the completed buildings.[32] The number of jobs provided by new factory employment is in excess of 200,000, and increased employment in the materials and building trades and in the utility and equipment industries has resulted directly from the new construction. The figures do not tell the whole story: increased employment generates employment in the service and other trades. Whereas in 1932 the number of unemployed in the Areas constituted 38 per cent of the insured workers, the figure in February 1950 had fallen to 4 per cent of a much larger insured population.[33]

Other Influences at Work

There is no disposition on the part of those who defend the Development Areas program to claim complete success, or even that the spectacular shrinkage in Areas unemployment is due solely to government activity. Many of the great staple industries that threw vast numbers into unemployment in the 1930's have come back into active production as part of the nation-wide war and postwar revival of industry and trade. Indeed, unemployment in the Areas, even at its greatly reduced rate, has remained at a level above the average for the nation as a whole, and within the Areas there are small pockets where unemployment is still distressingly high.

On the other hand, the picture is possibly more encouraging than is suggested by the statistics of unemployment. Many new industries have started in the Areas, bringing a diversification which should protect them in the future from

32. "Progress in the Development Areas in the Post-War Years," *Board of Trade Journal*, H.M.S.O., December 2, 1950, pp. 893–96. As of April 4, 1950, the President of the Board of Trade reported that 1,359 factories, representing a total building cost of £92 million, had been licensed within the Areas, that of these 986 (including 481 government financed schemes) had been completed, and that 279 factories, including some large iron and steel and chemical works, were then under construction. *Parliamentary Debates* (Hansard), House of Commons, Vol. 473, cols. 1023–24.

33. J. Sykes, *op. cit.*, p. 192; *Parliamentary Debates* (Hansard), House of Commons, Vol. 473, cols. 1026–27.

concentrated unemployment. This is particularly true because many of these industries are of the new, lighter types for which the prospects of expansion are great. Families, too, have been made more secure, as well as more prosperous because the newer industries are offering greatly increased employment for women.[34]

Criticisms of Policy

Two major criticisms of the government's distribution of industry policy and program have been advanced—(1) that the government's concern has been directed too exclusively to the Development Areas rather than to location of industry on a national scale, and (2) that no national plan for industrial location has been evolved or projected. A reasonable answer would seem to be that, although amelioration of the plight of the Areas has been uppermost in the minds of most of the Board's staff, industry in Great Britain is better distributed and located in 1951, from every pertinent point of view, than it would have been if government guidance, persuasion and restriction had been absent in the postwar years. To the charge that the interests of the rest of the country have been neglected, it may be answered that the government was properly concerned with first things first,

34. On the prospects generally of the Development Areas, see J. Sykes, *op. cit.*, pp. 190–92. Professor Sykes, consultant on location to the Board of Trade, points out that in case of need, the hundreds of new factories, "which are predominantly suited to house modern industries of lighter types, could be used as an agency of anti-unemployment policy set in motion by the state to provide work for persons displaced from industries vulnerable to fluctuations of world demand, e.g., shipbuilding, heavy engineering" (p. 192).

Professor Sykes names "psychological uplift" as another gain to the Areas, and finds it reflected in the readiness of workers to discard restrictive, job-preserving practices, and to work more vigorously (p. 192). For a descriptive survey of the impact of the government's program on individual Areas, see the series of articles on the Areas in the *Board of Trade Journal,* beginning with the issue of December 2, 1950 (see footnote 32, above), and continuing in the issues of December 9, 16 and 30, 1950, and January 6 and 13, 1951. For an earlier survey, see *Distribution of Industry.*

and that apparent neglect may in fact be due more to neglect of appearances than to neglect of substance.

Throughout Britain employment has steadily been "full" since the war, and on the average has been even better outside than within the Areas. Pockets of unemployment that have appeared outside the Areas have been due mainly to temporary or peculiarly local conditions, and in those instances where the problems have become acute, the regions have been scheduled as additional "Development Areas."[35] Where owners have closed factories outside the Areas, scarcity of labor has been the principal cause; there has been little transfer of established firms into the Areas from outside and it would seem to be an accepted aim of location policy to direct new firms into areas where employable labor is available. Licenses for construction outside the Areas have been available in volume, and most of the denials have been due to evidence that the necessary specialized labor was lacking in the locations first specified, or to conditions such as those in London and the Midlands that have prompted all students of the problem to urge an embargo on all save the most clearly necessary expansion. In short, under the circumstances obtaining in postwar Britain, it may well be that sound Development Area policy was also sound national distribution of industry policy.

The policy embodied in the act and embraced by the Board—bringing jobs to labor rather than requiring labor to go to the jobs—may seem to constitute a denial of the proposition that labor mobility generates and reflects industrial progress, but in the situation at hand certain modifying factors should be borne in mind. Labor in the Development Areas was already housed, housing elsewhere was scarce, and the cost of factory construction is substantially less than the cost of building new houses for a transferred force of workers. Labor was already located at points where it could contribute effectively to the development of desirable exports;

35. The Highland area of Scotland, South Lancashire and Merseyside have been added to the schedule of Development Areas listed in the 1945 act.

and finally, the Board has worked actively to promote desirable mobility of labor within the Areas and has done nothing to check the rather considerable voluntary movement of labor from the Areas to other regions.

From the viewpoint of the "economics" of location, there is no reason to suppose that the Board's efforts have contributed in any serious measure to mal-location. A large part of the new construction (as well as the large volume of extensions) came from firms already in the Areas. Most of the rest came from industries which, economically, are as much at home in one region as in any other. All parties had the help of far more (and far more illuminating) information than had ever before been available, and no industry was forced to go where, in its own enlightened interest, it did not want to go. The test will come in the years ahead when economic events determine whether or not the "persuaded" industries can live without further subsidies. On the present record it is not difficult to believe that the work of the Board has made an important contribution to a more economic use of Britain's scarce resources since 1945.[36]

Lack of a National Plan

The absence of an over-all national plan for the location of industry is a serious defect in both the immediate problem and in the whole matter of town and country planning. Even more serious, probably, would be lack of awareness of

36. The form of the analysis and much of the material in this and the preceding paragraph have been drawn largely from J. Sykes, *op. cit.*, pp. 192–99. *The Economist* has been critical of "the premise, which underlay the Act and has inspired every phase of the Government's policy for industrial location, that the development areas enjoy an inevitable and natural entitlement to new industrial projects"; and has raised "the purely economic issue whether the forced revival of areas which have lost part or whole of their economic *raison d'être* may not in the end prove more costly than the development of regions which have positive economic attractions" (October 30, 1948, p. 692). *The Economist* has also expressed concern over the "political" character of the government's determination on location (August 2, 1947, p. 186). See also the questions raised in *The Times* (London), April 27, 1950.

the need for a plan. It is too early to say with conviction, however, whether the absence of an over-all plan at this juncture represents a lack of comprehension and vision or, rather, possession of native economic and political sense.

Planning as an institution is new in Great Britain; it still has its way to make. Detailed plans are necessary to attain precise ends. For many years it will represent real achievement if goals described in very broad terms can be gained. It is quite possible that concern over, and preoccupation with, the preparation of elaborate plans would constitute an obstacle rather than a help to the realization of a planning program. The British, no doubt, have too frequently made a virtue of their propensity to muddle, and the location program (as well as the case of town and country planning) may be just another such instance. On the other hand, to this date at least, substantial identifiable gains have been made in the steering of industrial location, and the future of the program appears now to be no worse than uncertain. It is significant that on the occasion of the debate (April 4, 1950) on the second reading of the Distribution of Industry Bill, much of the controversy revolved about the credit that might be claimed, respectively, by the Conservative and Labor parties for the passage of, and accomplishments under, the act of 1945.[37]

37. The Distribution of Industry Act, 1950, 14 George 6, Ch. 8, gave the additional power to the Board of Trade, with Treasury approval, to make grants to firms in the Areas to assist in meeting early losses due to "green" labor, and also to make grants or loans to housing associations to provide dwellings for workers in the Areas. The Opposition "welcomed" the bill. See *Parliamentary Debates* (Hansard), House of Commons, Vol. 473, cols. 1023–1134.

CHAPTER 9

The National Health Service

So MUCH MISINFORMATION about Britain's health service has reached the American public that the temptation is overpowering to open a descriptive survey of the health service by a statement of what the service *is not*. The health service is not a socialistic aberration. It has grown from the national health insurance program instituted in 1911; its roots in Britain are deep. At the same time, its socialistic quality—found in the undertaking to provide medical, dental, nursing and hospital services to all persons almost irrespective of status and ability to pay—is more apparent than in any other single project in Labor's program. The national health service is at once indigenous and radical.[1]

Background of the Problem

Investigation after investigation and report upon report for decades have pointed up the high correlation between

1. "The National Health Service cannot be described outside of its context in the overall professional, economical, social and political conditions in Great Britain. . . . Its purpose is to supply hospitalization, preventive medicine, family medical, dental and nursing services, medicines, appliances, and all other requirements for complete, comprehensive medical services for everyone, financed by the national government in the same way as are the armed forces, general education and other necessities." W. C. Rappleye, *The National Health Service of Great Britain,* Josiah Macy, Jr. Foundation, New York, 1950, p. 3. One commentator refers to the act as the "most radical of the nationalization measures" because of the distinctive characteristic of its object, which is regarded "as an absolute good of such an essential nature that the standards of service to the least and poorest should be as high as to the greatest and most affluent. Here there was to be absolute (or, at any rate, very nearly absolute) equality." Robert A. Brady, *Crisis in Britain,* University of California Press, Berkeley, 1950, p. 354.

poverty and ill health in Britain, and have stressed the inadequacy of the national health services to meet this problem. Progress was made through the years in the control of epidemics, but even in this area the heaviest burden continued to fall upon the poor. Although the general level of health has been raised, the incidence of ill health from all diseases still weighs heavily and preponderantly on the lower income groups.[2] Undernourishment, malnutrition, insanitary conditions, overcrowding, ignorance—these make up the soil and climate where illness flourishes, and an effective program to eradicate the consequences must necessarily contemplate an attack upon the underlying causes. Such a program must include, as well, the provision of more and better distributed medical service than ever before existed in Britain. While a medical program alone cannot be expected to eradicate ill health among the poor, it can, if sufficiently imaginative and daring, go far in this direction. At the very least, it can be ameliorative.

The Labor government, through a wide range of activities, has instituted a general attack on poverty, insecurity, gross inequality in wealth, and on the undernourishment, ignorance, poor housing and ill health that flow from and reflect these conditions. Its direct attack on the problem of medical care for everyone must be seen against the background of this larger program—which itself is a vital part of the program for improvement of health.[3]

2. "There exists throughout society, if these data are correct, a vast submerged, undiscovered, and untreated incubus of illness, which lies so heavily on those in the lower income brackets that among them extended periods of good health are virtually unknown." Robert A. Brady, *op. cit.*, p. 362. Chapter 9 of this book contains an account of the conditions and forces leading to the adoption of the National Health Service Act, 1946, as well as an analysis of the act itself. See also *Report on the British Health Service*, Political and Economic Planning, London, 1937; and *Medical Services in Great Britain* (No. R. 1237), Central Office of Information, London, 1946.

3. "Whilst by other means this Government are actively engaged in improving the standards of nutrition, housing, clothing of the people, education and provision of employment in order to secure advances in the standards of life, to improve the health of our people,

Public concern over, and government action with reference to, health are not new phenomena in Great Britain. Preventive measures—sanitary sewage, water supply, control of epidemics, general sanitary provisions, provisions against infection—were undertaken during the century preceding the inauguration of the national health service. The legislation setting up these measures largely gave form to the local authorities that play a leading role in the administration of the health service as well as in the operation of local government generally.[4]

Early Health Measures

The National Health Insurance Act of 1911 was the first nation-wide effort to provide general practitioner services paid for by insurance funds. The scheme, administered by the government, insurance companies and "friendly societies," and financed by compulsory payments by workers, employers and the government, furnished medical care and sick pay for wage earners within certain income limits. The families and dependents of the wage earners were not covered, the plan fell far short of embracing the entire population, and coverage, of course, depended on contribution. Nonetheless, in establishing a set of arrangements under which individuals were entitled to receive medical treatment when and as needed rather than on a fee-for-service basis, the National Health Insurance Act of 1911 paved the way for the health service legislation of 1946.

Between 1911 and 1946 a number of statutes dealing with public health were passed. They gave evidence of growing popular acceptance of collective responsibility in this field, but since they related to food, sanitation, treatment of tuberculosis, maternity, and to the government structure of public health activities, they made no direct

---

it will, alas, always be necessary that we should give early and adequate attention to the onset of diseases, the results of accidents and the effects of increasing age." The Parliamentary Secretary to the Ministry of Health, in *Parliamentary Debates* (Hansard), House of Commons, Vol. 426, col. 392.

4. Robert A. Brady, *op. cit.*, p. 364.

contribution to the extension of general medical and specialist services. Medical care had long been available to the destitute sick, under the administration of local poor-law authorities.

Two types of hospitals were in operation: privately managed *voluntary* hospitals, supported by private endowments, contributions and voluntary schemes, sometimes associated with medical schools, sometimes highly specialized, and sometimes small and served by local practitioners; and *municipal* or *public* hospitals, supported by public funds, and originating in most instances from efforts to care for the sick poor.[5] There was no hospital "system" on a national basis, with centralized responsibility and direction. The facilities were distributed quite unevenly, and in several instances facilities were heavily concentrated in areas with the smallest needs.

The defects in the health services available to the people of Britain at the close of World War II have been summarized as follows:

(i) The limitations of National Health Insurance, which left large numbers of persons without free medical practitioner care, and gave those who were covered different benefits, owing to the varying resources of different "Approved Societies."

(ii) Geographical distribution of hospital and specialist services was uneven, and it was far from true that any person could get the service he required.

(iii) With the increasing specialization of centers of medical and surgical treatment, the need for general and area planning of provision was clear.

(iv) There was insufficient link between the various services.

(v) There was a large amount of preventable ill health and

5. In 1939 there were 900 voluntary hospitals in England and Wales, with 77,000 beds; and 220 voluntary hospitals in Scotland, with 14,000 beds. There were 70,000 beds in 140 general hospitals run by local authorities in England and Wales, and 60,000 beds in public assistance institutions. In Scotland there were 5,500 beds in nine general hospitals, and some 1,700 beds for the chronic sick in public assistance institutions. *Health Services in Britain* (I. D. 753 Revised), British Information Services, August 1948, p. 4.

subnormal health, with corresponding loss in efficiency and personal happiness.

(vi) Economic status rather than medical need was too often the criterion of eligibility for medical service.

(vii) There was too much divided authority, and there was no comprehensive national policy to guide legislative and other developments in the sphere of medical service. There were too many central and local bodies concerned with one or another aspect of the country's health services, and there was insufficient collaboration between statutory bodies and between statutory and voluntary bodies.[6]

Labor Moves to Solve the Problem

When Labor came to power in 1945, it lost no time in pressing the case it had urged continuously and with increasing emphasis for decades. Early in the century the Labor party at its annual conferences had passed resolutions looking toward nationalization of hospitals and dispensaries, free medical service to school children, medical service (including hospital and operative treatment) available to everyone, and organization and coordination of health services on a national basis. The general nature and import (together with at least some of the details) of Labor's program for health were well known long before the introduction of its Health Service Bill, and the arguments offered for the bill during the Parliamentary debate contained little that could not reasonably have been anticipated.[7] The Minister of Health built his case for the legislation—point by point—around the defects and inadequacies of the existing service together with the improvement to be anticipated from the proposed system.[8]

6. *Ibid.*, pp. 4–5. On the maldistribution of facilities and services, see the statement by the Minister of Health in *Parliamentary Debates* (Hansard), House of Commons, Vol. 422, cols. 44 and 53.

7. See *National Service for Health*, The Labour Party, London, 1943.

8. The Minister laid particular stress upon the planless and unsystematic character of the available services and the need to eliminate financial anxiety from the problem of medical care: "the first evil that we must deal with is that which exists as a consequence of the fact

Parliamentary opposition to the bill was scattered, mild and concerned mainly with details. The position (or positions) of the Conservative party had been largely determined by the history of the issue up to the outbreak of the war, the Beveridge report of 1942[9] and the White Paper of 1944, which proposed changes looking toward the coordination and strengthening of the health services by government action. The opening speaker for the Opposition introduced his remarks with the statement:

I am anxious to make clear our position on these Benches in regard to the principle of a national, comprehensive, 100 per cent health service. Of course we accept the principle today, as we accepted it in 1944, when the Coalition White Paper was published. . . . We accept the principle, and we accept the consequences that flow from it. We understand, for example, that once we are committed, as we are gladly committed, to the principle of a 100 per cent service, we require an enormous expansion and development in the health services as a whole . . . [and] to a far greater degree of coordination, or planning as it is usually called, than we have ever known before.[10]

His criticisms of the bill were that it destroyed the proper relationship between doctor and patient, menaced all charitable foundations and weakened the responsibility of local

that the whole thing is the wrong way round. A person ought to be able to receive medical and hospital help without being involved in financial anxiety . . ." *Parliamentary Debates* (Hansard), House of Commons, Vol. 422, col. 43. The debate on the second reading is reported in *ibid.*, cols. 43–149, 200–313, 356–412. The bill, introduced on March 19, 1946, was passed on the second reading, May 2, 1946 by a vote of 359–172. The bill was passed on the third reading, July 26, 1946, and received the Royal assent on November 6, 1946.

9. *Social Insurance and Allied Services,* Inter-departmental Committee on Social Insurance and Allied Services, H.M.S.O., 1942. In interpreting the stand of the Opposition, it should be remembered that during the period between the wars, several committees, both governmental and "professional" (such as committees of the British Medical Association) had reported in favor of an extension and coordination of medical service in ways involving greatly increased participation by government.

10. *Parliamentary Debates* (Hansard), House of Commons, Vol. 422, cols. 66–67.

authorities. Thereafter, while personal exchanges frequently were sharp, the debate proceeded along expected, formal lines, and the legislation was passed and the project launched. A "tooling up" period was provided before the "appointed day" (July 5, 1948) on which the service was opened.

Administration of the Health Service

At the apex of the administrative structure of the national health service for England and Wales stands the Minister of Health.[11] It is his duty under the act "to promote the establishment in England and Wales of a comprehensive health service designed to secure improvement in the physical and mental health of the people . . . and the prevention, diagnosis and treatment of illness, and for that purpose to provide or secure the effective provision of services" in accordance with the provisions of the act. The first of the named provisions is that the services "shall be free of charge, except where any provision of this Act expressly provides for the making and recovery of charges."[12]

A professionally constituted Central Health Services Council has the duty, whether requested by the Minister or not, to advise him "upon such general matters relating to the services" provided under the act or by the local health authorities "as the Council think fit" as well as upon any questions referred to them by the Minister.[13] The composition of the Council is set forth in the act, although it is provided that the Minister, after consultation with the Council, may vary its constitution.

The Council consists of forty-one members, of whom six are *ex officio,* the persons holding "for the time being" the offices of the President of the Royal College of Physicians of London, the President of the Royal College of

11. National Health Service Act, 1946, 9 & 10 George 6, Ch. 81, Sec. 1 (1). A separate administration, under the Minister of State for Scotland, is established for Scotland. National Health Service (Scotland) Act, 1947, 10 & 11 George 6, Ch. 27.

12. *Ibid.,* Sec. 1 (2).

13. *Ibid.,* Sec. 2 (1).

Surgeons of England, the President of the Royal College of Obstetricians and Gynaecologists, the Chairman of the Council of the British Medical Association, the President of the General Medical Council and the Chairman of the Council of the Society of Medical Officers of Health. The remaining members, appointed by the Minister, after consultation with such organizations as he may recognize as representative of those persons, are: (1) fifteen medical practitioners, two of whom have special knowledge of mental illness and mental defectiveness; (2) five persons, not medical practitioners, with experience in hospital management; (3) five persons, not medical practitioners, with experience in local government; (4) three dental practitioners; (5) two persons experienced in mental health services; (6) two registered nurses; (7) a certified midwife; and (8) two registered pharmacists.[14] The Council members, although appointed after consultation with their respective organizations, serve as individuals and not as organization representatives.

The Minister is empowered, further, to name standing committees, consisting of members of the Council and others to advise him and the Council on such services as he may specify. The Council itself may appoint committees, and the standing committees may appoint subcommittees. The standing committees may report directly to the Minister, provided the report is made available to the Council for an expression of the Council's views.[15] By the end of 1949, nine standing committees had been set up and members appointed.

14. *Ibid.*, Secs. 2 (1), 2 (2), and First Schedule.
15. The standing committees are under a duty to "advise the Minister and the Central Council upon such matters relating to the services with which the committee are concerned as they think fit and upon any questions referred to them by the Minister or Central Council relating to those services . . ." Sec. 2(4). The act requires that the annual report of the Council to the Minister be laid before Parliament, unless the Minister shall decide that it would be contrary to the public interest to make the report, or any part of it, public.

The extent of the professional influence now brought to bear on the administration of the service is indicated by the fact that although the Central Council, by a narrow majority, was prepared to advise the Minister that the medical, dental, pharmaceutical and ophthalmic standing committees should contain a "small element of lay representation," the Minister insisted that these committees, to which he wished to look "for purely technical advice," should be made up exclusively of members of the professions.[16]

In addition to his general powers and duties, the Minister is authorized to conduct, or assist others by grants or otherwise to conduct, medical research, and to provide a bacteriological service and a service for making available supplies of blood for transfusions and supplies of any other substances and preparations that he may have acquired.[17] The rest of the service falls administratively into three parts: (1) the work of medical and dental practitioners and the provision of pharamaceutical and supplementary ophthalmic services; (2) a group of health services provided by local health authorities; and (3) the services of hospitals and specialists.

16. *Report of the Central Health Services Council for the period ending December 31, 1949, preceded by a Statement made by the Minister of Health* (cited hereafter as *C.H.S.C. First Annual Report*), H.M.S.O., 1950, p. 2. In addition to the standing committees named above, the following have been established: nursing, maternity and midwifery, tuberculosis, mental health, and cancer and radiotherapy. The members are listed on pages 23–28 of the *C.H.S.C. First Annual Report*. During the period covered by the report, the Minister "remitted some 30 separate questions for the consideration of the Council and Committees, while these bodies have themselves originated more than a dozen further matters on which they have submitted advice . . .; the whole of this advice, including that dealt with in the first place by the Committees, has been reviewed and co-ordinated by the Council." *Ibid.,* p. ii. Most recently, the Council has appointed a committee under the chairmanship of the President of the British Medical Association to study general practice under the service. *The Times* (London), January 9, 1951.

17. National Health Service Act, 1946, Secs. 16, 17 and 18.

Functions of Local Bodies

The services of general medical and dental practitioners, together with pharmaceutical and supplementary ophthalmic services, are provided to the public under the immediate supervision of the local executive councils. With a few exceptions, one executive council is established for each county or county borough area. Each consists of a chairman appointed by the Minister, and twenty-four members of whom eight are appointed by the local health authority for the area, four by the Minister, seven by the local medical committee, three by the local dental committee and two by the local pharmaceutical committee.[18]

Doctors in established practice at the "appointed day" were free to join or to refrain from joining the service in their respective areas. Each was free, as well, to take private fee-paying patients in addition to the "public" patients on his lists. Every member of the public was free to select a practitioner from those who had joined the service, subject to the consent of the practitioner in each case. The practitioner is free to leave the service at any time, to refuse to accept as a patient any person whom he does not care to serve, and to have patients' names removed from his list. Patients are free to change doctors. Freedom of choice, with its important contribution to the essential personal quality of the doctor-patient relationship, has been protected.

It is the duty of the local executive council "in accordance with regulations to make arrangements with medical practitioners for the provision by them . . . of personal medical services for all persons in the area who wish to take advantage of the arrangements."[19] Most of the "arrangements" are prescribed by the "regulations." The councils do not employ the practitioners and they have no authority to direct them in the conduct of their professional activi-

18. *Ibid.*, Fifth Schedule. Part IV of the act governs the provision of these services. In practice, the local executive councils consist of professional and lay members.

19. *Ibid.*, Sec. 33.

ties. With slight exceptions the arrangements are uniform for all areas. The councils exercise general oversight, deal with disputes between practitioners and patients, and, with the advice of the local medical committee, play a part in determining the number of practitioners needed to serve their areas and in selecting new candidates to fill these needs.

Status of Practitioners

Entry into the service by doctors who were not practicing on the "appointed day," and entry into a new area by a doctor who was in practice when the service was instituted, offer two of the few opportunities, under the act, for control of the profession by the state. Since the "appointed day," areas may not be entered for the first time without the consent of the Medical Practices Committee—seven medical practitioners and two laymen appointed by the Minister. The committee is authorized to refuse an application to enter any area which in its judgment should be designated as "closed" because it already is served by a sufficient number of doctors. Permission may be given by the committee to enter a particular part of a closed area or to fill a vacancy.

In the case of "open" areas, permission is granted as a matter of course, except where the number of applicants exceeds the number of positions which the committee is prepared to recognize. In this situation, the committee will make its choice from the group of candidates, after consulting with the local executive council which offers advice after consultation with the local medical committee.[20] Ap-

20. *Ibid.*, Sec. 34. The act provides for the recognition within each area of a local medical (also a local pharmaceutical and a local dental) committee, representative of the "medical practitioners of that area"; and stipulates the occasions upon which the executive council must consult with the committee. *Ibid.*, Sec. 32. The second annual report of the Medical Practices Committee, issued in August 1950, disclosed that the number of general practitioners in England and Wales had increased by 330 during the year, and that "the distribution of family doctors is clearly moving, by voluntary choice, according to the needs of the public." *The Times* (London), August 31, 1950.

plicants who are denied permission to enter an area may appeal from the decision of the Medical Practices Committee to the Minister. The Minister has final authority to allow an applicant to enter an area; he has also the ultimate decision on applicants admitted by the committee, and even, with certain procedural safeguards, the authority to admit another candidate in the place of one approved by the committee.

Practitioners and the government disagreed strongly, of course, about remuneration—both the form and the amount—in the planning for establishment of the service. The amount of compensation will no doubt always occasion some dissatisfaction. Many doctors feared the possibility of full-time salaried service, and were hostile to any proposals which in their judgment looked in that direction. Following a report by the so-called Spens Committee[21]—composed equally of medical and lay members—the government offered those who entered the service the alternatives of payment on the basis of the number of persons on the practitioner's list (capitation fee) or, with the consent of the executive council, a combination of fixed annual payment plus a lower capitation fee for each person on his list. Doctors in practice when the act became operative were free to choose between these methods; those who entered practice thereafter were required to accept the second (annual payment plus capitation fee) method for three years, and thereafter were free to continue or to shift to the other basis.[22]

Remuneration of Doctors

The fixed annual payment, to be available in combination with a reduced capitation fee with the approval of the

21. *Report of the Inter-departmental Committee on the Remuneration of General Practitioners,* Cmd. 6810, H.M.S.O., 1946.

22. *Health Services in Britain,* p. 9. "The Minister undertook that no full-time salaried service would be introduced unless the question was reviewed by Parliament." *Ibid.,* p. 10. By March 31, 1949, fixed annual payments had been granted to 2,123 doctors, including a number granted on appeal.

practitioner's executive council, was set and has remained at £300. The capitation fee varies not only as between those doctors for whom it constitutes the sole payment and those who receive the capitation fee in addition to the basic annual payment, but also as between areas. The exact fee payable in each case is worked out in the following manner:

A central pool is formed by setting aside 18s. 0d. per head of 95 per cent of the estimated civilian population of England, Scotland, and Wales. An International Distribution Committee apportions this pool between England and Wales on the one hand and Scotland on the other.

From the central pool, a certain sum is set aside for mileage payments to doctors in rural areas. After this deduction, the English and Welsh portion of the pool is distributed quarterly on the advice of the Medical Distribution Committee in the form of local pools to the 138 Executive Councils in England and Wales. The distribution is made in proportion to the number of persons on doctors' lists in each area, adjusted by the addition of one third of the number of persons in each area who are not on doctors' lists.

In the year 1948–1949, the local pools were distributed to the doctors in proportion to the number of persons on their lists at January 1, 1949. Advances were made quarterly, and a final adjustment made with the payment on March 31, 1949.[23]

Doctors within the service are able to augment their regular stipulated income by any or all of a number of special payments. Mileage payments are made to rural practitioners to compensate for the time and expense involved in visiting patients. A fund has been provided, from which the Minister, after consultation with the Medical Practices Committee, may make "inducement" payments to doctors who practice in difficult, sparsely populated or unpopular areas. Doctors may receive grants for training assistants, plus the salary, boarding expenses and car allowance for the assistant.

23. *Remuneration of Doctors Under the National Health Service* (I.D. 906), British Information Services, September 1950, p. 2.

A fee of five guineas (in some instances seven guineas) is paid to all doctors for each maternity case undertaken for patients on their lists. Payments are made to practitioners for drugs and dressings which they must carry for immediate use, and additional payments are made where, by arrangement with his executive council, a doctor dispenses drugs and supplies. Finally, a doctor may receive remuneration from a hospital management committee for services rendered as a member of the staff of a "cottage" hospital or as a part-time medical officer of a convalescent home or other institution. In addition to these receipts from within the organization of the medical services, a doctor may receive fees for work in a local health authority clinic or for service on a medical board of a government department or private corporation. And, of course, any doctor may receive fees from private patients.[24]

A doctor with a list of 2,000 at a capitation fee of, say, 15s. 2d. each, would receive £1,516 annually from this source. His gross receipts, after adding his fixed payment of £300, would thus be £1,816. If his expenses were 40 per cent of his gross income, his net income would amount to £1,090. The larger the number of persons on a doctor's list, the larger is his gross income. Expenses absorb a somewhat smaller percentage of the gross for the larger practices. Estimates of net income for larger practices are: 2,500 list, £1,317; 3,000 list, £1,606; 3,500 list, £1,920; 4,000 list, £2,222. Dr. W. C. Rappleye states, "It is generally agreed that most general practitioners receive as much or more than they had previously."[25]

24. *Ibid.*, pp. 2–3. By the end of 1949, 56 doctors were receiving "inducement payments," and 512 doctors had been approved for grants for training assistants. General practitioners also benefit financially from the superannuation scheme established under the act. The doctor contributes 6 per cent of his net annual receipts from the general medical and pharmaceutical services and the Exchequer contributes 8 per cent of those receipts. After a qualifying period, a doctor (or his widow) becomes entitled to a wide range of benefits on the occasion of his retirement, incapacity or death, the amounts depending on the number of years he has contributed. *Ibid.*, p. 4.

25. W. C. Rappleye, *op. cit.*, p. 26.

Sale of Practices

A problem related to that of remuneration developed out of the government's determination to prohibit the sale by general practitioners of their public "practices."[26] The profession strongly opposed this loss of the "value" of their practices. Many doctors had paid substantial sums for good will when they had begun to practice, and most of them looked forward to the sale of their practices to help them financially in their retirement. On the other hand, under the new arrangements for distribution of practices and the listing of patients, the sale of practices would have been anachronistic, and the government decided to eliminate it.

As a compromise, and in the interest of fairness, the act provided that compensation be awarded to cover the loss of reasonable expectations held by doctors who were in practice on the appointed day. A global sum of £66 million was set up, for pro rata distribution to practitioners who joined the service, as compensation for loss of the sale value of their respective practices. Individual compensation from the fund was to be fixed, under the act and later regulations, by the Minister (with the advice, at his discretion, of the Practices Compensation Committee) on the basis of the "annual loss" suffered by the practitioner—taken as his average gross yearly receipts calculated by reference to the last two accounting years immediately preceding the appointed day.[27]

26. "Where the name of any medical practitioner is on the appointed day or at any time thereafter, entered on any list of medical practitioners undertaking to provide general medical services, it shall be unlawful subsequently to sell the goodwill or any part of the goodwill of the medical practice of that medical practitioner." National Health Service Act, 1946, Sec. 35 (1). The act permits a doctor who has withdrawn from the service, and who thereafter undertakes private practice in an area where his name has never been on an executive council list, to sell the good will of his practice in that area.

27. *Ibid.*, Secs. 36 and 37; and Charles Hill and John Woodcock, *The National Health Service*, Christopher Johnson, London, 1949, Chap. 7. Each claimant was to receive such proportion of the over-all £66 million as his "annual loss" bore to the aggregate annual loss.

In the bulk of cases, payment will be made on the death or the retirement of the practitioner, whichever occurs first, and in the meantime semiannual payments of interest, calculated at the rate of 2.75 per cent a year on the base sum will be made from the appointed day until the base compensation sum is finally paid.[28] Special provisions to deal with the intricacies of compensation in the case of partnerships were added in the legislation of 1949.[29]

Treatment of Complaints

An elaborate structure of committees, procedures and penalties was provided by the act and regulations established under the act, to deal with the wide varieties of complaints of nonfeasance and malfeasance that might be made by officials, patients and other practitioners against general practitioners, dental practitioners and persons undertaking to provide pharmaceutical and supplementary ophthalmic services.[30] These safeguards have been described as follows:

> Provision is made for the constitution by each Executive Council of Medical, Dental and Pharmaceutical Service Committees for the investigation of complaints; for the reference of certain matters involving wholly professional considerations to the Local Medical Committee (or the Local Dental or Pharmaceutical Committee); and for the consideration by the Tribunal appointed under Section 42 of the Act of representations that the name of a doctor, dentist or chemist should be removed from the Executive Council lists. Regulations prescribe the procedure to be followed before the Local Medical and other professional committees, the Service Committees, the Executive Council and the Tribunal and for appeals against the decisions of those bodies.[31]

28. *Ibid.* See also National Health Service (Amendment) Act, 1949, 12, 13 & 14 George 6, Ch. 93, Sec. 8.

29. National Health Service (Amendment) Act, 1949, Part I.

30. National Health Service Act, 1946, Secs. 42 and 47; *National Health Service (Service Committees and Tribunal) Regulations* (S.I. 1948, No. 507), 1948.

31. C. Hill and J. Woodcock, *op. cit.,* p. 127.

Provision was made for dealing with such complaints as excessive prescribing, errors in certification, inadequate clinical records, improper demand for fees, supplying and charging for substances not on the pharmaceutical lists, and unprofessional conduct such as failure to exercise reasonable skill and care, to visit or treat patients requiring treatment or to order or supply necessary drugs. Doctors may complain of the conduct of other doctors; and doctors may complain of the conduct of patients under treatment. The procedures established by the act and the regulations appear to be well designed to insure both ascertainment of facts and full protection of the legitimate interests of the accused, through requirements for notice, hearing and presentations, representation and appeal. Final decisions, on appeal, lie with the Minister, and penalties range from censure and withholding of remuneration to dismissal from the service. The several committees and tribunals before whom the accused is privileged to appear are heavily weighted with professional members.[32]

Dentists under the Plan

Arrangements covering dentistry differ slightly from those applied to general medical practice. Dentists "sign up" on the lists of local executive councils (indeed, a dentist may sign with more than one council); but patients do not register with particular dentists, and they are free to apply for treatment to any dentist, wherever located. The dentist may accept as many patients as he cares to treat; he is under no obligation to accept any particular applicant, and he is free to treat as many private patients as he is willing to take. It was explained to the public at the outset that because of the anticipated demand for dental work and the limited number of dentists, ordinary patients would undoubtedly experience difficulty in securing prompt treatment, and that priority under the service would be given to young people and expectant mothers. Dentists may leave the service by giving required notice.

32. For further details of disciplinary procedure and investigation of complaints, see C. Hill and J. Woodcock, *op. cit.*, Chap. 12.

Dentists are required to prepare a dental estimate form for each patient, including therein a statement of the full treatment which in the dentist's opinion is necessary, and of such part of the recommended treatment as the patient is willing to undergo. With reference to certain more or less standard items the dentist may proceed at once with the treatment and submit his bill to the Dental Estimates Board.[33] Before undertaking items of treatment not on the standard list, however, the practitioner must, save in case of emergency, present his estimate to, and receive the approval of the Dental Estimates Board.

Apparently because of the use of a different method of payment (stated fees for services actually performed rather than an annual capitation payment), coupled with errors in early predictions, dentists in Great Britain have been remunerated rather more generously than doctors. Dentists who join the service are under contract with their local executive councils, but the scale of fees is set on a national basis.

Within a few weeks after the service was begun, some 5,386 dentists—out of an estimated total of 10,000 available for active general practice—had signed with their executive councils, and in about eight months (by February 26, 1949) the number had reached 9,272. Original estimates of the extent to which the service would be used were embarrassingly modest: it was expected that the demand for dental treatment would run at an annual rate of about 4 million cases, whereas during the period ending March 31, 1949, the yearly rate was approximately 7 million cases.[34]

33. *Ibid.*, Chap. 14. The Dental Estimates Board consists of a chairman (dentist), and six dentists and two lay members. The board passes on estimates submitted by dentists and on bills submitted for payment. It submits monthly statements to executive councils of payments due to dentists on their lists.

34. *Report of the Ministry of Health for the year ended 31st March, 1949*, Cmd. 7910, H.M.S.O., 1950, p. 269. The demand at the peak was at the annual rate of 8.5 million cases, and at the end of the year cases were running at an annual rate of 8 million.

Early in the operation of the dental services it was evident that general dental practitioners were earning amounts substantially larger than those contemplated when the schedule of fees was adopted. The original schedule was set up in the light of a report by an interdepartmental (Spens) committee in which consideration was given to estimates of timings of different dental operations and ratio of expenses to net remuneration, etc.,[35] and it was intended to produce for the fully employed, experienced, unassisted dentist, a net annual income of about £1,778. Weekly chair-side time was taken at 33 hours, and expenses were estimated at about 52 per cent of gross receipts.

By October and November of 1948, a number of dentists were earning sums "out of all proportion with the recommendations in the Spens Report; and regulations were accordingly made on 23rd December and 17th January, the effect of which was to halve all earnings in excess of £4,800 gross in a full year, with effect from 1st February."[36] An investigation in the early winter of 1949 of the earnings of 5,078 dentists showed that 1,066 were grossing more than £6,000 from their public practice, and that, of these, the gross receipts of 333 were above £8,400. In an order superseding the earlier selective cut, the Minister promulgated a new schedule of fees, effective June 1, 1949, designed to reduce gross fees by about 20 per cent.[37] Studies of timing of dental operations and of dental expenses were instituted, but before definite conclusions were drawn from these, and in advance of any agreement with the dentists, the Minister announced another interim across-the-board re-

35. *Report of the Inter-departmental Committee on the Remuneration of General Dental Practitioners,* Cmd. 7402, H.M.S.O., May 1948.
36. *Report of the Ministry of Health for the year ended 31st March, 1949,* p. 269. In announcing the measure in Parliament, the Minister said, "I am adopting a temporary arrangement whereby fees are reduced by half after a dentist reaches an income of £4,800 gross—or £1,000 in excess of the point at which the Spens Committee said the risk of bad dentistry began." *Parliamentary Debates* (Hansard), House of Commons, Vol. 459, col. 71.
37. *The Times* (London), May 20, 1949.

duction of 10 per cent in the remuneration of dental practitioners, to be effective May 1, 1950.[38]

Ophthalmic Services and Pharmacy

Part II of the act, relating to the provision by the Minister of hospital and specialist services, contemplated the organization and furnishing of complete ophthalmic services. Pending the establishment of this service, however, the act (Sec. 41) provided, under the heading of "Supplementary Ophthalmic Service," for the testing of vision and the supplying of optical appliances under the direction of the local executive councils. Every person is entitled, upon the recommendation of any general practitioner, to have his eyes tested by an approved ophthalmic optician and, if glasses are recommended, to obtain them without cost to himself, from the optician or any other approved dispensing optician.[39]

38. *The Times* (London), April 28, 1950. This action was debated in Parliament on May 15, 1950, at which time it was pointed out that to institute an across-the-board cut would have the effect of penalizing the more careful practitioners because some members of the profession had made exorbitant earnings by rushing their patients. The government indicated its willingness to consider proposals designed to mitigate this effect. The basic criticism of the Opposition was directed to the whole structure of the dental services which it said operated to divert service from the real priority classes—school children and expectant mothers. *Parliamentary Debates* (Hansard), House of Commons, Vol. 475, cols. 911–54. See also *The Economist*, May 20, 1950, pp. 1113–14.

There have been two reductions in the remuneration paid to ophthalmic opticians and practitioners, and a reduction to 16 per cent in mark-ups allowed to chemists. *The Times* (London), April 25, 1951.

39. C. Hill and J. Woodcock, *op. cit.*, Chap. 13. "For spectacles within an approved range and for replacements and repairs not necessitated by lack of care no charge will be made, the whole cost falling on the State," *ibid.*, p. 157. *The Times* (London), May 1, 1950, reported that "from today there will be four varieties of spectacles supplied by opticians without charge, and there will be a range of 14 frames toward the cost of which payment will be made by the patient. Payments will vary from 2s. to 12s. 3d." The recommendation of the

Local administration of the service is in the hands of an Ophthalmic Services Committee, set up by the local executive council. It consists of eight members of the council other than those appointed by the local medical committee, one medical practitioner appointed from those members of the council appointed by the local medical committee, and three other medical practitioners, three ophthalmic opticians and one dispensing optician appointed in each case by their respective professional organizations. To qualify for the service, practitioners must first apply to, and be approved by, a central professional committee and thereafter apply for inclusion in the local list. Fees for testing and dispensing are established on a national basis, and are paid through the executive councils.

The final general task laid by the act (Sec. 38) upon the local executive councils was that of arranging for the supply of pharmaceutical services—"of proper and sufficient drugs and medicines and prescribed appliances to all persons in the area who are receiving general medical services, and of prescribed drugs and medicines to all persons in the area who are receiving general dental services." Qualified persons or firms may apply to be included on the "Pharmaceutical List" drawn up by each executive council, and are required to supply such drugs or appliances as may be prescribed by doctors or dentists on official forms. Doctors have complete discretion in prescribing drugs; dentists may prescribe only those set out in official schedules. Dentists may not prescribe appliances, but doctors may prescribe appliances that are scheduled.

All drugs, if officially prescribed by doctors and dentists in the service, are furnished free of charge to the patient, and until recently this was true as well of all appliances. Patients who receive their prescriptions from doctors to whom they pay fees under private arrangements, however, are required to pay, as well, for their medicines and appliances. Under the terms of the Amending Act of 1949,

---

medical practitioner is required only on the occasion of the first visit, and under some circumstances may be dispensed with entirely.

charges may be made for such pharmaceutical services as the Minister may direct, but in his Budget speech on April 18, 1950, the Chancellor of the Exchequer announced for the government that the policy of free drugs and appliances would be continued.[40] In the Budget speech a year later the Chancellor proposed that a charge of about one half of the scale fee be made for dentures and for the cost of all spectacles for adults.[41]

Pharmacists present their bills, and are paid monthly by their executive councils. Prescriptions and orders which he has filled under the service are presented by the pharmacist to the pricing bureau for his region (there are thirteen regions for England and one for Wales), whose function it is to "price" the prescriptions and orders and to certify to the councils the amounts due to each claimant. A joint pricing committee coordinates the work of the bureaus. Local pharmaceutical committees, if found representative of those furnishing pharmaceutical services in the area, are recognized by the Minister for certain advisory duties.

Local Health Authorities

The second general sector of health service administration is concerned with the establishment of health centers and provision of special services by local health authorities. Here, even more strongly than in the case of the activities of the local executive councils, the emphasis is on local control as distinct from centralized bureaucracy. The local health authority as constituted by the act "shall for each

40. National Health Service (Amendment) Act, 1949, Sec. 16; *Parliamentary Debates* (Hansard), House of Commons, Vol. 474, col. 60.

41. *The Times* (London), April 11, 1951. Up to mid-December 1949, some 12,874 artificial limbs, 10,004 optical eyes, 8,913 wigs and 48,000 hearing aids had been furnished. *Some Statistics on the National Health Service* (I. D. 1002), British Information Services, March 1950, pp. 2–3. It was announced in April 1951 that over 20 million pairs of spectacles had been supplied by the service. *The Times* (London), April 25, 1951.

county be the council of the county and for each county borough be the council of the county borough."[42]

Authorities are required to submit proposals for carrying out their specified duties to the Minister for approval. If any authority fails to submit proposals, the Minister on his own initiative may make proposals that shall be put into effect by the authority. Nonetheless, most commentators have been impressed by the uncoordinated autonomy of local health authorities. The fact that these governmental units, as the underlying structure, not only bear no logical relation to the services required of them by the new system, but are outmoded for the performance even of their traditional government functions, means that the prospects of this branch of the service are definitely limited.[43]

Health Centers

The first of the two broad sets of duties placed by the act upon the local health authorities is "to provide, equip and maintain to the satisfaction of the Minister premises, which shall be called 'health centres,' "[44] at which facilities are to be available for the provision of general medical, dental and pharmaceutical services, specialist and other services for out-patients, and any of the services which the health authorities are required or empowered to provide. Necessary staff is to be maintained, but the authorities are

42. National Health Service Act, 1946, Sec. 19. Part III of the act, comprising sections 19–30, inclusive, covers "Health Services Provided by Local Health Authorities." Each authority is required to establish a health committee (a majority of the members must be members of the authority), to refer all matters, except those requiring immediate action, to the committee for consideration and report, and is empowered to delegate most of its operative duties to the committee. *Ibid.*, Fourth Schedule.

43. It seems apparent that the arrangements represent an open concession to those opponents of the national health service who feared "centralized bureaucracy," and that their presence in the act is to be explained largely on grounds of political expediency. In this connection, see Robert A. Brady, *op. cit.*, pp. 390–92.

44. National Health Service Act, 1946, Sec. 21.

specifically forbidden to employ medical and dental practitioners to render their respective services at health centers.

The health centers were to be a bright new experiment. They would furnish facilities and equipment for the use of general practitioners beyond their ability to provide for themselves, and would serve as local centers for health education and development of programs for the advancement of public health. It was expected that various types of centers would be devised and placed in operation and that out of the broad range of experience the very best in group and community practice and service would develop.

To date, however, experience is almost wholly lacking. It was originally stipulated that proposals for the provision of health centers were to be submitted by November 30, 1947, but the deadline was postponed and later canceled. A few schemes were submitted, in instances where existing establishments were being continued, but as of the most recent report, only one scheme has been approved for the construction of a new center. The program has been delayed by the severe shortages in building materials and labor, and also by reason of its novelty and the attendant uncertainty as to just what is desirable in design and operation.[45]

Nursing and Other Services

The second set of duties that local health authorities are required to perform consists of arranging for the provision of care for expectant and nursing mothers and young children, of domiciliary midwife services, of health visiting and home nursing services, of vaccination and immunization services and of ambulance service. In addition, the authorities are empowered to arrange for domestic help for households where such help is required because of illness

45. "No authority has yet put forward a comprehensive programme in a scheme under this section, and it would be undesirable to confirm such a programme, if one were submitted, in view of our present inexperience in this field. Nevertheless, much exploratory work is in progress. . . ." *Report of the Ministry of Health for the year ended 31st March, 1949*, p. 121. See also *C.H.S.C. First Annual Report*, pp. 4–5.

or the presence of young children and to adjust any charges for the service in line with the ability of the household to pay. Authorities are permitted wide discretion in selecting the "arrangements" to be employed in providing the services, ranging from the use of existing organizations of various types to proprietary action by the authority itself.

The first year's operation of these several services was marked by a heavy demand for ambulance service and help in the home. In both cases the facilities were overworked and the costs were high. There was evidence of abuse, but the Ministry was inclined to believe that the demand indicated a great pent-up need hitherto unsatisfied.[46] There were transitional maladjustments and misunderstandings in moving the services to the authorities, but these were expected and the change seems to have been effected without great public reaction, either favorable or unfavorable.

Hospitals Nationalized

Nationalization entered the British health service in the form of government ownership and operation of the nation's hospitals. The structure is a curious mixture of centralization and local authority, of political and professional control, and of state service and voluntary workers.

Voluntary hospitals ranged in size from the great teaching hospitals to small cottage hospitals of less than ten beds. They varied greatly in functions and traditions, and in the structure and character of their organization and their voluntary governing boards. Public hospitals were supported and run by local authorities or by joint boards representing several local authorities, and in many cases their services were principally the care of the poor and the feeble-minded. Typically they were managed by committees of county councils or other local authorities.

46. *Report of the Ministry of Health for the year ended 31st March, 1949,* p. 122. "[The home help service] has played a most important part in enabling the elderly chronic sick, who require care rather than active treatment, to remain at home and lead fuller lives in their family circle than they can in a hospital ward, which is so apt to become their permanent abode."

Part II of the National Health Service Act of 1946 made it the duty of the Minister to provide—to such extent as he might deem necessary to meet reasonable requirements—hospital accommodations, medical, nursing and other services required at or for the purposes of hospitals, and the services of specialists at hospitals, health centers and clinics or at the home of the patient; and under the terms of the act the Minister took over the ownership of all the hospitals in the country, with the exception of a few which he disclaimed for special reasons.[47] England and Wales were divided into fourteen regions, and the hospitals in each (with the exception of the "teaching" hospitals) were placed under the control of a regional hospital board responsible to the Minister. So-called teaching hospitals were named—one in each of ten regions, and a total of 26 in the four metropolitan (London) regions—each to be controlled by a board of governors. Teaching hospitals were to be so constituted as to provide necessary clinical and research facilities to the universities with which each was connected. This has meant that many of the teaching hospitals have had other hospitals attached to them in order to meet this need.

Teaching hospitals are run directly by their respective boards of governors, but all other hospitals are in the hands of hospital management committees, each of which is in charge of a large hospital or a group of smaller hospitals. The regional boards, the members of which are named by the Minister, appoint the members of the management committees for the hospitals, as the boards choose to group them, in their respective regions.[48] The method of appoint-

47. Some 2,688 hospitals were taken over, with beds (including 50,-000 unstaffed) totaling 504,209, as of December 31, 1948. The Minister disclaimed 207 establishments. *Some Statistics on the National Health Service*, p. 3.

48. The Third Schedule to the National Health Service Act, 1946, provides for the constitution of the several hospital governing bodies as follows:

Regional Hospital Boards. A chairman, appointed by the Minister together with such other members (similarly appointed) as the Minis-

ment of the members of the two top governing boards
(regional boards and boards of governors), with the final
selection in the hands of the Minister after consultation
with many groups, both professional and political (elected
"authorities"), made it possible to secure a balanced blending of interests in hospital control. The regional boards
have varied in size from twenty-two to thirty-three members, and while individual qualities of appointees rather
than representation of interests has always been stressed in
the Minister's selections, "interests" are certainly present
and are bound to make themselves felt.[49]

ter thinks fit, to include persons appointed after consultation with the
university with which the board's hospital and specialist services are to
be associated, after consultation with representative medical organizations, and after consultation with local health authorities in the area
and any other organizations which appear to the Minister to be concerned. The original board was also to include persons appointed after
consultation with organizations representative of voluntary hospitals
in the area.

Hospital Management Committees. A chairman appointed by the
regional hospital board, together with such members (similarly appointed) as the board thinks fit after consulting with the following:
local health authorities, executive councils, senior medical and dental
staff at the hospitals concerned, and any other organizations concerned. In the case of voluntary hospitals, the original committees
were to include persons appointed after consultation with the erstwhile governing body of the hospital.

Boards of Governors of Teaching Hospitals. A chairman appointed
by the Minister, together with such members (similarly appointed) as
the Minister thinks fit, and of those members not more than one fifth
are to be nominated by the associated university; not more than one
fifth are to be nominated by the regional hospital board; not more
than one fifth are to be nominated by the medical and dental teaching
staff of the hospital; and others are to be appointed after consultation
with such local health authorities and other organizations as the Minister finds are concerned. The original boards were to contain persons
appointed after consultation with the erstwhile governing bodies of
any voluntary hospital comprised in the teaching hospital.

The several boards and committees are "bodies corporate with perpetual succession."

49. "The Hospital Service: System of Management," *Planning*,
September 26, 1949, p. 97. In mid-1949 the 364 members of the 14 regional boards included 120 doctors, 10 hospital matrons and 2 practicing dentists. *Ibid.*, p. 101.

The grouping of hospitals by the regional boards raised the issue of *locality* versus *function*. In the main the issue seems to have been resolved "by a fairly judicious blending of the principles of functional self-sufficiency and relationship with a locality or localities."[50]

One study of the new service has pointed out that whereas it was intended—and the intention was emphasized—that hospitals, with the exception of the teaching hospitals, should be under a two-tier administration, a four-tier structure has in fact developed.[51] Primarily because of its financial responsibility, the Ministry of Health has been forced to concern itself with details which it had been expected would be dealt with almost exclusively by the regional boards and, under the boards, the management committees.[52] At the other extreme, "house committees" have grown up, more or less informally, under the management committees, to concern themselves with the domestic affairs of individual hospitals.

50. *Ibid.*, p. 89. Hospital groups of varying size and varying pattern were decided upon. In some instances, institutions geographically remote were joined under the same management committee in order to bring a particular specialty into the group. "Some comparatively large groups of 2,000–2,500 beds were permitted, more particularly in the large urban areas, while the bigger mental hospitals were for the most part given their own management committees. In some cases sanatoria and mental hospitals were grouped functionally." *Ibid.*, pp. 89–90.

51. *Ibid.*, pp. 90 ff.

52. "The Regional Boards are responsible for the general planning of the Hospital Service within their region. They receive financial grants from the Treasury and allocate them among the various groups; they appoint the chairmen and members of the H.M.C.s themselves, as well as the specialists and consultants working with particular hospitals, and have general supervision of the work of the groups. Nevertheless, the H.M.C.s are intended to be at the centre of gravity of the new Service. They have powers to appoint and dismiss all staff (with the exception of consultants), to maintain all land and premises under their control, and to acquire and maintain equipment, furniture and other movable property . . . [Decisions of the Regional Boards] on clinical and functional matters are normally taken only after consultation with the Management Committees, who alone can implement such decisions." *Ibid.*, pp. 91–92. See also National Health Service Act, 1946, Secs. 11 and 12.

The Chancellor of the Exchequer was empowered by the act to take over the endowments of voluntary hospitals. The Minister of Health decided, however, to leave all teaching hospitals with their fiscal endowments, and to give them power to make medical education freer than in the past. In addition, about £32 million belonging to the voluntary hospitals was reserved for them to spend over and above the funds provided by the state. The money was left in the hands of the regional boards, with the power to distribute it to the local management committees of the hospitals, so that the hospitals could be responsive to local influence as well as to central direction. The regional boards, given an annual budget, have freedom within that budget to make their own allocations.[53]

The management committees of the hospitals, receiving operating funds from the regional boards, have virtually full spending powers for salaries and wages (except for consultants), for drugs, appliances and equipment, utilities, maintenance, repairs and renewals. They make monthly requisitions on their boards for cash. Estimates on a yearly basis are prepared by the management committees; these are reviewed by the regional boards and, together with board estimates, are sent to the Minister who has the overall task of reviewing and fitting the total estimates to a pattern acceptable to the Treasury and Parliament.

Specialists and Consultants

Employment by the Boards of specialists and consultants has raised one serious problem—but one that is neither new nor peculiar to a nationalized service. The remuneration and conditions of employment of medical specialists are relatively so favorable that recruiting students to train for service as general practitioners seems likely to become increasingly difficult unless readjustments are made. Before the service was instituted, the career of the specialist was something of a financial speculation, so that a decided con-

53. The Minister of Health, in *Parliamentary Debates* (Hansard), House of Commons, Vol. 422, cols. 62–63.

centration of specialists occurred in centers where large numbers of fee-paying patients were present. There was a shortage of specialists and they were badly distributed. Under the new dispensation, specialists as a group will lead more comfortable lives, with greater security and higher pay. *The Times* tells the story:

They are virtually guaranteed net incomes from all sources of about £2,000 a year at the age of thirty-two, rising to £3,000 a year at forty; and a third of all specialists are promised considerably more. The standard starting salary for the full-time services of the newly qualified specialist at thirty-two is £1,700, to which must be added the State superannuation contribution of £136. . . . From thirty-two until forty the specialist is to receive automatic annual increases so that at and beyond the age of forty he can rely on a "basic" salary of £2,750 with £220 added to his superannuation account.[54]

In addition to salaries and pensions, specialists now receive paid holidays, paid leaves for study, continuance of salary during illness, and payment of many expenses. There are available to them, as well, "distinction awards," to be distributed on the recommendation of a committee of eminent medical men, which will add £500 to the annual salary of one specialist in every five, £1,500 to one in every ten, and £2,500 to four in every hundred. *The Times* continues:

The lowest rate for the youngest specialist represents roughly the highest rate the really conscientious general practitioner can hope to earn from the service if he restricts his practice to 2,500 patients in order to do good work and undertakes a good deal of midwifery and other duties to make up his income. . . . Only by undertaking the care of 3,000 or 4,000 patients, which is out of the question for most doctors and intolerable to the best, can he hope to approach the incomes now offered to specialists of more than three or five years' standing.[55]

54. *The Times* (London), March 17, 1949. The terms of remuneration for specialists were fixed by the government following the report in May 1948, of the Inter-departmental Committee on the Remuneration of Consultants and Specialists, Cmd. 7420, H.M.S.O., 1948.

55. *Ibid.* *The Times* goes on to point out that a revision of other professional remuneration, both of doctors and others, is likely to

Those who use hospital accommodation or the services of specialists or consultants, at the recommendation of their doctors, need make no payment. Even semiprivate and private rooms are available without cost to the patient if his condition requires such accommodation. On the other hand, if the patient chooses semiprivate accommodations he must bear a part of the cost of the room and hospital service, and if he chooses a private room he must bear the whole cost. Patients are not permitted to select the hospital at which they will receive treatment. If their condition warrants it they may receive specialist services at their homes, but neither they nor their practitioners are permitted to choose the specialist who is to attend. Specialists may serve private patients for pay.[56]

The really notable and moving fact in the whole set of arrangements, however, is that patients may have the full range of hospital and specialist service if required by their condition, without financial worry; and practitioners may feel entirely free to recommend for their patients the fullest treatment required for their needs, irrespective of the financial circumstances of the patient.

Acceptance of the Service—and Its Cost

The "tooling-up" period between the passage of the act (November 6, 1946) and the "appointed day" (July 5, 1948)

result. Appointments to specialist posts are limited in number and, if the pay of general practitioners is regarded as unsatisfactory the profession as a whole will be less attractive to potential entrants. The problem of limited opportunities was raised dramatically by the Ministry's announcement in the fall of 1950 that the number of registrars in training in hospitals for specialist positions was to be reduced from 2,800 to 1,700. *Ibid.*, November 25 and 28, 1950 and January 1, 1951.

56. One anomaly in arrangements for charges has been pointed out. "The patient who obtains general practitioner service privately is not denied hospital and specialist services (including medicines) at the public expense. Conversely, the patient obtaining general practitioner service at the public expense may obtain hospital or specialist service privately. But the patient obtaining general practitioner treatment at his own expense cannot obtain drugs and medicines at the public expense." C. Hill and J. Woodcock, *op. cit.*, pp. 200–01.

produced much disagreement, but adjustment proceeded and the service went into effect on schedule. It was, in fact, well organized, well staffed and equipped—and well received. The service has developed into an accepted, going enterprise. As of the beginning of 1950, some 41.2 million persons (95 per cent of the population) had joined doctors' lists in England and Wales; and approximately 88 per cent of the doctors and 95 per cent of the dentists and virtually all of the nation's pharmacists had entered the service.

Many points of disagreement and dissatisfaction remain —some will continue to remain—and many of these are important matters of policy. Yet the positions taken officially by the major political parties in the General Election of 1950 and in Parliamentary debates, together with the tenor of articles in medical and opinion journals suggest no present prospect of a return to the old system or even a significant modification of the system now obtaining.[57] There are defects; changes will certainly occur and new defects will appear; but the philosophy and the general structure of the health service are not likely to be disturbed.

A major criticism of the service grows out of the heavy burden of cost. Alarm is expressed not only over the magnitude of the cost, but also over the fact that it was not anticipated either by the public or, apparently, by the government or the Ministry itself. Only a small portion of the total cost of the service is covered by contributions from national insurance. Most of the burden is borne by the general taxpayers.

The original official estimate of the net cost of the service

57. The attitude of the British public is accurately and pointedly described by the title of an article on the British health service appearing in *Newsweek*, August 7, 1950, p. 46: "Britons OK Health Plan Despite Beefs."

The controversy that occurred during the passage of the health service legislation and the subsequent negotiations between the government and the medical profession is reminiscent of that occasioned in 1911 by the institution of national health insurance. See Roy Lewis and Angus Maude, *The English Middle Classes*, Knopf, New York, 1950, pp. 187–88.

to the general taxpayer for the first nine months was at the annual rate of approximately £200 million; the final estimate came to £278 million. The original estimate for the year 1949–1950 was £260 million; the revised estimate totaled £359 million. The original estimate for 1950–1951 is now set at £393 million.[58] The estimate for 1950–1951 for each of the main branches of the service, together with the corresponding figure in the revised (final) estimate for 1949–1950, is shown in Table 5.

TABLE 5

HEALTH SERVICE COSTS: ESTIMATES FOR 1949–1950 AND 1950–1951
(In Millions)

Main Branches of the Service	Revised Estimate 1949–1950	Original Estimate 1950–1951
Grants to local health authorities	£ 15.4	£ 18.5
General practitioner service	47.1	48.2
Pharmaceutical service	35.3	31.0
Dental service	48.6	46.6
Supplementary ophthalmic service	25.1	28.2
Advances to hospital boards	243.3	274.3
(Including maintenance expenditures)	(232.8)	(262.6)
Other health service expenditures	34.4	33.8
Total gross cost to taxpayer	£449.2	£480.6
Less offsets and appropriations-in-aid	90.7	87.7
Total net cost to taxpayer	£358.5	£392.9

Source: The Economist, April 1, 1950, p. 699.

Note: Publication of civil appropriation accounts for 1949–1950 showed that although the revised estimate for the health services was £449.2 million, the actual expenditure was only £436 million. The Times (London), January 30, 1951.

58. Seventh Report from the Select Committee on Estimates (Session 1948–1949), H.M.S.O., 1949, p. viii; The Economist, March 11, 1950, pp. 520–21; The Times (London), March 15, 1950. It was estimated that the gross expenditure of £464.5 million on the service for 1950–1951 would be reduced by appropriations-in-aid of £71.5 million. The figures given here include Scotland, together with England and Wales.

The estimates first announced for 1951–1952 were about £5 million higher than for 1950–1951; the net cost to the taxpayer was to be about £398 million. The cost of hospital maintenance and operation, specialist and ancillary services showed an increase of £15.6 million, but charges to be imposed for the first time would effect a large saving in dental and ophthalmic services. It was later announced that the figure of £398 million would be raised to £400 million.[59]

Although more might be spent to make the health service all that could be asked for or, in fact, is asked for, there is a growing realization that the claims of other services and goods on the national income must be given a sympathetic hearing. In the Parliamentary debate of March 14, 1950, on the supplementary estimate of £98 million for the year 1949–1950, the Opposition charged wasteful overspending. The government pleaded the need for service. Both sides agreed on the wisdom of reasoned expenditure in the light of limited resources and competing needs.

The Chancellor of the Exchequer was called to task by the Opposition for failure to enforce in his own departments the injunction he had issued earlier in the year "that only in special cases, such as, for example, major changes of policy, can any supplementary Estimates in future be permitted." In reply, the Chancellor pointed out that the estimates for hospital and specialist expenditures were made by the hospital management committees in August 1948, that the committees were at that time without experience and without adequate staffs and records, and therefore they could not reasonably have been expected to be accurate in their forecasts. The only way in which actual expenditures could have been kept within the estimates would have been to reduce hospital beds and essential services—an unthinkable course. Specialists' salaries had been negotiated after the making of the estimates, the price of supplies had risen, and no one could have foreseen the extent of the pent-up demand for dental, supplementary and pharmaceu-

59. *The Times* (London), March 28, 1951 and April 25, 1951; *The Economist*, March 31, 1951, p. 729.

tical services that had in fact developed and was responsible for the great increase in cost.

The government conceded the presence of some waste and inefficiency, but related most of it to the newness of the service, the frankly tentative character of its organization and procedures, and the inexperience of the great numbers of persons, both voluntary and paid, who were engaged in administering the new venture. The Chancellor announced that the estimates for the forthcoming year would constitute an absolute ceiling on expenditures, and stated that some way must be found to associate the Minister of Health more directly with the regional boards and management committees in financial matters, and that there would be consultations with these bodies.[60]

The problem of cost cannot, of course, be considered independently of the detailed items of each part of the service for which the expenditures are incurred, and of the structural organization that conditions the operation of the service. Much, both official and unofficial, has been published on these matters, expressing the views of individuals, committees, associations and agencies.[61]

60. See *Parliamentary Debates* (Hansard), House of Commons, Vol. 472, cols. 916–1038. The government treated the Opposition motion on this occasion as a vote of censure, and in the balloting won by a vote of 308–289. The Liberals did not join the Opposition. For an earlier debate, on February 17, 1949, along much the same line, see *ibid.*, Vol. 461, cols. 1351–1462. In his Budget speech, April 18, 1950, the Chancellor reiterated his decision to permit no expenditures beyond the estimate. The period of initiation is over, he said, and "It is clear that it is not possible in existing circumstances to permit any over-all increase in the expenditure on the Health Services. Any expansion in one part of the Service must in the future be met by economies or, if necessary, by contraction in others." *Ibid.*, Vol. 474, cols. 59–60.

61. See, particularly, the *Seventh Report from the Select Committee on Estimates* (Session 1948–1949); the *Twentieth Report* from the same committee, H.M.S.O., 1949, containing the Departmental Reply to the *Seventh Report;* the *Third Report from the Select Committee on Estimates* (Session 1950), H.M.S.O., 1950; W. C. Rappleye, *op. cit.;* the Autumn 1949, Special Issue of *The Practitioner* on "The National Health Service Act in Great Britain: A Review of the First Year's

Defects May Be Remedied

The elaborate superstructure of boards, committees and subcommittees, with the inevitable conflicts of jurisdiction, interests and personalities has aroused criticism; and the general tripartite structure that was adopted in order to blend central control with local autonomy has produced difficult problems of its own. The point is frequently made that hospital management committees should be held strictly to long-term, over-all limits of expenditure, but that within those limits they should exercise their own discretion without restraint by the Ministry. There is great dissatisfaction over the obvious lack of coordination in the ambulance service and in the services involved in maternity cases, where regional boards, local authorities and executive councils all are involved.[62]

Of all of the complaints voiced by doctors, other than those concerned directly with underpay, the most persistent relates to certification—a task for which the service itself is not directly responsible. Medical and health certificates are required of the British people to qualify them for participation and benefits in a long list of activities and schemes, and the paper work involved in preparing the necessary records, reports and certificates has become a very irritating burden. Participation in the work of the seemingly endless array of committees and subcommittees is also cited by practitioners and specialists as a particularly annoying and frustrating type of nonmedical activity, and here the service must admit its share of the responsibility.

Practitioners have increasingly claimed that rates of pay, never really satisfactory, have failed conspicuously to keep pace with the rising cost of living. For many months a movement has been under way looking toward a general withdrawal of practitioners from the service unless the Minister adopts a more sympathetic attitude toward the representa-

Working"; *C.H.S.C. First Annual Report; Planning,* September 26, 1949 and February 13, 1950; *The Economist,* July 1, 1950, pp. 5–6, and March 24, 1951, p. 677; and *The Times* (London), March 2, 1951.

62. See the *Report of the Select Committee on Estimates,* reported and discussed in *The Economist,* September 22, 1951, p. 670.

tions that have been made to him over a long period. Matters reached a crisis early in 1951, but after a satisfactory meeting with the new Minister of Health,[63] followed by his letter recognizing the existence of a good prima facie case for an immediate review of the adequacy of general practitioners' remuneration, the tension eased and a special conference of the representatives of local medical committees passed a resolution welcoming the "new attitude" of the Ministry. A continuation of negotiations was arranged, but in the meantime the possibility of a general withdrawal of doctors from the service was not precluded.[64]

None of the criticisms leveled against the service constitutes an attack on its basic philosophy; and all of them—except those that are mutually contradictory—are capable of being dealt with without impairing the existing basic structure. It may be that too much was undertaken "too soon";[65] it may be that too much attention has been given to a standard of perfection and too little to cost and to "competing claims on the nation's purse."[66] Changes in organization will certainly be made and, in time, remade. Complaints over details—which, of course, do not appear to the complainants as mere "details"—will never cease. The significant facts in the present situation are that the idea of medical service for all is completely accepted in Great Britain,[67]

63. See p. 224.

64. *The Times* (London), December 23, 1949; June 30, July 14, 1950; February 23, 28, March 29, 30, 1951. The whole problem of absolute and relative earnings of general practitioners, dentists and specialists is discussed in a special article, "Health Service Pay," in *ibid.*, February 28, 1951. Later developments include a demand by the doctors for arbitration of their claims for increased pay, and a conditional acceptance by the Minister. *The Economist,* June 23, 1951, p. 1497; August 11, 1951, p. 330.

Chemists, too, have grown restive in the matter of remuneration. *The Times* (London), July 1 and August 31, 1950.

65. For a reasoned denial of this contention, see W. C. Rappleye, *op. cit.,* p. 9.

66. See *The Times* (London), March 15, 1950.

67. Despite his tiredness and his individual grievances, the conscientious practitioner knows that the service is making it possible for him to provide, and for his patients generally to receive, a better type

and that those who are responsible for the conduct of the service seem to be fully aware of its problems and to be disposed to meet them.

Responsibility for housing was removed from the Ministry of Health in January 1951, and at the same time the Minister who had been at the helm from the beginning (Aneurin Bevan) was shifted to the Ministry of Labor and National Service. With the coming of the new Minister of Health (Hilary Marquand) who, it may be assumed, will not be handicapped by any "pride of authorship," it may be easier for desirable changes to be made.[68]

The new Minister received his baptism of fire soon after he assumed office when he defended in Parliament the government's decision to depart from its principle of a universally free health service by imposing charges for dentures and for spectacles for adults. It was imperative, said the Minister, to secure money to cover expanded service and rising costs, and the proposed charges (which might be expected to yield £25 million in a full year) would provide the necessary revenue without affecting those who were seriously ill, and with a minimum cost of collection. In addition, the charges might have a deterrent effect on excessive demands. The government's proposal threatened to produce a major split in the ranks of Labor, and did, indeed, result in the resignation of two Labor ministers, but the Opposition supported the government in Parliament, and the controversial measure passed its second and third readings without a division.[69]

---

of practice than ever before. See W. C. Rappleye, *op. cit.*, pp. 12–13. *The Economist* (May 20, 1950, p. 1114) argues that "In the long run some direct contribution from the public towards [the cost of the health service] seems inevitable."

Referring to the health service and education the Conservative manifesto for 1951 states simply, "For the money now being spent, we will provide better services, and so fulfill the high hopes we all held when we planned the improvements during the war." *The Times* (London), September 29, 1951.

68. *The Times* (London), January 18, 1951.

69. The measure was altered in the House of Commons to restrict the duration of the new charges to April 1954 unless they are con-

It is much too early to attempt conclusions as to the actual effect of the new service upon the public health. Statistics alone do not tell the story. Apart from the fact that natural conditions affecting health do not remain constant, the general environmental conditions affecting health (housing, nutrition, distribution of wealth, etc.) have undergone material changes at the hands of the government in the past five years. It is a matter of record that more people in Great Britain are calling for medical service, and are calling for it more frequently and for longer periods. This may be taken to mean more illness; it may also mean simply that more people can afford to be ill and to report their illness and have it treated.[70]

tinued by affirmative resolution of both Houses for further periods of one year at a time. *The Economist,* May 12, 1951, p. 1090; *The Times* (London), April 25 and May 8, 1951. See p. 208, footnote 41.

70. *The Times* (London), April 21, 1950.

CHAPTER 10

Housing

THE DEVASTATION WROUGHT by World War II has forced housing—for decades a major problem in Britain—into the forefront of contemporary public and government concern. The construction and provision of dwellings has been a principal project of the Labor government, as it would have been of any postwar government in Britain.

Nature of the Housing Problem

About one third of Britain's 13 million homes were damaged by enemy action, and of these about 475,000 were rendered uninhabitable. During the five years preceding 1939, new dwellings constructed averaged over 360,000 a year; but between September 1939 and May 1945 the overall total amounted only to 220,000 houses, and most of these had been under construction at the outbreak of war. Repair and maintenance work was kept at a minimum during the six years of hostilities and the resulting deterioration of existing buildings rendered the shortage even more acute. The situation was made still more serious by the wartime increase in marriage and birth rates; during the decade 1939–1949, the population of the United Kingdom increased by two and a quarter million.

Not only was there a general shortage of housing but more houses were needed in particular districts to accommodate the movement of the working population that the government was trying to encourage in certain industries, such as agriculture and coal mining.[1] The war years made desperate

1. See *Housing in Britain* (R. 1901), Central Office of Information, London, March 1950, pp. 4–6; *The Times* (London), February 17, 1950. The factual presentation in the present chapter follows closely the material and arrangement in *Housing in Britain*.

an age-old problem in Britain and forced an immediate, positive program to provide simple shelter as well as a plan for the provision of really adequate housing. Yet building materials were in short supply, the building labor force had dwindled during the war, building costs were twice their prewar level, and the nation had many demands upon its limited resources.[2]

Responsibility for Housing

Since the Cabinet changes of January 1951, housing policy for England and Wales has been in the hands of the newly created Ministry of Local Government and Planning; for the preceding five years the Ministry of Health was primarily responsible. (The Secretary of State for Scotland remains responsible for policy in Scotland.) Responsibility for the total program has always been shared by a number of other government departments. The Ministry of Works and the Ministry of Supply control building supplies and equipment, and the Ministry of Works, in addition, "is responsible for general building efficiency, for relations with the building industry, for the programming of building resources and for the operation of the licensing system, for which it uses the local authorities as its agents."[3] The Ministry of Agriculture advises on the use of possible agricultural land for housing, the Board of Trade controls the distribution of timber and the Ministry of Labor is concerned with the flow of labor to the building industry. Supervision of local planning authorities who advise on the choice of sites and layout, and whose approval of housing projects is required, is now a responsibility of the Ministry of Local Government and Planning; prior to January 1951, supervision was exercised by the Ministry of Town and Country Planning.

Executive responsibility for provision of housing is borne by the local authorities in their respective areas—councils

2. For the background of the postwar housing situation, see M. Bowley, *Housing and the State, 1919–1944*, Allen and Unwin, London, 1945.

3. *Housing in Britain*, p. 6.

of county boroughs, of boroughs, of urban districts and of rural districts in England and Wales; town and county councils in Scotland; the London County Council and the City of London. These authorities are also responsible to the Ministry of Works for the local operation of the licensing system.

The powers and duties of local authorities in England and Wales for housing are set forth under the consolidating Housing Acts of 1936 and 1949. Supplementary legislation was provided in the Housing (Financial and Miscellaneous Provisions) Act of 1946.[4] Under the first of these acts—the product of a Conservative government—local authorities were empowered (and in certain instances required) to secure the repair of, or to destroy, insanitary houses; to undertake the clearance and redevelopment of unhealthy and congested areas; to abate overcrowding; and to provide housing accommodation for the working classes.[5] The term "working classes" has been interpreted broadly, particularly since the shortage of housing consequent upon World War II became a universal problem. The legislation of 1949 deleted the restrictive references to the working classes in most of the sections of the 1936 act.[6]

Under the Housing Act of 1936 it became the duty of every local authority to review "the housing conditions in their district and the needs of the district with respect to the provision of further housing accommodation for the working classes . . . [and] to prepare and submit to the Minister [of Health] proposals for the provision of new houses for the working classes."[7] The authorities were empowered to acquire land (including buildings), and to erect houses, to convert existing buildings into residences, to acquire houses and to alter existing houses; and to supply

4. Housing Act, 1936, 26 George 5, and 1 Edward 8, Ch. 51; Housing Act, 1949, 12 & 13 George 6, Ch. 60; Housing (Financial and Miscellaneous Provisions) Act, 1946, 9 & 10 George 6, Ch. 48.
5. Housing Act, 1936, Parts II–V.
6. Housing Act, 1949, Part I, Sec. 1.
7. Housing Act, 1936, Part V, Sec. 71.

them with all requisite furniture, fittings and conveniences. They may, with the consent of the Minister, provide and maintain recreation grounds, shops, and other land and buildings that will serve a "beneficial purpose" in connection with their houses.[8] Local authorities are responsible for the management of their housing properties, including selection of tenants, the establishment and collection of rents, and the maintenance and preservation of suitable conditions.[9]

Antecedents of Present Housing Policy

Private enterprise has always played an important part in the provision of housing in England and Wales.

Before World War I private enterprise was responsible for practically the whole of the building undertaken, both of houses to let and for sale. In the inter-war period private enterprise continued to provide the majority of houses built in England and Wales, but, as a normal rule, for sale rather than to let. During this period a major part in the provision of houses to be rented was played by local authorities. In all, over 4 million houses were built in England and Wales between the wars, about three-quarters of them by private enterprise. In Scotland the majority of houses built between the wars were built by the local authorities.[10]

For a long period prior to the advent of the Labor government, programs were in effect in Britain to make housing available to lower-income tenants who could not afford to pay rents covering full costs. From 1919 to 1939, subsidies from the national government and also from local taxes were employed to make it possible for local authorities to rent their houses at the low levels their tenants were able

8. *Ibid.*, Sec. 72, 73 and 80. Under the Housing Act of 1949 local authorities may provide meals and laundry services, and may sell furniture to their tenants. Sec. 7, 8.

9. Housing Act, 1936, Part V, Sec. 83–87.

10. *Housing in Britain*, p. 8. Housing was provided also by so-called "Housing Associations," consisting of "persons interested in the provision of houses for people in low income groups." *Ibid.*, p. 8.

to pay. Treasury contributions were used to relieve the housing shortage resulting from the first world war, to clear slums and to reduce overcrowding. "The capital cost of houses provided by local authorities was met from loans and to a very small extent from housing revenue and rate fund monies. The current expenditure, including interest on repayment of loans, was met from rents, state subsidies and contributions from the rate funds."[11] Public funds in relatively small amounts were provided for loans to private builders, both landlords (individual and institutional) and owner-occupiers.

The housing program, already under way in its preliminary stages during the closing days of the war, was taken over enthusiastically by the Labor government. The central problem was the same as that encountered by all major economic projects in postwar Britain—inadequate resources in the face of conflicting extraordinary needs. The task of appraising the relative importance of housing in the light of other demands upon the nation's budget, and of organizing and prosecuting the production drive with imagination and efficiency provided a severe test for the new government.

The peculiar contributions of the Labor government were its identification and acceptance of the project as an exercise in "planning" (both in the matter of fitting housing into its total economic "plan" and in its ordered distribution of housing between areas and occupants), in its heavy reliance upon building by, or to the order of local authorities for renting, and its determined effort to keep rent payments by tenants at a minimum. Its performance will be judged in terms of the impact of the housing program upon other sectors of the economy, and the cost and quality, as well as the absolute number, of the housing units constructed.

Shortages of Labor and Materials

The limiting forces were, of course, labor and materials. It is estimated that, at the outbreak of the war, some 350,000

11. *Ibid.,* p. 9.

men were employed in building new houses; in July 1945, the labor force engaged in site preparation and construction of houses amounted to only 26,000. A year later the figure had risen to 191,000, and by the summer of 1947, to 257,000. In September 1949, 544,000 men were employed on all types of housing work, of whom 228,000 were engaged on site preparation and construction of new houses.[12] The increase in the labor force was accomplished by the early release from the armed forces and munitions industries of building and building-materials workers and technicians; by transfer (by invitation) from other industries of workers formerly employed in building; by the use of prisoners of war; and by special training schemes for the building industry.[13]

Wages in the building industry have been determined on a national basis, with district variations in the standard rate as agreed upon by employers and workers. The hourly rates are reviewed annually and adjusted on a retail price sliding scale. During and following the war, a number of changes in working conditions and wage arrangements were made: holidays with pay, a guaranteed work week (changed in 1947 to payment for time lost for causes beyond control of the parties, and a minimum weekly payment), and incentive payments.[14]

12. *Ibid.*, p. 17.
13. *Ibid.*, p. 17. By the end of 1947, the government's vocational training scheme had trained for building trades over 50,000 men whose earlier training had been interrupted or who were unable to return to their prewar occupation. This was arranged in consultation with the Building and Civil Engineering Labour Advisory Panel, consisting of representatives of employers and workers. The Building Apprenticeship and Training Council (set up in 1943 by the Ministry of Works and composed of representatives of employers, workers, educational and professional institutions, and interested government departments) advises on recruitment, education and training of young persons for craftsmanship and management. The National Joint Apprenticeship Scheme for England and Wales is administered by a standing committee of the National Joint Council for the Building Industry. *Ibid.*, pp. 17–19.
14. *Ibid.*, pp. 19–20. Wages of building workers are subject to negotiation and are also linked to the cost-of-living index. See *The*

The most serious bottleneck in materials since 1945 has been timber. Since Russia and other European sources needed their softwood for their own construction, Britain was forced to rely upon dollar countries for its supplies, and because of the delicate foreign trade position has had to proceed with great care and calculation. Before the war Britain imported about a fifth of its softwood timber from dollar countries; in 1947 nearly half came from these areas, but the need to economize on dollars forced a continuous reduction that brought the proportion to less than a third in 1949. Timber is imported exclusively by the Board of Trade, and is resold by the Board to timber merchants.[15]

Other materials requirements were met from home production and while serious shortages were present at the outset, production gradually caught up with demand.[16] In November 1948, it was possible to rescind the Control of Building Materials (No. 1) Order of 1947, governing the distribution of certain materials, and other controls were relaxed in succeeding months. Many materials and items still remain in short supply, however, and overordering with consequent maldistribution and local shortages has resulted

Economist (December 30, 1950, p. 1221) for a description and analysis of an incentive wage system worked out by the building unions and the National Federation of Building Trades Employers, under which a bonus is paid if workers exceed a "target" rate of construction. It has been estimated that where incentives have been used (use is optional with the employer), costs have been cut by at least £15 a house.

15. *Ibid.*, pp. 20–21. See also *Report of the Ministry of Health for the year ended 31st March, 1949,* Cmd. 7910, H.M.S.O., 1950, p. 320. For a criticism of the "bulk buying" of timber, see R. S. Russell, *Government Bulk Buying,* Empire Economic Union, London, 1948, pp. 65–66. See also the suggestions for a general overhauling of the entire system of buying, distribution and price control of timber in the *Seventh Report from the Select Committee on Estimates* (Session 1950) as reported in *The Times* (London), November 15, 1950.

16. *Housing in Britain,* p. 20. In May 1945 the output of bricks was less than one seventh of prewar output; at the beginning of 1946 the building materials industries together had less than half their prewar labor force and were producing, as a whole, less than half their prewar output.

in interruptions even though over-all stocks were adequate.[17]

How Programs Are Made

The programing of housing has been almost exclusively a matter of national government action since Labor took over in 1945 (as well as during the war, of course). All building work involving an expenditure above a stated minimum requires permission from the licensing authority (local authorities, under the Ministry of Works), and compliance with regulations governing the flow of scarce materials. The Cabinet makes an over-all allocation of national resources for housing, and within this limit the Ministry of Health has set the allowable proportion of private building to that by local authorities.

The emphasis throughout has been on the building of "suitably sized" houses by local authorities for rental, with special consideration to housing for miners and agricultural workers.[18] The reasons given for relying on local authorities

17. The National Federation of Building Trades Employers complained, in their annual report, of cement and brick shortages in 1949: "there was an almost complete breakdown in supplies in the northeast," *The Times* (London), January 23, 1950. The building industry was reported as "seriously concerned" about the softwood position in 1950, following difficulties in the government's negotiations with Sweden. *The Times* (London), May 5, 1950. In the debate in the House of Commons, May 22, 1950, the Minister of Works argued that although the current timber stocks were lower than the desirable minimum, there would be no stoppage if "licensing authorities behave with discretion and if the merchants do not demand more than they ought to have, and if it is not spread about that there is an unusual shortage." *Parliamentary Debates* (Hansard), House of Commons, Vol. 475, col. 1689.

18. From April 1, 1947 to March 31, 1950, a total of 36,393 new permanent and temporary houses built by local authorities in England and Wales was let to miners; the total for agricultural workers from April 1, 1945 to March 31, 1950, was 23,107. Corresponding figures for Scottish local authorities and the Special Housing Association in Scotland, for the period January 1, 1945 to March 31, 1950, were 12,544 and 2,897 respectively. *Housing Return for England and Wales, 31st*

234 BRITISH PLANNING AND NATIONALIZATION

(whose work is done by private builders under contract)
rather than on private enterprisers in carrying out the housing program, are that

> . . . local authorities are considered to be in a better position
> than private enterprise to build houses to let and within the
> reach of tenants who could not afford to buy; that local author-
> ities are able to select tenants according to need; and that the
> activities of local authorities are more easily planned than those
> of private enterprise.[19]

Private houses may be built only under license, only to order
and not for speculation, and are normally restricted to a
floor area of not more than 1,500 square feet.[20] From the
outset until October 1949 (except for the period August
1947–June 1948) licenses in England and Wales were held
to a maximum of one privately built house to four houses
built by local authorities. Licensing was suspended in October 1949, and resumed as of February 1950 at a maximum
private-local authority ratio of one to ten. The former ratio
of one in five was restored in May 1950, with provisions for
exceeding the figure in exceptional cases and for the issu-
ance of "mobile" licenses.[21]

March, 1950, Cmd. 7938, H.M.S.O., 1950, p. 8; and *Housing Return
for Scotland, 31st March, 1950,* Cmd. 7939, H.M.S.O., 1950, p. 8.

19. *Housing in Britain,* p. 11. See the discussion of housing in the
1950 election campaign later in this chapter (pp. 245–46) for an
elaboration of Labor's position on this matter.

20. *Ibid.,* p. 12. Other conditions fix the maximum selling price and
rental. The Control of Building Operations (No. 15) Order of 1950
continued for the year beginning July 1, 1950, the limit of £100 as
the amount of work that may be done on any dwelling without a
license. *The Times* (London), June 20, 1950.

21. *The Times* (London), May 5, 1950. A "mobile" license is one
issued to an applicant who wishes to build a house for his own occupation in a district other than the one in which he is now living. It is
issued by the authority in the district where the house is to be built,
but is chargeable against the quota of the applicant's present district.
Although not satisfied, *The Times* hailed the announcement of the
provisions as "tardy concessions to common sense."

High Costs and Subsidies

A major difficulty encountered by the housing program has been the high and rising costs of house construction. Various estimates have been made of the amount of the increase, by official committees and others. *Housing in Britain*, basing its figures on the July 1948 report of a committee appointed by the Minister of Health, gives the cost of a typical local authority house as approximately three-and-a-quarter times as high as its counterpart built in 1938 and 1939. The 1947 house required twice as much labor and a third more material. The average 1947 house was larger than the 1938–1939 house, and superior in construction and fittings. On identical standards, the 1947 house would have cost 140 per cent more than in 1938–1939. Materials had increased in price by 125 per cent (excluding timber, about 97 per cent), wages by about 69 per cent, and there had been a decline in labor productivity of approximately 30 per cent.[22]

The second report of the Minister's committee, in May 1950, showed a further increase in costs despite an improvement in the productivity of building labor.[23]

22. *Housing in Britain*, p. 14.

23. Discussing the report, *The Times* (London), May 22, 1950, notes rises in land, site development and professional fees of £36 a house in the two years. By using simpler plans and fittings, costs had been cut by £40 per house; on the other hand, increased size of the 1949 houses added £15 to their cost. The labor cost in 1949 was £407, as against £416 in 1947, "yet even in 1949 five men were still needed to do what four men could have done before the war." The materials in the 1949 house cost £785—an advance of £86 over the cost two years earlier. For additional estimates and analyses of housing costs, see *The Economist*, January 14, 1950, pp. 63–65; and the debates on March 13, 1950, in *Parliamentary Debates* (Hansard), House of Commons, Vol. 472, cols. 754–874; on May 22, 1950, in *ibid.*, Vol. 475, cols. 1664–1790. *The Economist, loc. cit.*, notes that the Minister of Health "has sedulously declined to give any figures of housing costs either for the regions, or the country as a whole, on the pretext that this would deter contractors from lowering their tender prices." See also "Economics of the Council House," *Planning*, January 23, 1950, p. 185. *The Economist*,

In order that houses constructed by local authorities under conditions of higher cost might be made available to
tenants at rents they could afford to pay, increased subsidies
were provided in the legislation of 1946 and 1949. The 1946
legislation set a general standard subsidy of £22 yearly per
house for 60 years (the estimated amount of the annual
deficit on a standard house, assuming an average net rent,
exclusive of rates, of 10s. per week). The Treasury contribution was fixed at £16 10s. annually, and the balance was to
be met by the local authority.[24] Special rates of subsidy were
established to meet special situations, such as agricultural
housing, housing in "poor areas," flats on "expensive sites,"
flats requiring lifts, and expensive construction to guard
against cave-in of land.[25]

The act also provided a capital payment to be made to
local authorities for houses built by "non-traditional" methods, on proposals approved before the end of 1947.[26] It was
estimated that the cost of this special grant would amount
to £27 million for the years 1947–1950. The estimated cost

(February 17, 1951, p. 357) gives index figures of 215 for wholesale
prices of building materials and 211 for average hourly earnings in
building in April 1950, against 100 in 1938; a figure of 260 for housebuilding costs per square foot in 1949 (100 in 1938–1939); and 75 for
building productivity in 1949 (100 in 1938).

It is estimated that the cost of the average three bedroom local
authority house will be increased by £30 as a result of wage increases
negotiated in the winter of 1951. *The Times* (London), February 9,
1951. A government order issued in the spring of 1951 permits local
authorities to build three-bedroom houses below the hitherto existing
minimum of 900 square feet provided that the size of individual rooms
is not reduced. Housing authorities were also released from the obligation to submit plans to the Ministry, provided certain standards are
maintained. *The Economist,* May 5, 1951, p. 1029.

24. The Housing (Financial and Miscellaneous Provisions) Act,
1946, Secs. 1, 2 and 5.

25. *Ibid.,* Secs. 3, 4 and 6.

26. *Ibid.,* Sec. 17. The purpose was to encourage the use of these
methods (factory-built houses) by meeting the extra costs they would
involve at the outset. It was expected that these costs would fall with
increased output and experience.

of the housing subsidies to the Treasury and the local governments for the year 1948 was £43 million.

In calculating the total burden of the subsidies, however, account should be taken of the actual deficits incurred by local authorities in their building accounts. In the case of the London County Council, for instance, the annual average deficit over the six months January to June 1949, was £14 12s. 2d. per house for 3,424 houses. "This means that instead of a statutory subsidy of £22 per house a year, the actual subsidy is £36 a year or all but 14s. a week."[27]

The Housing Act of 1949 added a new subsidy—for residential hostels provided by local authorities, new-town development corporations and by housing associations—together with financial assistance to local authorities and private individuals for the improvement of existing housing.[28]

Kinds of Housing Provided

Provision of housing by improvement and conversion rather than by new building has been an important feature of the postwar program; by the end of 1948 about 34 per cent of persons rehoused had been taken care of in this

27. *The Economist,* January 14, 1950, pp. 63–64. A 1949 survey by Political and Economic Planning of 162 local authorities in England and Wales showed that 72 per cent were charging less than the rent required to meet expenses even after deducting the full subsidy; "Economics of the Council House," p. 187. Note, however, that this was true of 41 per cent of the authorities even in 1938–1939, *ibid.,* p. 188. *The Economist* (February 17, 1951, p. 358) refers to housing subsidies that "totalled £75 million in 1949 compared with £23 million in 1938."

28. Housing Act, 1949, Sec. 40 and Part II. In the case of improvements by local authorities, the Treasury provides payments over twenty years equal to three quarters of the estimated loss to the local authority. Approved improvements by individuals falling within the limits of £100 to £600 may be reimbursed by the local authority up to half of the estimated cost; the Treasury in turn will pay to the local authority for twenty years an annual sum equal to three quarters of the loan charge on its grant to the individual.

manner. In July 1945, only 9 per cent of the housing labor force was employed in new building; the rest was engaged in repairing war damage. The building force had increased to 49 per cent at the end of August 1947. At the end of 1948 the distribution of the housing labor force was: war damage repairs, 75,000 men; other house repairs and maintenance, 179,000; conversion and adaptation, 45,000; new housing, 222,000. By the end of September 1949, the corresponding figures were 67,000; 191,000; 36,400; and 223,000.[29]

In order to meet pressing immediate needs the government undertook for a short period to provide temporary housing of the nontraditional (factory-built) single-story, two-bedroom type. The program, comprising 157,146 houses provided by the Ministry of Works for erection on sites furnished by local authorities, was complete in England and Wales by the end of 1948, and in Scotland in March 1949. The cost was approximately £220,000.[30] Nontraditional houses were used, as well, in the government's permanent housing program.

Shifting Targets—and Accomplishment

The government's building efforts have been aimed at a shifting target; indeed *The Times* argues that housing has suffered from "targetology":

In the spring of 1947, when Ministers still dreamed of working steadily up to an output of 400,000 houses a year, the goal for the year was set at 240,000, of which only 98,000 were finished. Nine months later it was planned to reduce house building steadily to no more than 140,000 a year by the middle of 1949. Three months after that, in the spring of 1948, this plan too was given up, and by the end of 1948 there was talk of building 180,000 to 190,000 a year. In July, 1949, Mr. Bevan raised the figure to 200,000, but in October Sir Stafford Cripps cut it again to 175,000, and from then on private building was severely restricted. By Budget day of this year the total was back to 200,000—until the next change of policy. No "target" yet has

29. *Housing in Britain*, p. 31.
30. *Ibid.*, p. 26.

lasted as long as was needed to finish the houses it brought into being.[31]

Nonetheless, the government's accomplishment has been substantial—805,568 new permanent houses and flats, and 157,146 temporary houses had been provided by the end of November 1950 in Great Britain by the postwar housing program; existing premises had been repaired and converted to add another 333,302 units to the grand total.[32] As *The Economist* put it, "There are many objections that can be, and have been, brought against Mr. Bevan's housing policy. It has been erratic, expensive and, in some respects, unjust. But judged by the paramount test, that of numbers of dwellings completed, it has succeeded."[33]

Rents and Rent Control

The setting of rents for local authority houses ("council houses") and the statutory control of rents charged by private landlords are essential parts of the government's overall housing program. The government has proceeded on the theory that an annual subsidy of £22 for each house was required to bring the rent on council houses down to 10s. a week (2s. 6d. above the average prewar net rent), an amount it was felt most families could afford. The subsidy, taken as a whole, has proved inadequate, and local authority rents have risen substantially and unevenly, since 1945, both for prewar and postwar houses.

The Political and Economic Planning survey of 162 local authorities in 1949 showed an average gross rent (including

31. *The Times* (London), May 5, 1950. Successive "targets" are set out in the *Economic Survey: for 1947*, p. 25; *for 1948*, p. 39; *for 1949*, pp. 58–59; *for 1950*, pp. 33, 47–48; and in *Capital Investment in 1948*, Cmd. 7268, H.M.S.O., 1947, pp. 8–10.

32. *Housing Summary, 30th November, 1950,* Cmd. 8114, H.M.S.O., 1950, p. 21. Of the new permanent houses and flats, local authorities had provided 622,084; private builders, 123,648; housing associations, 5,729; and government departments, 12,265. Local authorities had rebuilt 9,167 war-destroyed buildings, and 32,675 had been rebuilt under license.

33. *The Economist,* January 7, 1950, p. 3.

rates) of 15s. per week for prewar houses, and of 21s. per week for postwar houses. In the case of prewar houses, a third of the authorities charged rents of 12s. 6d. or less, and one seventh charged rents over 17s. 6d. Gross rents of postwar houses varied even more widely: half of the rents were 20s. or less (47 per cent were between 15s. 1d. and 20s.), and a sixth were over 25s.[34]

It is apparent that rent policy must steer a careful course in order to avoid inequities as between the occupants of prewar and postwar council houses, and also to enable subsidies to be enjoyed by those in need rather than indiscriminately by the whole body of tenants irrespective of their individual incomes. Some of the local authorities have consolidated their prewar and postwar rents and pooled their subsidies, and even fewer have introduced rebate schemes to help tenants by relating rent to need. Yet the rent policy currently in effect for public housing seems largely to reflect immediate political and administrative convenience.

Control of rents for private houses is fully as confused and inequitable as the rental situation in the case of public housing. Rent regulation began in 1915, and has continued, through a series of acts, agencies, devices, adjustments, decontrols and recontrols, to produce in 1950 a veritable hodgepodge of restrictions, exceptions—and rental figures.

The Ridley committee estimated that in Great Britain there were, in 1945,

(1) About 4 million houses of a ratable value not above £35 in London and Scotland, and £20 in the provinces, which had been built before 1919 and continuously controlled on the basis of 1914 rents plus a 40 per cent permitted increase on the net rent. The average net rent of these was about 6s. a week (9s. in London).

34. "Economics of the Council House," p. 187. These figures represented increases in weekly net rents on the part of 88 per cent of the authorities: most were 2s. 6d. or less, 24 per cent were between 2s. 6d. and 5s., and 15 per cent were over 5s. Rates had also risen in the case of 95 per cent of the authorities, bringing the gross rent up to the levels shown above. *Ibid.*, p. 187.

(2) About 4½ million similar houses which had been decontrolled. The average net rent of these was about 30 per cent more than before decontrol (50 per cent in London), although rents varied widely.

(3) A further 1½ million local authority houses (mostly post-1918), not controlled, whose average net rents were 7s. a week (10s. 6d. in London).

(4) Finally, 3 million post-1919 private enterprise houses, mostly owner-occupied. Those to let had average net rents "appreciably higher" than pre-war houses. These rents were not controlled until 1939.

To these must now [1949] be added:

(5) About half a million post-1939 local authority houses (not controlled).

(6) Eighty-three thousand post-1939 private enterprise houses, of which about one-eleventh are for letting. These have in practice been subject to some measure of rent and price regulations as a condition of the licence to build and are coming into formal control as they are referred to the tribunals.

(7) Some seventy thousand dwellings made available by conversion or adaptation, an unknown number of which are for letting for the first time and subject to control by the tribunals.[35]

The acts limit the rent (including any premiums) which may lawfully be charged, and give security of tenure to the tenant. Landlords are given protection against undue increases in rates of mortgage interest and against the calling in of mortgages "so long as they pay the restricted interest due."[36] Rents are established by reference to rents payable on certain dates in the past, adjusted by statute, and also by

35. "Rent Control Policy," *Planning*, November 7, 1949, pp. 127–28. See also *Report of the Inter-departmental [Ridley] Committee on Rent Control*, Cmd. 6621, H.M.S.O., 1945; *Rent Control in England and Wales*, Ministry of Health, H.M.S.O., 1946; and *Housing in Britain*, pp. 35–38. Rent control acts now in force, wholly or in part, consist of nine laws passed between 1920 and 1939, collectively entitled Rent and Mortgage Interest Restriction Acts, 1920 to 1939, together with the Building Materials and Housing Acts, 1945, the Furnished Houses (Rent Control) Act, 1946, the Housing Act, 1949, and the Landlord and Tenant (Rent Control) Act, 1949.

36. *Housing in Britain*, p. 36.

determination of rent tribunals, 80 of which have been set up in England and Wales, and 29 in Scotland. In addition to allegations that returns on rented property generally have been held to uneconomically low levels, there are many charges of inequity as between owners of properties constructed and first rented at different dates.[37]

Criticisms of the Accomplishment

It is clear that Britain, in deed as well as philosophy, accepts housing as a public problem, to be dealt with very largely by government measures and agencies. That this is so is evidenced by the record of public action on all aspects of housing since the middle of World War I, and also by the conduct of the General Election of 1950, in which party responsibility for adequate housing was loudly proclaimed. There are, nonetheless, sharp differences of responsible opinion on a wide range of basic issues growing out of housing policy and practice.

The Labor government has built houses on a gigantic scale, but the size of its program has produced criticism that represents two conflicting points of view. Sometimes these opposite criticisms come from the same source. It has been argued, for instance, that the grandiose program undertaken at the outset produced bottlenecks, disorganization and rising prices that prevented the completion of houses under construction, and reacted adversely upon the rest of

37. During the year 1948–1949 the disposition of cases referred to the tribunals was: outside the tribunals' jurisdiction or withdrawn, 4,318; rent reductions (averaging 30 per cent), 6,633; rent increases, 129; rent approved, 1,727; and dismissed, 1,605. Of the adjudicated cases later referred for reconsideration on grounds of changed circumstances, 313 were invalid or were withdrawn, 95 were dismissed, rent was approved in 191 cases, rent was reduced (by an average of 15 per cent) in 115 cases, and in 915 cases rent was increased. *Report of the Ministry of Health for the year ended 31st March, 1949*, pp. 329–30. As a result of rent control and subsidies, "the average rent charged for new houses has risen only from 7s. 7d. a week in 1939 to 16s. 5d. in 1949." *The Economist*, February 17, 1951, p. 358.

the economy. Conversely, it was argued as late as the spring of 1950 that to reduce the housing program below an annual figure of 200,000 houses (indeed, not to raise the program above that figure) was to betray the country.[38]

The varying size of the program has also brought forth complaints from those who have feared the effect upon the stability of the building and the building-materials industries. In the sort of economic circumstances that Britain has faced since the close of the war, flexibility in programs is as desirable as it has been inevitable; on the other hand flexibility carried to the point of vacillation becomes the antithesis of effective planning.

The cost of housing has produced the most pointed attack, principally because those who allege extravagance and inefficiency are able to link their claims with advocacy of a "return to private enterprise." Private builders, it is urged, bidding and operating in a speculative market would have every incentive to promote efficiency and economy, whereas under what amounts to a cost-plus arrangement under government contract, waste and soldiering are inevitable. This is a contention that is difficult to appraise. The government has been aware of wastes and high costs, and has recognized

38. *The Times* (London), commenting on this proposition (May 5, 1950), said: "It is easy enough to say this figure is too low; it is less easy to reconcile a much higher figure with the clamant needs of the schools, the hospitals, and industrial and other consumers of all sorts. Until the Opposition has produced an investment programme which reconciles these claims in different and better proportions than those chosen by the Government, its complaints about the quantity of houses are bound to sound less convincing than its criticism of their cost." Noting that in the second quarter of 1951 the number of houses under construction had increased greatly while the number completed remained stable, *The Economist* (August 18, 1951, p. 388) expressed fear that "the building programme is again getting out of control."
Any appraisal of the need for housing in postwar Britain must take into account that some of the increased demand for housing flows from the increased general productivity of the British people, and that some of it is the product of rent controls, housing subsidies and, indirectly, of food subsidies.

its responsibility for their elimination.[39] It has been inclined to lay much of the blame at the door of the building industry as it developed during the decades prior to the beginning of World War II—small scale, disorganized, nonmechanized, and plagued by "rings" and self-imposed restrictions.

Wherever the truth lies, there cannot be a test of the merits of private speculative building *versus* building to large-scale government order unless the general conditions of trade and employment are substantially the same in the two cases. There has been waste and inefficiency since the war. It is not entirely clear, however, how much of the excessive cost is to be attributed to the leading role played by the government, and how much to the fact that full employment does not strongly stimulate labor and managerial efficiency.

The government's subsidy and rental programs have both aroused serious criticism and, unless political considerations prove overwhelming, both are due for substantial revision. The rents for council houses and the rents imposed by law upon private housing are inequitable in their impact, and the degree and incidence of the inequity is largely fortuitous. The effect on occupancy and use of houses is open to question. There is reason to believe, as well, that the level of rents is too low to permit—certainly to induce—desirable repairs and maintenance in the case of private landlords.

Subsidies are attached to houses, whereas to serve any purpose for which the government purportedly stands, they should be attached to persons. Many proposals for their correction are now prevalent. Remedies in this area, even if they could be quickly decided upon, cannot be put into effect overnight without producing a host of wholly undesirable results. The existing system is clearly in need of a careful revision, gradually applied, and designed to offer

39. A working party on the building industry, set up by the government, has made two reports; the Ministry of Health has established a committee of inquiry into the costs of housebuilding (two reports); and the building industry itself has sent a "productivity team" to the United States. *The Times* (London), May 5, 1950.

assistance only where it is really called for and to serve the over-all purpose of providing, maintaining and allocating housing on an economical basis.[40]

Private Enterprise or More Nationalization?

The criticism of the government's housing policies and program offered by the Conservative candidates in the 1950 election campaign was general in character and not particularly penetrating. In the main it consisted of taunts directed at high costs and indifferent results. Emphasis was placed on the desirability of permitting private enterprise to play a larger part in the program—an emphasis that has been repeated in later Parliamentary debates.[41]

The Opposition has employed housing as the subject of three of the many "no confidence" votes it has forced in the House of Commons since Labor's narrow retention of Parliamentary power in 1950. The debates on these occasions produced the usual charges and countercharges, but with the exception of the most recent, the proceedings were neither novel nor particularly spirited.[42] Plenty of spirit was in evidence, however, when the government was challenged on housing in November 1950 for the third time in eight months. At the Conservative party conference in October 1950, a motion demanding the building of 300,000 houses

40. For analyses and proposals for change in housing, subsidy and rental policy, see the following: *The Economist*, January 7, 1950, p. 3; January 14, 1950, p. 63; April 22, 1950, p. 874; and May 6, 1950, p. 991; "Rent Control Policy," *Planning*, November 7, 1949, p. 125; "Economics of the Council House," *Planning*, January 23, 1950, p. 185; "A New Policy for Housing Subsidies," *Planning*, April 24, 1950, p. 257; F. W. Paish, "The Economics of Rent Restriction," *Lloyds Bank Review*, April 1950, p. 1; *The Times* (London), February 17, 1950, May 5, 1950, May 22, 1950, and November 13, 1950.

41. The housing programs of the Labor and Conservative parties are outlined in a special article in *The Times* (London), February 17, 1950.

42. The government prevailed in the vote of March 13, 1950, 314–289. *Parliamentary Debates* (Hansard), House of Commons, Vol. 472, col. 870; and on May 22, 1950, 299–293. *Ibid.*, Vol. 475, col. 1784.

a year was carried with great enthusiasm,[43] and the Opposition rallied to this figure when, in November, it moved in Parliament to attack the government's policy and record on housing. The resulting debate, with both Mr. Bevan and Mr. Churchill at their vitriolic best, was extremely lively, although, as might have been anticipated, it contributed little that was new. The government withstood the attack, 300–288.[44]

43. *The Times* (London), October 14, 1950. Critical of the Conservative pledge, *The Times* (October 17) observed that "Political parties are seldom sweetly reasonable when spoiling for an electoral fight." Government leaders referred to the demand as a "cynical and irresponsible attempt to exploit the housing difficulties of our people" (Morrison, in *The Times* (London), October 17, 1950); and as "disgraceful" (Bevan, in *The Times* (London), October 23, 1950). Even *The Economist* (October 21, 1950, p. 617), in an article entitled "Houses in the Air," took the position that "The resolution was moved as the result of a purely demagogic agitation among the delegates," and added, "On a cool calculation it is difficult to see how it is possible to build an extra 100,000 houses a year and still retain the rest of the investment programme without seriously adding fuel to the flames of inflation."

44. *Parliamentary Debates* (Hansard), House of Commons, Vol. 480, cols. 605–718. *The Economist* (November 11, 1950, p. 724) commented that "It is hard to take seriously the debate on whether the Conservative housing programme is practicable . . . The case against promising to build 300,000 houses a year is not that it is impracticable but that it is irresponsible. Certainly the houses can be built—if enough other things are sacrificed." In a pamphlet written by E. Marples, Secretary of the Conservative Parliamentary Housing Committee and published early in 1951 by the Conservative Political Centre, the goal of 300,000 houses annually is superseded by "As far as is humanly possible we intend to build as many houses as possible." The pamphlet, as reported in *The Economist* (March 24, 1951, pp. 673–74), attacks the government's temperamental changes in policy with consequent disorganization of the materials industries; extravagance in standards; excessive controls and delays; failure to amend the rent control statutes; and lack of competition and incentive. *The Economist* reports gaps, however, in the treatment of such points of general policy as the role of local authorities, the ensurance of adequate standards, and of how "to prevent the demand for houses from eating up the resources required by industry." In its latest manifesto (1951), the Conservative party promises

Delegates to the annual conference of the National Federation of Building Trades Operatives, representing 500,000 members of building trades unions, voted unanimously on June 21, 1950, to accept their executives' proposals for nationalization of the building industry. "No improvement could be expected of an industry with 125,000 firms of all sorts and sizes, each pursuing casually evaluated profit-making in competition with the rest, each grasping for contracts and able to build only in accordance with its random equipment."[45] Details of the proposal and methods for carrying it out were not elaborated; and it is not likely soon to find its way into the official program of the Labor party or the government. In fact, at the October 1950 conference of the Labor party, the then Minister of Health, Mr. Bevan, reputedly one of the government's most vigorous champions of nationalization, spoke strongly against extending nationalization to the building industry.[46]

to give housing a priority second only to national defense, and reiterates that its target is 300,000 houses a year. More freedom is to be given to the private builder, but there is to be no reduction in the number of houses and flats built to let. *The Times* (London), September 29, 1951.

45. *The Times* (London), June 21 and 22, 1950.

46. *The Times* (London), October 6, 1950.

CHAPTER I I

Agriculture

BRITISH AGRICULTURE IN 1951 constitutes an epitome of democratic government planning and control in an area of free enterprise. The conflicts of ends, the tangle of sanctions and persuasions, the high purpose and the self seeking, the ebullient enthusiasm and the red tape, the frustration and the accomplishment—all are here.

Britain's Dependence on Food Imports

Agriculture occupies a very special place in the British economy. Britain depends for its life upon imported food supplies. Because of the threat to British shipping and hence to imports in the two world wars, the government instituted programs in both wars for increasing food production at home. The program for an expanded home agriculture was permitted to collapse after World War I—perhaps mistakenly, in the light of the appeal that was to be made again to British farmers when, in twenty years, British shipping lanes were once more under submarine attack.

The second wartime program has been continued—restimulated and strengthened—since the conclusion of hostilities, because of the continuing danger of insufficient food. Britain needs dollars to buy food, and dollars have been painfully scarce in London since the close of the war. Almost in desperation, Britain has undertaken to change the pattern of its domestic economy to meet the crisis brought about by the war-generated disruption of the international economy. The food that cannot be bought must be produced at home. Britain hopes by 1952 to increase the net value of the annual agricultural output "to about 50 per cent above pre-war, that is, about 20 per cent above the 1946–47 level and 15 per cent above the wartime peak of 1943–44."[1]

It is natural to think of Great Britain (particularly England) as a nation of factories, mines and shops; yet 48 million of the 60 million acres of land in England, Wales, Scotland and Northern Ireland are used in agriculture, and farming in this area employs over a million and a quarter people. In England and Wales, there are some 290,600 separate holdings farmed as single units of five acres or more of crops and grass. Three quarters of these (30 per cent of the total area) are less than 100 acres in size; most of the rest range in size from 100 to 300 acres. One per cent of the farms exceed 700 acres each. Types of farming differ in the several regions, but in most of them dairying is predominant, or important.[2]

Changing Patterns of Agriculture

The history of agriculture in Great Britain is characterized fully as much by a changing pattern as by changing volume. The loss of tariff protection in 1846, the growth of the great foreign grain areas and the development of cheap transportation all left their mark; through the period 1870–1940, there was a persistent trend "away from an agricultural industry based on cereals, especially wheat, to an agriculture based on livestock and livestock products and, among crops, an increasing emphasis on vegetables."[3] Prices of farm products followed the general downward movement of all prices during the long agricultural depression in the late 1800's, but prices of livestock and livestock products remained much firmer than other agricultural prices. Butter and meat imports from the Empire, Argentina and

1. *Agriculture in Britain* (I.D. 945), British Information Services, November 1949, p. 5. For an informative and critical treatment of British agricultural and food policy, see R. A. Brady, *Crisis in Britain,* University of California Press, Berkeley, 1950, Chap. 11.
2. *Agriculture in Britain,* pp. 10–11.
3. *Ibid.,* p. 12.

Denmark increased, and production in Great Britain moved gradually, through a number of phases, toward emphasis on milk, eggs and vegetables.

During the decade preceding World War II, there was marked increase in livestock, livestock products and horticultural output. British agriculture was moving away from primary production and was becoming a processing industry—concentrating on livestock and its products, and even importing a substantial proportion of animal feed, including fresh grass and hay. At the outbreak of the war, Britain was producing about half of its meat supply, 90 per cent of its vegetables, all of its fresh milk and 67 per cent of its eggs, but only 12 per cent of its cereals, 25 per cent of fruit, and under 12 per cent of sugar.

The effect of this development on the character of British land use was pronounced: "in the seventy years before the Second World War an area greater than that of the whole of Wales was lost to the plough and the proportion of arable land to permanent grass was almost reversed. In England and Wales the arable land was almost halved and in Scotland it was reduced by about 15 per cent."[4]

War demanded a drastic change. Wheat and potatoes for direct human consumption were required from British farmers, and the production of livestock and livestock products was markedly lessened. Meat output in the United Kingdom in 1945 was 30 per cent below the prewar figures, while the amount of wheat was 32 per cent higher than the prewar level. In the same period barley production increased 176 per cent, oats 67 per cent, potatoes 101 per cent and vegetables by 37 per cent. A start was made late in 1944 toward a return to a long-term policy of increasing emphasis on the production of meat, but the world-wide food shortage that persisted after the close of the war made it necessary in 1946 to continue the wartime stress on production of cereals.

4. *Ibid.*, p. 14. The decrease between 1870 and 1937 in acreage devoted to cereal crops was 47 per cent, to root crops 46 per cent, and to rotation grasses 19 per cent.

Agricultural Legislation Not New

Concern over agriculture and government measures to deal with agricultural problems are not recent phenomena in Great Britain, nor are they to be associated peculiarly with the Labor party. Most of Britain's industries suffered severely from depression throughout the twenty-year period between the wars, and agriculture was among those hardest hit. The agricultural price index fell from 292 in 1920 (1913 = 100) to 107 in 1933; the number of persons employed on farms declined by 83,000 between 1921 and 1931; and the number of acres of land under tillage and temporary grass fell by 25 per cent between 1919 and 1933. Because of the general fall of consumer purchasing power, there was a weakened demand for food; and because of world surpluses, foreign products were available in Britain at distress prices.

In 1932, the government reversed its century-old policy of free trade and substituted a program of mild, conditional protection for those industries that gave indications of willingness to curb, or to submit to restrictions on, all-out competition in the domestic market. Agriculture was given only a slight measure of direct protection by the Import Duties Act of 1932, but this was augmented by Empire arrangements, subsidies, and a provision in the Agricultural Marketing Act of 1933 that gave authority to the Board of Trade to restrict imports if this action were required to make effective any marketing scheme set up under the act. The marketing schemes contemplated by the 1933 act and its predecessor, the Agricultural Marketing Act of 1931, played an important part on the agricultural stage until the government reorganization that followed the outbreak of war, and, in altered shape, they have been prominent ever since.

The 1931 act adopted a policy similar to that which was later applied to virtually all of Britain's industries. It provided for the organization of producers in the various branches of agriculture into marketing boards to restrict production of their respective commodities by setting quotas, and to secure for the members the benefits of a stronger bargaining position, more market information, better credit standing and the results of cooperative research. If two thirds of the producers of a recognized commodity could agree upon a plan which, in turn, was approved by the Minister of Agriculture, a marketing board whose actions would bind the entire group might be established. Only one marketing scheme, however, was approved under the act—for hops, where producers were already well organized and relatively prosperous. Farmers apparently were not eager for long-term remedies for their difficulties; and schemes for restriction that gave them neither protection against, nor compensation for, the inflow of cheap farm products from foreign countries held little attraction.

Two years later, in the Agricultural Marketing Act of 1933, the government offered additional inducement for acceptance of officially sanctioned "self-government" for agriculture, and producers, weakened by two more years of depression, began nibbling at the bait. The act strengthened the control that the boards could exercise over supply —a direct quantity limit, based on his past sales, might be placed on the sales of any producer. It conferred power on the government to restrict imports of these commodities, the domestic producers of which were organized under marketing schemes. The act was hailed by producer groups, but only a few actually submitted to board control. In order to gain import protection from the government it was necessary only to take steps to prepare a marketing scheme— not to bring the scheme to the point of acceptance and operation. Producers began to benefit from other protections as well (quota arrangements with foreign countries, tariffs, subsidies, etc.), simply on the showing of the existence of distress in the affected industry and without any commitment for the overhauling of its marketing methods.[5]

5. "British farmers disliked co-operation, and were only prepared to submit to the discipline of marketing schemes insofar as they were rewarded for so doing by protection of their prices from the effect of the bargaining power of organised middlemen or by protection from foreign competitors. Where such protection could be obtained either in the form of subsidy or limitation of foreign supplies without the

Marketing Schemes and Commodity Commissions

Marketing schemes were, in fact, established and marketing boards set up, but the range of covered commodities was small and the results were indifferent. Four commodities were involved:

. . . for three of the products (hops, milk and potatoes) . . . the home producer had a virtual monopoly of the market and it only required a marketing scheme to make this fully effective. In these cases organisation under the Acts served a vital short-term purpose in providing a practical recipe for price amelioration. For hops this objective was secured by means of production quotas; for potatoes, by prohibiting sales of tubers below a prescribed size; for milk, it was achieved by enforcing a system of discriminating prices for supplies disposed of for different uses. In the case of pigs and bacon, however, where home production accounted for a relatively small part of the total supply, the drastic restriction of bacon imports, supplemented later by a Government subsidy, was the essential feature of the whole arrangement from the pig producer's standpoint. Indeed, in many respects, the marketing scheme proposed by the Reorganisation Commission and accepted by producers proved, in time, so defective as to be almost unworkable.[6]

During the immediate prewar period the government introduced another device, somewhat similar to the marketing boards, to aid distressed farmers. Commodity commissions were set up by Parliament for wheat (1932), sugar (1936) and livestock (1937); and proposals, later withdrawn, were made for a milk commission and a poultry commission. Membership on the commissions was by government

---

necessity of setting up a marketing board, producers on the whole preferred to do without a marketing board." *Report of the Committee Appointed to Review the Working of the Agricultural Marketing Acts* [*Lucas Report*], Ministry of Agriculture and Fisheries, H.M.S.O., 1947, p. 13.

6. *Ibid.*, pp. 9–10. During the period 1932–1939 there were instituted three schemes for potatoes, four for pigs and bacon, seven for milk and milk products, and a single scheme each for hops, eggs and fat stock. The several schemes covered various geographic and political areas. Several schemes were submitted, but were either defeated or withdrawn.

appointment, the members in some instances being independent, and in others representative of the industry. The commissions were first intended to serve as agencies for handling subsidies provided by the government for the affected industries. The subsidy was central; the commissions were part of the subsidy machinery. It was the function of the wheat commission to make deficiency payments to home growers of wheat, from the proceeds of a levy laid by the commission upon all millers and importers of flour. Payments to growers were equal to the difference between a standard price fixed by the Minister of Agriculture and the average price received for the crop, adjusted to permit higher returns for producers of better quality wheat. The commission also handled the subsidies for oats and barley, and in 1939 was given power to make loans for the encouragement of research and education on "the growing, marketing and utilisation of wheat."[7] Operation of the wheat legislation was discontinued soon after the beginning of the war.

The sugar commission, provided for in the Sugar Industry (Reorganisation) Act of 1936, was given a variety of supervisory and regulatory functions. It was required to prepare a scheme for the compulsory amalgamation of the factory companies (an agreement for the voluntary amalgamation of the companies into the British Sugar Corporation, Ltd., was reached); to supervise, and in case of disagreement to specify the terms of contracts covering the purchase of sugar beets from home growers by the corporation; to prescribe maximum global and individual contract acreages (it did not, in fact, prescribe individual acreages); to register refiners and to be prepared to institute a licensing scheme; to oversee the corporation's production and marketing program; and to advise the Minister of Agriculture on the conditions and rate of financial assistance to be given to the industry. With the coming of war, control

7. *Ibid.*, p. 37. The information given here and in the following paragraphs on marketing boards and commodity commissions is drawn largely from the *Lucas Report*.

of the industry was given to the Minister of Food, and in 1942 the remaining functions of the commission were suspended or transferred to the Ministries of Food and Agriculture.

The livestock commission arrived late (1937) on the scene, as the agency for carrying out the government's program of assistance to and improvement of the livestock industry. The Livestock Industry Act of 1937 provided for:

(i) assistance from public funds to producers of fat cattle

(ii) the regulation under certain circumstances of imports of livestock and meat

(iii) measures designed to secure efficiency and economy in the marketing of livestock

(iv) trial of methods of slaughter and processing which had proved successful in other countries

(v) the promotion by the various sections of the industry of "service schemes" for their mutual benefit.[8]

Other legislation was put into effect during this period, all of which, together with the measures already discussed, presents a picture of increasing government aid, direct and indirect, fumbling and tentative attempts to encourage efficiency, some government direction, and—in common with developments in manufacturing, mining and distribution —increasing reliance upon industry self-government of the restrictive, cartel type.[9] This was the Conservative prescription for the problems of British agriculture, but there is no evidence, despite broad doctrinaire advocacy of general structural reforms, that Labor was dissatisfied with this prescription or, indeed, that it had more than a casual interest in the whole matter at this time.

Controls Strengthened for War Purposes

Like all British industry, agriculture and food were closely controlled throughout the war. Two thirds of Brit-

8. *Ibid.,* p. 40. The commission's responsibilities in the direction of "rationalizing" the industry's production and marketing processes were apparently greater than in the case of wheat and sugar.

9. See R. A. Brady, *op. cit.,* pp. 456–59.

ain's food supply was imported, and food accounted for nearly half of all the imports. Shipping was under attack and shipping space was badly needed for war supplies. The government's wartime food program envisaged an increase in the over-all home output (with emphasis upon crops with the greatest food value), the regulation of consumption by rationing, and reduction of imports.[10] New administrative lines were set up, and a framework of control that was to continue after the war was erected to achieve (1) the production and sale off farms of the greatly increased quantities of food, and (2) its flow into channels which would ensure its proper use.

Execution of the government's program was in the hands of the Ministry of Agriculture and the newly created Ministry of Food. The level and pattern of the production program were the responsibility of the Minister of Agriculture. County committees were tentatively selected in 1938 and 1939, so that when the emergency came and the appropriate orders were issued the organization went into action with little delay. There were 62 of these county war agricultural executive committees, each with from eight to twelve volunteer members appointed by the Minister, representing county councils, landlords, farmers, laborers and the government. Each had a paid executive officer with a staff of technical assistants. Counties were divided into districts— 474 in England and Wales—and each of these had its volunteer committee to carry out the work of the county committees on a local level. The Minister set crop quotas by counties, and it was the task of the county and district committees to see that the quotas were met.

The Ministry of Food bought the produce of farmers, either directly or through licensed agents, at guaranteed prices set a year in advance by the Minister of Agriculture

10. *The Economist* (November 29, 1941, p. 643) took issue with the program, on the grounds that home production at best could be increased only slightly, that an overstimulated industry would be hard hit when trade opened again after the war, and that precious manpower would be wasted in agriculture.

after consultation with the National Farmers' Union and
the Food Price Committee representing interested government departments. Farmers were promised that guaranteed
prices would continue for at least a year after the end of the
war. The government paid subsidies to farmers for plowing
grassland and increasing crop acreage, for growing designated crops, and for capital installations and land improvement. Credit facilities and the results of accelerated research projects were made available to farmers. The county
committees surveyed all farms in Britain in an effort to determine the qualities of every farm and farmer as a basis
for the formulation and enforcement of quotas. Farmers
were expected to grow the kinds of crops requested by their
committees; in the event of disagreement the committee's
decision was final and enforceable by legal penalties. Committees had power, as well, to supervise farming operations
and to remove tenants and even farmer-owners from their
holdings, for inefficiency. Price incentives and persuasion
were usually sufficient to induce compliance with committee requests, and drastic steps were taken in relatively few
cases.[11]

The government took steps to provide and maintain an
adequate supply of agricultural labor. It relieved farm
workers from the draft, forbade factories to hire men with
agricultural experience, and empowered county committees to require farmers to remain on their farms. The committees organized pools of temporary workers from which
farmers could draw seasonal and emergency help. In addition, wage increases sponsored by the government played a
part. The Central Agricultural Wages Board was established in 1940, and thereafter, in consultation with labor
and the Minister, proceeded to set gradually increasing
minimum levels for wages. Agricultural wages more than
doubled between 1939 and 1945. In 1939, a total of 607,129
persons were employed regularly or as casuals in agricul-

11. Some 3,000 operators who could not (or would not) meet minimum standards of efficiency were ordered off their farms.

tural occupations; in 1945 the corresponding figure was 812,000, not including prisoners of war.[12]

The formal existence of most of the prewar marketing boards and commodity commissions was terminated by the war, but their activities continued without too complete a break under the Ministry of Food. The Ministry was responsible for all stages of marketing, utilization and distribution beyond the farm. The Ministry was the sole purchaser of some home-grown commodities; producers sold others to buyers licensed and controlled by the Ministry. "In all cases as much use as possible was made of pre-war marketing facilities and personnel, the extent of the modifications depending on the nature of the commodity and the marketing organisation already in existence."[13] Control points, such as government slaughterhouses, collecting centers and packing stations were established for some commodities; for others licensed buyers and merchants were designated; in the case of fruit, pre-emption of the crop was employed. The Ministry assumed control of food processing undertakings as well, thus taking over direction of quantity, kind and quality of manufactured or processed

12. See *War-Time Organisation of Agriculture,* Ministry of Agriculture, H.M.S.O., 1946, for an account of the government's activity throughout this period. See also D. Skilbeck, "War-Time Changes in British Farming," *Lloyds Bank Review,* July 1947, p. 60.

13. *Lucas Report,* p. 45. Indeed this policy was carried so far that, as of 1947, the report stated that "The Ministry of Food is a distributors' Ministry recruited largely from men drawn from the distributive trades. Inevitably it has become distributor minded." *Ibid.,* p. 57. As one critic has put it: "The Ministry of Food . . . was controlled by the very people who had been responsible for the development of the marketing boards and commissions . . . [it] became a central agency for coördinating all the various trade associations . . . engaged in the food trades by converting them into official or semiofficial representatives of the government. In this capacity they were charged with the duty of carrying into effect instructions given them by the government which were, almost in their entirety, consonant with the ideas and objectives of the superseded marketing boards and commissions themselves." R. A. Brady, *op. cit.,* p. 460. However, Brady notes (p. 460) that "regulations restricting supply gave way generally to formal policies for expanding supply."

foods and regulating their course to the consumer. Various arrangements were made by the Ministry at the level of wholesale and retail distribution. Consumer rationing was its responsibility; it employed associations as well as individual firms to get the goods into the hands of distributors. It fixed prices at all stages, and paid subsidies where necessary to introduce incentives that were incompatible with appropriate prices to purchasers.

How the War Left the Agricultural Problem

The government's program for changing the pattern of agricultural production was substantially achieved. The relative position of cereals, potatoes and vegetables was improved, while that of meat and meat products declined. A significant gain was made also in total output. Crop acreages expanded greatly, the value of net output (in constant prices) increased by about 35 per cent and food, in terms of food value, by about 70 per cent.[14] The annual savings in shipping space reached approximately a million tons. These achievements were costly. Indirect aids in the form of tax rebates and preferential rail rates supplemented direct subsidies for land improvement, acreage increase, capital expansion, etc. To all of these must be added the government cost of food subsidies involved in the fight against inflation. The Ministry of Food deliberately ran a deficit in its "trading account" as a result of its policy of selling commodities to consumers (or for resale to consumers) at prices below those which it paid to farmers. How much of this loss should be charged as aid to agriculture and how much as aid to consumers is a question, but the total cost to the government of all subsidies, aid and guarantees in 1945 has been estimated at £308 million.[15]

The agricultural situation facing Britain in the months following the close of the war may be simply stated: Prior to the war Britain had imported two thirds of its food sup-

14. *Economic Survey for 1947*, Cmd. 7046, H.M.S.O., p. 24. Output per man-year rose by 10 to 15 per cent.

15. *The Economist*, February 28, 1948, p. 334.

ply, and food and feeding stuffs had constituted nearly half of the United Kingdom imports. Twenty per cent of Britain's total prewar imports were paid for by income from foreign investments. During the war, these investments had been liquidated to a point where they would cover only about 4 per cent of Britain's total imports.

It was necessary, thus, for Britain to increase exports and reduce imports. Shortage of exchange rather than of shipping was now the moving force, but it was no less insistent. Food imports had to share in the cut, and home agriculture therefore had to produce more to fill the gap and to raise the standard of consumption above the war and immediate postwar levels.

Agricultural Policy of Labor Government

There was every reason for the Labor government to continue, and even to expand and intensify the wartime program of its Coalition predecessor, and this is what it has done. As early as the fall of 1945, the Minister of Agriculture (Tom Williams) announced that pending the enactment of legislation for peacetime agriculture, his office would support a program embracing: (1) development to the fullest extent of home production of food; (2) assured markets and guaranteed prices for principal products; (3) annual price reviews (prices to be set well in advance of harvests); (4) continued wage regulation; (5) continuance of devices and measures to increase efficiency (technical advice, supervision of farm operations and removal from farms, subject to review by an independent tribunal, of inefficient farmers); and (6) continuance of the structure of county committees.[16]

Labor's program for agriculture, embodying all the features outlined nearly two years earlier by the Minister and dovetailing perfectly with existing procedures, came formally into existence on August 6, 1947.[17] The provisions of

16. *Parliamentary Debates* (Hansard), House of Commons, Vol. 415, cols. 2333–38.

17. Agriculture Act, 1947, 10 & 11 George 6, Ch. 48.

the Agriculture Act are familiar; indeed, the opening sections deal with "guaranteed prices and assured markets," the purpose of which is declared to be the promotion and maintenance of

. . . a stable and efficient agricultural industry capable of producing such part of the nation's food and other agricultural produce as in the national interest it is desirable to produce in the United Kingdom, and of producing it at minimum prices consistently with proper remuneration and living conditions for farmers and workers in agriculture and an adequate return on capital invested in the industry.[18]

Price arrangements under the act cover about 75 per cent of all farm products, and include such items as fat cattle, sheep and pigs, milk, eggs, wheat, barley, oats, rye, potatoes and sugar beets. After a review of the industry participated in by farmers' representatives, the Minister of Agriculture, the Secretary of State for Scotland and the Home Secretary[19] act together annually to fix prices at levels designed to induce the desired volume and balance of output. At the same time, with the participation of the Minister of Food, assured markets—through purchase by, or under the control of, the Ministry of Food—are established. As a result, farmers know the *actual* prices and the size of the assured markets for crops at least eighteen months prior to the harvest, and for livestock prices twelve months ahead. For livestock products, *minimum* prices and size of market are announced from two to four years ahead.[20] Special reviews of prices

18. *Ibid.,* Sec. 1.

19. The price and market provisions of the act apply to England and Wales, Scotland and Northern Ireland. Orders issued under these provisions are subject to approval by the Treasury.

20. On March 23, 1950, after consultation and review, the government announced increases in the prices to be paid for milk, fat cattle, fat sheep and fat pigs, effective April 1, 1950. Acreage payments for potatoes and rye were to be discontinued, but prices would be higher for the main crop and second early potatoes. *The Times* (London), March 24, 1950. The guaranteed *minimum* prices for fat stock, milk and eggs for the years 1952–1953 and 1953–1954 were listed by *The Times* on August 31, 1950.

Results of the 1951 price review and negotiations which established

occur when unforeseen circumstances render an earlier decision inequitable. Prices are of several types—a guaranteed fixed price, an acreage payment, a subsidy, or a price based on a cost formula.

Enforcement of Efficient Farming

Farmers are expected to maintain a minimum level of efficiency in their operations, and the act stipulates, by provisions very similar to those existing throughout the war, that the Minister may enforce standards of good husbandry by direction, supervision and even by dispossession. He proceeds through the familiar county committees—now designated county agricultural executive committees[21]— and it is his duty to act with reference both to maintenance of farm equipment and the manner of farming, e.g., the maintenance of pasture, the cropping of arable land, proper stocking, protection from disease and infestation, preservation of harvested crops, etc. The Minister may dispossess an owner or a tenant who fails to improve his standards or who disobeys directions, subject only to appeal by the affected party to the Agricultural Land Tribunal.[22] Short

---

schedules applicable from April 1, 1951 and for crops of the 1952 harvest were announced March 29, 1951. Prices generally were increased to help farmers meet increased costs, and meat prices were given a special raise to encourage greater production. The total increase in payments to farmers was estimated at £43 million, a considerable part of which was expected to be reflected in higher retail prices. *The Times* (London), March 30, 1951; *The Economist,* April 7, 1951, p. 783.

21. These committees, consisting of 12 members, five appointed directly by the Minister, and three from panels nominated by farmer interests, two from worker panels and two from landowner panels, act as the Minister's agents, in a continuation of the effort to combine central direction with decentralized administration. The arrangements in Scotland and Northern Ireland are slightly different.

See the proposals for change in the functions and operations of the county committees made by the Committee on the Organisation of the Ministry of Agriculture, as reported in *The Economist,* May 5, 1951, p. 1029.

22. The Tribunal consists of an independent legal chairman appointed by the Lord Chancellor, and two other members appointed

of dispossession, the Minister may enter upon land, carry out the required work, and recover the reasonable cost of the operation from the occupier.

The Minister may also give directions as to the use of land, including the manner of use and the products to be grown, when he finds that the national interest requires such direction; but his finding in this regard depends upon approval by both houses of Parliament. Directive powers had been used some 349 times by the close of 1949, mainly to force into production idle lands close to urban centers. Through the remainder of its 111 sections and 13 schedules (118 pages), the act provides an array of devices and measures designed to improve the quality of land management and the efficiency of farming. An Agricultural Land Commission is established to advise the Minister on management matters and to manage land vested in the Minister; a system for making small holdings available to experienced agricultural workers without capital is also established. Security of tenure for tenants was dealt with in provisions subsequently repealed and re-enacted together with amplifying provisions in the Agricultural Holdings Act of 1948.[23] County councils held 467,000 acres in 1949, and provided some 28,700 holdings.

The government has undertaken through other legislation and departmental action to improve the conditions of farm life and to stimulate and make possible more and better production. Research and education are carried on both broadly and intensively; houses for agricultural workers have been given a favored position in the government's housing program; agricultural wages have been steadily increased under the agricultural wages boards;[24] labor and

by the Minister from panels named respectively by farmers and landowners. The decision of the Tribunal is final. In the case of dispossession of an owner, the action takes the form of compulsory purchase; in the case of a tenant by termination of his tenancy. Only 40 dispossessions occurred between 1947 and 1949, and in April 1949, only 62,286 acres were under government control.

23. Agricultural Holdings Act, 1948, 11 & 12 George 6, Ch. 63.

24. Minimum wages for men on farms were raised to £5 a week in the fall of 1950.

farm machinery pools are available to farmers through their county committees; and a wide variety of government contributions, grants and subsidies are offered to induce and to aid the provision of desired facilities and the employment of desired measures.[25]

Food Distribution under Labor

The Ministry of Food carries out its functions of procurement and distribution of food under the Labor government in very much the same manner as during the war under the Coalition. It still employs as its agents associations of producers, manufacturers, wholesalers and retailers, and it has formed a number of companies owned by members of industry and subject, in matters of major policy, to control by the Ministry. Employees of the Ministry are recruited in large measure from the interested industries, and many draw their industry salaries in lieu of salaries from the government.[26] The purchasing activities of the Ministry include "bulk purchase" of foods from foreign producers and foreign governments as well as from home producers.

25. Grants are made, for example, to improve land drainage, to develop cooperative grass drying, to improve the quality of livestock, to improve marginal land in upland areas suited primarily for rearing cattle and sheep, and for a variety of other purposes. For a catalogue of legislation and measures, see *Agriculture in Britain*, pp. 21–56. An interesting example of the in-and-out use of grants and subsidies is found in the introduction, following the annual price review in 1950, of subsidies to small farmers to aid in supply of feeding stuffs, of grants toward the cost of fertilizers applied to grasslands, and grants made to offset the increased cost of gasoline used in farm machines; and the withdrawal of all of these a year later because "full use is not being made of them in all cases, and there are certain unavoidable weaknesses in their administration, with the result that they have had almost as many critics as friends." *The Times* (London), June 29, 1950; July 1, 1950; *The Economist*, December 2, 1950, p. 935; Agriculture (Miscellaneous Provisions) Act, 1950, 14 George 6, Ch. 17; *The Times* (London), February 23, 1951.

26. See R. A. Brady, *op. cit.*, pp. 459–66, for a discussion of the facts and implications of this " 'privatization' of public functions." See also p. 258, footnote 13.

The old marketing boards are beginning once more to stir, but the position of the Labor government toward reviving them is still uncertain. The Lucas committee, set up by the Labor Minister of Agriculture in 1946 "to review the workings of the Agricultural Marketing Acts, to consider . . . modifications . . . and to make recommendations," proposed in the following year that "the primary responsibility for marketing strategy" for major agricultural commodities should be entrusted neither to a government department nor to statutory boards set up and controlled by producers, but to independent commodity commissions. These commissions, which would resemble public utility corporations, would be constituted by members appointed by the Ministers of Agriculture and Food who would not be limited in their selections to nominees of the industries; and would be financed from public funds. A commission would acquire control of a commodity from its producers and would thereafter arrange, either through existing private channels or (if these were not efficient and economical) through its own trading powers, for "the disposal of the supply in the most efficient and economical manner possible."

Prices paid to producers would be determined in three stages: (1) negotiations between the National Farmers' Union and the agricultural departments of a global figure representing an appropriate agricultural income for the nation's farmers; (2) negotiations between the same parties of an allocation among the several commodities; and (3) a breakdown of each commodity allocation into a schedule of prices by the commodity commission and representative organizations of the producers involved. The commissions would sell either at freely determined market prices or at below-the-market prices set by the government to aid consumers. The commissions, although acting as sales organizations of home producers, would be essentially "agents of the tax-payer." Any losses incurred by reason of prices paid to producers above the market level would be regarded as the cost to the taxpayer of maintaining British agriculture;

losses due to authorized sales below the market would be a straight consumer subsidy. The Lucas committee favored, as well, the establishment of producer-controlled marketing boards for each important commodity—to represent producers in negotiations and to promote measures to raise productive efficiency.[27]

The attitude of the Labor government toward the Lucas committee recommendations is obscure, but there is no indication of enthusiasm for the report or, indeed, of any desire for pronounced change in existing arrangements. The government's marketing legislation,[28] in the references to marketing boards established under the acts of 1931 and 1933, provides that where, after prescribed investigation, the Minister of Agriculture finds any act or omission of a marketing board—such as restriction of use or output, regulation of price or limitation of the classes of persons to or through whom commodities are sold—contrary to the public interest, he may order such action as he deems necessary to prevent the result or mitigate the damage.[29] Increased activity among producers looking toward the establishment of new schemes, and the reactivation of old ones, is becoming evident.[30]

Output Goals and Progress toward Them

The purpose of the drive for stability and efficiency was to increase home production to fill the gap between the food

27. The committee's recommendations both on commodity commissions and producers' marketing boards will be found in the *Lucas Report*, pp. 58–68. The proposals have been criticized by the Conservatives. The position both of the committee and the Conservatives is discussed in Brady, *op. cit.*, pp. 487–92.

28. Agricultural Marketing Act, 1949, 12 & 13 George 6, Ch. 38.

29. *Ibid.*, Secs. 2 and 3. Other sections deal with board organization and procedures for assessing penalties for contravention of board schemes, and with details of even lesser moment.

30. See *The Times* (London), January 11, 1950 and February 12, 1951 (milk); July 17, 1950 (wool and tomatoes); and the *Midland Bank Review,* February 1951 (tomatoes and cucumbers). See also the statement by the president of the National Farmers' Union in favor of producer-controlled marketing boards, together with a critical editorial in *The Times* (London), December 5, 1950.

required for an acceptable standard of living and the
food economically available through imports. In 1947 the
government named an exact goal for its program—output
targets to be achieved by British farmers by 1952-1953—
and published its objective for the world to read. A report[31]
of the Economic Cooperation Administration summarizes
the production program as follows:

Compared to prewar, the program is designed to produce,
at home, enough food and feed so that imports could be cut
by the equivalent of $400 million per year the first two years
and as much as $520 million by 1952 (at 1947/48 prices). In
terms of imports volume, foods and feed are to be roughly
three-quarters of prewar volume. . . .

The goal of the United Kingdom long-term food and agriculture program—compared to prewar—is about as follows:

Expand wheat production by more than half; double the
coarse grain production for livestock feed; double potato output for the first two years and then ease off to about one-half
above prewar; increase sugar beets a third, milk a fourth, poultry a half, and meat cattle by 10 per cent. Sheep will be reduced
about a sixth and hogs 8 per cent from prewar, although both
are to be increased over present numbers. Over-all this means
about 50 per cent increase in total output over prewar, and 15
per cent over the peak wartime production. Important individual goals are as follows:

Item	1952 Production as a Per Cent of Prewar (1936–1939 Average)
Bread grains	157
Other grains	199
Potatoes	158
Sugar beets	132
Milk (dairy cattle)	123
Eggs (chickens)	152
Beef and veal	110
Mutton and lamb	83
Pork	92

31. *Report of the E.C.A. Mission to the United Kingdom*, Vol. 2,
London, 1948, pp. 149–50. See also *European Co-operation* [*Long-
Term Programme of the United Kingdom*], Cmd. 7572, H.M.S.O.,
December 1948, pp. 15–17; and *Economic Survey for 1948*, Cmd. 7344,
H.M.S.O., March 1948, pp. 33–36.

The British expect to achieve this goal in yearly stages
. . . about as follows:

Year	Per Cent of War Production
1948–1949	128
1949–1950	135
1950–1951	143
1951–1952	150

Performance has been substantial. Progress was made in
the crop year 1948–1949 under favorable conditions, and
improvement has continued in later years. "For 1950–51
the net output of British agriculture has climbed to about
21 per cent above that of 1946–47 (when the weather was
bad). At 40 per cent above the prewar output it is higher
than ever before."[32]

Attitudes toward the Program—The Subsidy Issue

So far as the main lines of the agricultural production
program are concerned, there is little articulate dissent.
The Labor, Conservative and Liberal parties are all on record in favor of "guaranteed prices and assured markets."[33]

Outside of official party circles questions as to the future
of the farmer are raised—whether he may be riding for a

32. *The Economist,* April 7, 1951, p. 782. *The Economist* adds, "It
is not physically possible to bring about a further rapid increase in
the output of British agriculture." See also the *Economic Survey for
1950,* Cmd. 7915, H.M.S.O., pp. 26 ff.

33. Relative to the 1950 General Election, *The Economist* (February 18, 1950, p. 358) commented: "Agricultural policy is *not* an important issue in the election tussle. The reason is that the main parties
are committed to maintaining the system of guaranteed prices and
assured markets and to raising the output of British agriculture as
a means of saving dollars. They all promise to the farmer security and
prosperity, and assistance in increasing his production." See also the
official party manifestos issued for the 1950 election: *Let Us Win
Through Together* (Labor); *This Is the Road* (Conservative); and
No Easy Way (Liberal).

The Economist (October 6, 1951, p. 787) refers to the 1951 Conservative proposals for agriculture as "blatantly restrictive," and as
"written exclusively from the producer's point of view, and on a
narrow interpretation of the producer's interest at that."

fall when free world markets open again and whether the proper commodities are selected for accelerated home production. The free market seems far away, however, and the immediate need to conserve dollars, the ever-present cloud of possible war, and the political power of farmers and landowners are far more potent than abstract economics in determining the outlines and the details of Britain's mid-century agricultural policy. *The Economist,* pointing out that the average farmer now gets five times his prewar income for less than one and a half times his prewar output, questions whether "the nation should go on using methods that procure comparatively little extra food for a very high cost."[34]

There is a good deal of controversy over the food subsidy, but this device possesses an ambiguity that greatly confuses the issue of its cost and its efficiency as a stimulus to farm production. Farmers are paid guaranteed prices by the Ministry of Food, which in turn sells the purchased produce (ultimately to consumers) at prices lower than the prices it has paid. The resulting loss is the subsidy, but it is not entirely clear how much of the subsidy is a payment to sustain high-cost farming and how much of it is a payment to underwrite low-cost consumption. The extent to which the guaranteed prices are above the levels at which food could regularly be imported into Britain from world suppliers may be regarded as the measure of the subsidy to farmers. In this connection the comparative figures published by *The Times* are suggestive, but it should be realized that they constitute a shifting and questionable basis for exact conclusions. (See Table 6.) The exact over-all cost of the subsidies depends on the complete trading account (profits and losses) of the Minister of Food, including his purchase of food from foreign sources, and the calculation of other payments to farmers. The most recent approved figures total approximately £425 million for 1949–1950. These cover the entire cost of food subsidies for the year, including

34. *The Economist,* April 7, 1951, p. 782.

TABLE 6

COMPARATIVE AVERAGE PRICES OF DOMESTIC
AND IMPORTED AGRICULTURAL PRODUCTS,
SEPTEMBER 30, 1949—MARCH 31, 1950

Product	Home-Produced Supplies, per Ton	Imported Supplies, per Ton (C.I.F.)
Beef	£145 ex slaughterhouse	
Frozen fore and hind quarters		£100.90
Boned and boneless		100.30
Lamb and mutton	226 ex slaughterhouse	107.50
Bacon	289 ex factory	235.30
Wheat	23.62 ex farm[a]	28.20
Barley	23.72 ex farm	20.23
Oats	19.48 ex farm	17.56
Linseed	59 ex farm	54.22
Shell eggs[b]	7.417 ex packing station	4.07

Source: The Times (London), May 22, 1950, p. 2.
a. Plus acreage payment costing £1.075.
b. Per box of 360.

crop acreage payments and the fertilizer subsidy.[35] The cost of the food subsidies in the Minister's trading accounts (after a profit of some £26.3 million on certain commodity groups) was £394,417,510 compared with £453,419,891 in 1948–1949. In the early summer of 1950 the Minister reported to Parliament the profits and losses in his trading account. (See Table 7.) In presenting his budget in the spring of 1950 for the ensuing year, the Chancellor of the Exchequer, while defending the principle of subsidies, set the maximum (which he emphasized was also a minimum) figure for the food subsidy for 1950–1951 at £410 million—a reduction from the maximum announced for 1949–1950 of £465 million.[36] He stated the government's determina-

35. The Times (London), February 14, 1951.
36. The Times (London), April 19, 1950. The reduction was to be attributed, the Chancellor said, to economies introduced during the preceding autumn—elimination of certain direct subsidies, certain price increases and administrative savings.

tion to hold subsidies beneath this ceiling even though this should make it necessary to raise prices to consumers, and subsequent action has tended to confirm the seriousness of the government's purpose.[37] The same limit (£410 million) was announced in the Budget speech in 1951, and an even greater rise in retail food prices was predicted.[38]

TABLE 7

PROFITS AND LOSSES IN TRADING ACCOUNT OF
MINISTER OF FOOD, 1946–1949

(*In Millions*)

Year Ending	Profits Made in Bulk Purchase of Food	Losses Incurred on Subsidized Foods[a]
March 31, 1946	£ 4.8	£2.03
March 31, 1947	8.0	2.57
March 31, 1948	28.0	3.23
March 31, 1949	17.6	3.83

Sources: For profits, *Parliamentary Debates* (Hansard), House of Commons, Vol. 476, cols. 185, 262; for losses, *ibid.*, Vol. 477, cols. 1355–56.

a. Not necessarily bulk purchased.

Mild objections have been raised against the guaranteed price-subsidy arrangement as a device for encouraging production on the grounds that it gives unnecessary profits to many farmers, since as farmer income rises the effect is to induce lethargy rather than efficiency. Maximum security, it is argued, is neither a condition nor a prescription for maximum efficiency; increased efficiency and production could be better achieved by giving direct grants to farmers to encourage capital investment, improvement of land and buildings, and the like. As an aid to consumers, the food

37. For example, the Minister of Food announced increases in retail prices of bacon, effective September 10, 1950, "in accordance with the policy of adjusting the rate of the food subsidies to maintain the total of £410 million as both a ceiling and a floor." *The Times* (London), September 1, 1950.

38. *The Economist*, April 14, 1951, pp. 877, 884.

subsidies are questioned primarily on the ground that they are indiscriminate in their effect and hence wasteful; direct allowances should be given by the government to needy, low-income families, and the prices of food should then be allowed to find their own level in the free market.[39]

Is Land Nationalization in Prospect?

Cries are raised, of course, against the "regimentation" of farmers inherent in the program, and also against high administrative costs. So far as regimentation is concerned, the controversy seems to be at a stand-off. Many are critical of the lenient attitude which the farmer-dominated county committees adopt toward the indifferent and inefficient practices of the farmers whose operations the committees are expected to oversee and control. However, "regimentation" by one's peers is not an unusual or recent feature of British economic activity in any area or at any level. The Ministries of Food and Agriculture have instituted in-

39. The most dramatic of recent attacks on subsidies to farmers came from within the government. Mr. Stanley Evans, then Parliamentary Secretary to the Ministry of Food, expressed his views at a press conference, March 17, 1950, to the effect that "We must be very careful not to cosset any section of the population at the expense of the community as a whole. We must . . . avoid a situation in which consumers become the milch cow to be milked irrevocably and continuously by our friends of the countryside." Later he raised the question whether high subsidies did not conceal "a good deal of agricultural inefficiency and inertia," and offered the conclusion that "no other nation feather-beds its agriculture like Britain." On April 16, 1950 came the expected announcement that the Prime Minister had accepted Mr. Evans' resignation. *The Times* (London), March 18 and April 17, 1950. Mr. Evans later made a spirited defense of his position in Parliament. *Parliamentary Debates* (Hansard), House of Commons, Vol. 475, cols. 1040–50.

The Economist (May 26, 1951, pp. 1214–16) attacked the administration of the guaranteed price plan as "inflexible," and argued that "the established expectations of the farming community count for more in determining the result of the price review than do the economic objectives of the Government."

quiries and reforms looking toward a reduction in overhead costs, but many of the farmer members of the county committees are still critical of book work and administrative red tape.

Much criticism is directed at Britain's system for distribution of agricultural goods, and the Ministry of Food and the marketing boards are the principal targets. The principle of industry self-government that has characterized all British industry for many years has been embraced with enthusiasm in food processing and distribution. It raises questions that are essentially philosophical, as well as practical issues of monopoly profit and monopoly restrictions on efficient methods and innovation. Many find it remarkable that Labor is not strongly set against these developments, but, properly or otherwise, British Labor seems to be following its traditional course. The forerunner of nationalization in coal, steel, and the public utilities was industry self-government of the sort which seems now to be so firmly established in agriculture and food; and Labor was officially indifferent to the phenomenon in those cases.[40]

Labor is on record in favor of nationalization of the land in Britain—but not at this time. It did not ask for and it did not receive a mandate for this step either in 1945 or in 1950. There is latent support for the move—on the grounds of need in agricultural industry for more capital than individuals can furnish, and for larger holdings in order to permit the use of large-scale methods of operation. In addition, over 65 per cent of Britain's farmers are tenants, and the government has already moved deeply into the industry through financial aid, controls and ownership of marginal land. On the other hand, there is no widespread popular support for land nationalization, and little that is apparent to the observer in the councils of the Labor party.

40. The sugar manufacturing and refining industry which adopted self-government with great enthusiasm in the middle 1930's is on the government's schedule for nationalization, according to its 1950 manifesto.

Labor's agricultural program in 1951 amounts to a series of improvisations, differing only in degree and detail from the program that any other party in power in Britain today would probably sponsor. It remains to be seen to what extent Labor's lack of a basic plan for agriculture is due to the bankruptcy of Labor idealism, to tiredness or to pragmatic acceptance of a system that "works," and how much to shrewd political sense and a willingness to wait.

CHAPTER 12

In Conclusion

SUPPORTERS AND CRITICS of Labor have been drawing conclusions since the hour when Labor first assumed the responsibilities of His Majesty's government. Every improvement in British circumstances has been hailed as a demonstration of the validity of Labor's thesis; every setback as proof of the blighting effect of socialism and the welfare state. Labor has pointed with pride to results that might equally have occurred under a different government; and has been held to account for conditions that it did not produce, and for failing to keep promises that it never made.

There is nothing unusual or alarming about all this, but it serves to point up one solid proposition: it is much too early to attempt a definitive appraisal of British planning and nationalization. The most that is warranted at this time and in this book are some general observations, offered tentatively, in an effort to promote further understanding of the major Labor projects described and discussed in the preceding chapters. These projects, it should be emphasized, do not constitute necessary and integral parts of a carefully conceived, tightly constructed program. Any one of them could be substantially altered or even discontinued without making any less symmetrical the very interesting, but quite unsymmetrical pattern that the Labor government has woven since 1945.

Planning Is Pragmatic

The British economy in 1951 is "planned" neither in structure nor in operation. Britain has no master plan. Indeed, the lack of a bold, imaginative over-all plan, to point the way and to quicken and control the development of

275

major projects such as distribution of industry and the re-
making of towns and countryside, is regarded in many quarters as a basic defect in Labor's course of action. It has made
many people less fearful of Labor, but it has also tempered
the enthusiasm of many who might have been attracted by
a more confident and direct display of precise purpose.

The kind of planning that goes on in Britain reflects no
starry-eyed, single-minded search for Utopia. It is eminently
pragmatic, and is much more the offspring of immediate
pressures than of deeply held ideological convictions. It is
experimental in its approach (although it may prove to be
somewhat less experimental in the matter of withdrawal!).
In its variety, confusion and contradictions, its boldness and
caution, its perception and blindness, its carefully considered measures and improvisations, its idealism and dema-
goguery, British postwar planning is reminiscent of our own
early New Deal. Its background and immediate goals are,
of course, quite different, but the atmosphere that sur-
rounds it and emanates from it is very similar. Here is no
coolly calculated, finely drawn socialist blueprint; this is
plain, democratic muddling—of a fairly high quality. This
is the way democracies behave in the face of the formidable
problems of organized living-together in the middle of the
twentieth century.

The need to resort to direct as well as to indirect controls
over phases of the British economy was recognized even by
the Coalition government in its famous 1944 White Paper
on employment policy. The "planning" (such as it is) and
the controls embraced by the Labor government are different from those anticipated in 1944, but they sprang from
forces and pressures that were even more immediately insistent and which, to say the least, strongly suggested the
nature and direction of the steps properly to be taken. Britain's books of account in 1945 showed limited and battered
resources, a confused internal and international situation,
and an urgent and generally recognized need to meet certain
major, well-defined investment, production and trade demands squarely and with full force. Given the time and

circumstances, it is difficult to believe that any government, regardless of its make-up, could have refrained from an attempt to budget and direct the use of the nation's scarce resources, at least in major categories.

Resource budgeting by the Labor government has been done tentatively, hopefully and with little pretense. The direct controls employed—price fixing, rationing, licensing —have been extended from the wartime emergency to the peacetime emergency, but they are not a basic feature of any long-run program the Labor government has yet disclosed. During 1949–1950 the controls were appreciably relaxed, but the intensified defense effort at the beginning of 1951 halted the movement and dictated the reimposition of some of the controls which had earlier been taken away. Such controls are irritating—just as the resource shortages they reflect are irritating—and it may be that Labor was unwise, both economically and politically, in its failure to move more energetically after the close of the war to eliminate them. This should be considered, however, as an issue of day-to-day operating policy; there is nothing to indicate that Labor looks upon extensive direct controls as a permanent part of its program.

Labor's Program Thoroughly British

The Labor government must bear the political responsibility (and is entitled to the political credit) for the program which it sponsors, but the program—including controls, reform and reconstruction—is not Labor's alone. Its roots go deeper than World War I; it was taking shape between the wars; virtually all of its parts at one time or another and in varying degrees have drawn open support from Conservatives and Liberals. It is thoroughly British.

Labor came into power at a critical point in British history, and its program was instituted under conditions and circumstances that added greatly to its difficulties. Even the survival thus far of its major projects is something of an achievement. It is almost certain that many of them will live far into the future. Others must improve in performance to live, and this will take time and opportunity—and more. It may be argued that Labor was ill-advised and even ruthless to load its burden of reforms on to the back of a weakened economy. Labor's answer might be, first, that these very conditions were responsible for its call to govern, and the only time a political party can prosecute its program is when it is in office; and, second, that the measures Labor has introduced, if only their roots can become established, will add strength and character to the economy.

Labor has risked much (both for itself and for Britain) by its bold (rash?) program of nationalization on so extended a front. Nationalization of large-scale, far-flung industries adds problems of responsibility to those of organization and control. Industries under private ownership and management, broken into separate (even if not always fully competitive) units and firms, are difficult enough to operate. Lines of authority, incentives, centralization *versus* decentralization, etc., are continuing problems under either private ownership or nationalization. Under nationalization, however, monopoly takes the place of competition (formal or real); the entire industry becomes a single unit; problems of the firm merge with problems of the industry, and these, in turn, merge with problems of the economy—with final, almost terrifying economic responsibility resting on those persons who at the same time bear the responsibility of the political state.

Economic Responsibility Now More Personal

Responsibility for operation of the economy is present under any organization of the economic system. Individual mistakes under private ownership may easily be wide in their effect; the interlacing and interdependence of economic phenomena are increasingly a characteristic of modern life, whether industrial property is privately owned or nationalized. But under private ownership responsibility to society is difficult to assign; it cannot be located in or identified with any single person or group less than society itself or, possibly, the entrepreneurial group as a whole.

Under socialism, and in a lesser degree under selective nationalization, individual economic decisions stand out in clear relief. Public awareness of processes and effects hitherto accepted as "given" tends to focus responsibility on the government in power; the public can, and does, fix blame on persons instead of on "the system." The burden carried by those in authority under extensive nationalization is heavy indeed, and their positions are precarious. To advocate nationalization, one must foresee great gains; to participate actively in its institution and to accept accountability for its operation one must be prepared to sacrifice heavily.

It may be argued that Labor's risk was politically necessary; clearly, it was a calculated risk. It is almost certain that public opinion in Britain would have demanded nationalization of coal, railways, electricity distribution, gas, airways and the Bank of England within the first ten or fifteen years after the war, whether by a Labor government or by a government of different complexion. Nationalization of road haulage and steel are the only really controversial cases, and Labor's action here is at least easy to understand, even if not wholly to support. It should not be difficult for Americans to realize that if railways are taken over by the government, nationalization of road haulage cannot be far behind. Do we, in fact, have any convincing rationale for government regulation of motor bus and truck rates in the United States other than the fact that railway rates were first placed under close regulation? The substantive arguments advanced by Labor for government ownership of steel cannot be rejected as frivolous, but it is probably true that steel nationalization is a reflection more of emotional ideology than of severely practical economic considerations. But, in the light of what we know of the cartel-ridden, government-regulated steel industry under private ownership, how shall we judge the Conservative cry for "free enterprise" in steel? It is understandable, too, that a "socialist" government should want to socialize one relatively successful, going industry for the sheer sake of testing its socialist professions in a favorable setting.

Results So Far Inconclusive

The results of nationalization are just beginning to appear and they are, thus far, inconclusive. The records of the several industries are uneven as, indeed, they were under private ownership. On the score of productivity, investment and mechanization, labor relations, and financial returns there is nothing startling to report. Financial results in coal and electricity are satisfactory, but not good enough; in railway transport they are definitely unsatisfactory, but, under the circumstances, not surprising. Costs and prices are up in all cases; problems of efficiency, organization and reorganization, and labor incentives continue to be baffling. The government is well aware of the difficulties involved in mixing efficiency, responsibility and politics, and is working actively to keep them in hand. Clearly, nationalization per se is no panacea; just as clearly, British experience has not demonstrated that its possibilities are illusory. A convincing record, for or against nationalization in Britain has still to be made.

Sustained attacks on Labor's other projects have been directed principally against administration and details of structure. Town and country planning invites opposition, on one hand, because it lacks an over-all plan and is too loose in its requirements, and, on the other hand, because its requirements are irritating and time consuming and because its charges operate to deter development. It is probable that a change in government would produce substantial relaxation all along the line and, possibly, even virtual abandonment of the town and country planning program, although it must be remembered that the basic scheme was shaped mainly by experts serving under Conservative and Coalition governments.

Both major parties in Britain accept housing as a prime government concern, but the Conservatives promise more houses than the number for which Labor is willing to allocate resources, and they propose to turn over the task of supply more largely to private builders operating in a freer market.

Agricultural controls would undergo no significant changes at the hands of a Conservative government; but the government as bulk-buyer of foods would almost certainly be supplanted by business firms buying on private account. The Labor government has made no friends in its capacity as sole provider of imported meat for British consumers.

The location of industry under government influence and restraint is generally acceptable to the British public; at least irritations on one side are matched by impatience on the other

The principle of the national health service is now firmly implanted in Britain. Practitioners are concerned over the scale of pay and excessive demands upon their time, but there is no evidence of a revolt against, or any appreciable movement away from, the service. A Conservative government would undertake to lighten the administrative load and would probably move to increase the cost to the patient somewhat above the level reluctantly established in 1951 by Labor. Labor will do its best to restore the service completely to a "no charge" basis. Time and general economic improvement will unite Britain's parties behind the service.

The Economic and Political Future

From an economic point of view, what Britain really needs is an industrial and commercial rebirth—inventiveness, mechanization, daring and drive. The government knows this, but its efforts to achieve it are scattered and only faintly promising. Its plans for industrial development are pointed in the right direction, but it has yet to take hold with firmness and imagination. It is very conscious of the problems of organization in the nationalized industries, but it has been more apparently successful in achieving organization for responsibility than organization for efficiency.

It is easy to say that "security" and "fair shares" are bound to lessen incentive, but this will not be convincing to those who know something of British industrial and commercial life and performance for the quarter century preceding Labor's advent to power. The form of government and the relationship of government to economic life at all levels and at all points of contact are very important in this connection, but there are other considerations and forces at work, as well. There is little in the professed platforms of any of Labor's political rivals to give assurance that their success at the polls would bring about a regeneration of British industry and commerce. In short, it is worth suggesting that the test ahead is fully as much of people as of governmental forms and programs. Whether Britain can forge ahead in the economic steeplechase will depend fully as much upon the British people as upon whether Labor or one of its rivals is in the saddle.

As of mid-1951 the British public appears to look upon the program and record of its Labor government with something less than complete and enthusiastic favor. The immense parliamentary majority that Labor enjoyed during its first postwar term in office was reduced in the election of 1950 to such slender proportions that only the utmost vigilance and loyalty has enabled Labor to cling to its precarious parliamentary position. In a long and aggravating series of tests since the spring of 1950, Labor has yet to sustain a defeat on a significant legislative issue. Labor has experienced severe, and potentially dangerous, differences within its ranks, but it has presented a solid front to all challengers from the outside. Public opinion surveys suggest that Labor has lost ground even since February 1950, and that the coming election will bring the Conservative party back into power. The tone of the British press is entirely consistent with this view. Without accepting either press or opinion surveys as infallible counsel, it is still safe for an outsider to predict that Labor will be fortunate indeed to hold its present slight majority in the forthcoming test at the polls.

The swing of public support away from Labor is not simple to interpret. Certainly it is due in part to that element present in every political contest—desire for a change. It is also true that many independent voters feel that Labor's program has been concerned too little with production of wealth and too much with its redistribution, and that the redivision has left them among those deprived rather than with those who have benefited. Some are disgusted with what they regard as fumbling inefficiency. Some are disturbed that Labor has gone so far in an attempt to remake Britain; others (including erstwhile passionate supporters of Labor) are disgruntled that Labor has proceeded so cautiously, and with so little drive and imagination.

Projects as wide and varied as those Labor has set in motion are likely to invite attack at each of their many points of contact, and the attack spreads easily to other projects and to the program as a whole. However, since each is not an integral part of an undivided, self-contained and self-consistent program, its acceptance by those who find it good does not insure enthusiastic over-all support for the party that has sponsored it. Those who do not like the health service are probably opposed to Labor; those who like the health service are in favor of health service, but not necessarily in favor of Labor. Similarly, to assume power and to use it is to risk defeat. It is easier for any party to get into office on promises and hopes than to remain in on performance.

All in all, however, a loss of the coming election by Labor would probably indicate a desire by the electorate to rid the country of the Labor government much more than a positive desire to embrace a government by Conservatives. Much of what Labor has contrived and launched will remain even though the Labor government is forced to retire. Even at their election-campaign extremes, Labor and Conservatives in Britain are not widely apart, and the minimum working programs which each is willing to accept and claim as its own have much in common.

The Economic Picture in 1951

The 1951 picture of Britain's economic status and prospects is not clear. There is virtually no unemployment, work interruptions are minor and scattered, and production is rising in most industries. Export and import objectives have been brought into sight during Labor's years in office, but at the moment are seriously threatened. Britain no longer receives Marshall aid. Wealthy Britishers still live as wealthy people generally live, but with somewhat less than their former ostentation; the middle classes are not faring too well; the lower income groups are enjoying a relatively improved standard of living.

It would be silly to pretend, however, that all is well in Britain, that Britain's future is sure and bright, and that Labor has found and is employing a sure-fire formula for national well-being. Conditions in Great Britain are grim, and the present need to intensify defense efforts has brought the clouds even lower.

It is quite possible that since 1945 Labor has taken on a larger job than any peacetime government can handle—too much and too quickly. It may be that its tax program will prove to be so severe as to be self-defeating. The government itself could stand some streamlining. There have been mistakes, wastes and excesses in the health program. The position of labor in industries nationalized by a Labor government raises serious problems that have still to be carefully identified and worked out. In taking over coal and railways the government has saddled itself with heavy financial burdens. The British people are tired; they are irked by controls and restraints even though they know that controls and restraints cannot be lifted and that they must now, of necessity, be increased. There is much in the British situation that is disheartening, and much in British policy that is difficult to defend. There is much, too, that is fine and promising in Britain, not the least of which is the pride, courage and independence of the British people, and their willingness to tackle new problems in new ways.

Great Britain's economic position and condition are different from those of any other country, but the devices and measures that the nation is trying are of the greatest concern to the rest of the world and, particularly, to all of those who pin their faith on democracy. The British program runs the gamut of attitudes, approaches, policies and methods characteristic of, and available to, democracies. Quite apart from the substantive merits of the British program or any of its parts or phases, the British way is the democratic way. Whether under Labor or under Conservatives, Britain stands as a testing ground for democratic collective action, and as a bulwark against totalitarian dictatorship.

Bibliography

THIS LIST OF books, monographs, articles and government reports is intended to help the reader who wishes additional information on particular phases of British planning and nationalization. It is offered as suggestive rather than exhaustive. Many of the items contain still further suggestions.

In general, anyone who cares to keep in touch with current developments in Great Britain can enjoy a balanced fare by following *The Times* (London), *The Daily Herald* (London), *The Economist,* and government publications and reports obtainable through the British Information Services, 30 Rockefeller Plaza, New York 20. The B.I.S. publishes the quarterly *Labor and Industry in Britain,* as well as memoranda and bibliographies on special topics, and acts as the agent in the United States for His Majesty's Stationery Office, the publisher of official government documents. Some recent articles from *The Economist* are included in the following list, but only two items each from *The Times* (London) and *Labor and Industry in Britain.*

The publications and pronouncements of Great Britain's major political parties can be obtained, respectively, from the Conservative and Unionist Central Office, Abbey House, Victoria Street, London, S.W. 1; the Liberal Party Organisation, Merton House, 8 Gayfere Street, London, S.W. 1; and the Labor Party, Transport House, Smith Square, London, S.W. 1.

I. PLANNING AND NATIONALIZATION IN GENERAL

A. GOVERNMENT PUBLICATIONS

Britain, 1950–51, Central Office of Information, London, 1950. A handbook of information about the British government and economy.

Capital Investment in 1948. (Presented by the Chancellor of the Exchequer to Parliament, December 1947.) Cmd. 7268, H.M. S.O., 1947.

Economic Survey for 1947, Cmd. 7046; *for 1948,* Cmd. 7344; *for 1949,* Cmd. 7647; *for 1950,* Cmd. 7915; *for 1951,* Cmd. 8195, H.M.S.O. Britain's annual review and "plan."

Employment Policy, Cmd. 6527, H.M.S.O., May 1944. The Coalition government's "White Paper" that set the stage for subsequent peacetime controls.

European Co-operation [Long-Term Programme of the United Kingdom], Cmd. 7572, H.M.S.O., December 1948.

Monopolies and Restrictive Practices Act, 1948: Annual Report by the Board of Trade for the Period Ending 31st December 1949, H.M.S.O., March 1950.

"Price Control in Britain," *Labor and Industry in Britain,* British Information Services, March 1951.

Report on the Supply of Cast Iron Rainwater Goods, Monopolies and Restrictive Practices Commission, H.M.S.O., 1951.

Report on the Supply of Dental Goods, Monopolies and Restrictive Practices Commission, H.M.S.O., 1950.

Statement on Personal Incomes, Costs and Prices (Presented by the Prime Minister and First Lord of the Treasury to Parliament, February 1948). Cmd. 7321, H.M.S.O., 1948.

"Survey of Existing Controls," *Labor and Industry in Britain,* British Information Services, December 1950.

B. BOOKS AND MONOGRAPHS

Beveridge, W. H. *Full Employment in a Free Society,* Allen & Unwin, London, 1944; Norton, New York, 1945. The second of the famous Beveridge reports.

Bowen, I. *Britain's Industrial Survival,* Faber & Faber, London, 1947.

Brady, R. A. *Crisis in Britain,* University of California Press, Berkeley, 1950; Oxford University Press, Oxford, 1950. A thoroughgoing, critical study of Britain's postwar program. Separate chapters deal with all of the areas covered in the present book.

Chester, D. N. *The Nationalised Industries: A Statutory Analysis,* Institute of Public Administration, London, 1948. An excellent brief survey of the framework of the nationalized industries.

Cowles, V. S. *No Cause for Alarm,* Harper, New York, 1949.

Dalton, H. *Practical Socialism for Britain,* Routledge, London, 1935. An early statement.

Davies, E. *National Enterprise,* Gollancz, London, 1946.

de Jouvenel, B. *Problems of Socialist England,* Batchworth Press, London, 1949. Observations by a foreign observer.

Devons, E. *Economic Planning in War and Peace,* Manchester Statistical Society, Manchester, 1947.

———. *Planning in Practice,* Cambridge University Press, London, 1951.

Durbin, E. F. M. *Problems of Economic Planning,* Routledge & Kegan Paul, London, 1949.

Finer, H. *The Road to Reaction,* Little, Brown, Boston, 1945.

Franks, O. S. *Central Planning and Control in War and Peace,* Harvard University Press, Cambridge, 1947; Longmans, London, 1947.

Gordon, L. *The Public Corporation in Great Britain,* Oxford University Press, Oxford, 1938.

Harrod, R. F. *Are These Hardships Necessary?,* Hart-Davis, London, 1947.

———. *And So It Goes On,* Hart-Davis, London, 1951.

Hayek, F. A. *The Road to Serfdom,* University of Chicago Press, Chicago, 1944; Routledge & Kegan Paul, London, 1944.

Henderson, H. D. *The Uses and Abuses of Economic Planning,* Macmillan, New York, 1947; Cambridge University Press, London, 1947. A classic among the postwar pamphlets.

Hutchison, K. *Decline and Fall of British Capitalism,* Scribner, New York, 1950.

Jay, D. P. T. *The Socialist Case* (2d edition), Faber & Faber, London, 1947. A recent statement from a source close to the center of the Labor party.

Jewkes, J. *Ordeal by Planning,* Macmillan, London, 1948. Probably the best known of the recent attacks on planning and controls.

Labour Believes in Britain, The Labor Party, 1949. The Labor platform, 1949.

Let Us Face the Future, The Labor Party, 1945. The Labor platform, 1945.

Let Us Win Through Together, The Labor Party, 1950. The Labor platform for the 1950 election.

Lewis, B. W. *Price and Production Control in British Industry,* University of Chicago Press, Chicago, 1937; Cambridge University Press, London, 1938. An outline of British industrial self-government in the 1930's.

Lewis, R., and Maude, A. *The English Middle Classes,* J. M. Dent, London, 1949; Knopf, New York, 1950.

Lewis, W. A. *The Principles of Economic Planning,* Allen & Unwin, London, 1949.

Lipson, E. *A Planned Economy or Free Enterprise* (2d edition), Black, London, 1946. Historical and analytical.

Meade, J. E. *Planning and the Price Mechanism,* Macmillan, New York, 1948; Allen & Unwin, London, 1948. An excellent analysis.

No Easy Way, Liberal Party, 1950. The Liberal platform for the 1950 election.

O'Brien, T. H. *British Experiments in Public Ownership and Control,* Allen & Unwin, London, 1937; Norton, New York, 1938.

Robbins, L. C. *The Economic Problem in Peace and War,* Macmillan, London, 1947. A classic statement of the problem of planning.

Robson, W. A. (Editor). *Public Enterprise,* University of Chicago Press, Chicago, 1937; Allen & Unwin, London, 1937.

Rostas, L. *Productivity, Prices and Distribution in Selected British Industries,* Macmillan, New York, 1948; Cambridge University Press, London, 1948.

This is the Road, Conservative Party, 1950. The Conservative platform for the 1950 election.

Thomas, I. *The Socialist Tragedy,* Macmillan, New York, 1951. A former socialist attacks socialism in theory and practice.

Ulam, A. B. *Philosophical Foundations of English Socialism,* Harvard University Press, Cambridge, 1951; Oxford University Press, Oxford, 1951.

Williams, F. *Socialist Britain,* Viking Press, New York, 1949. A readable account, by a Labor stalwart.

Wootton, B. F. *Freedom under Planning,* University of North Carolina Press, Chapel Hill, 1945; Allen & Unwin, London, 1945.

Young, M. D. *Labour's Plan for Plenty,* Gollancz, London, 1947.

C. ARTICLES

Beacham, A. "Nationalization in Theory and Practice," *Quarterly Journal of Economics,* November 1950.

Bird, R. "Public Bodies and Public Accountability," *Lloyds Bank Review,* January 1950.

Brand, R. H. "Private Enterprise and Socialism," *Economic Journal,* September 1948.

Bunbury, H. "The Public Corporation," *Public Administration,* Summer 1944.

Clay, H. "Planning and Market Economy," *American Economic Review* (Papers and Proceedings), May 1950.

"Controlling the Giants," *The Economist,* November 4, 1950.

Crowther, G. "British Socialism on Trial," *Atlantic Monthly,* May 1949.

"Design for Drift," *The Economist,* April 1, 1950.

"Dividends under Control," *The Economist,* July 28, 1951.

"Economic Policy: A Discussion of Planning Techniques," *Planning,* April 3, 1950.

"Economic Survey for 1950," *The Economist,* April 1, 1950.

"Economic Survey for 1951," *The Economist,* April 7, 1951.

"Emergency Powers Since 1945," *The Economist,* November 11, 1950.

"End of the Middle Way," *The Economist,* March 3, 1951.

Finer, H. "Planning and Nationalisation in Great Britain," *International Labour Review,* March and April 1948.

Fischer, J. "Insomnia in Whitehall," *Harpers Magazine,* January 1950.

Fleming, M. "Production and Price Policy in Public Enterprise," *Economica,* February 1950.

"Government and Industry," *Planning,* September 18, 1950.

"Government Control over the Use of Capital Resources," *Midland Bank Review,* August 1950.

Hanson, A. H. "Parliamentary Questions on the Nationalised Industries," *Public Administration,* Spring 1951.

Heilbroner, R. L. "The Socialist Devils of England," *Harper's Magazine,* October 1951.

Henderson, H. D. "The Price System," *Economic Journal,* December 1948.

Henderson, P. D., and Seers, D. "1949: Forecast and Fact," *Bulletin of the Oxford University Institute of Statistics,* January and February 1950.

Jewkes, J. H. "Second Thoughts on the Employment White Paper," *Manchester School of Economic and Social Studies,* January 1948.

――― and Devons, E. "The Economic Survey for 1947," *Lloyds Bank Review,* April 1947.

Kahn, R. F. "Professor Meade on Planning," *Economic Journal,* March 1949.

Morrison, H. "Economic Planning in Britain," *Public Administration,* Spring 1947.

————. "Public Control of the Socialised Industries," *Public Administration,* Spring 1950.

Myrdal, G. "The Trend Towards Economic Planning," *The Manchester School of Economic and Social Studies,* January 1951.

Political Quarterly, April–June 1950 issue. Articles on various phases and problems of nationalization by D. N. Chester, E. Davies, P. S. Florence and G. Walker, J. A. G. Griffith, W. A. Lewis, W. A. Robson, and A. Salter.

"Resort to Price Control," *The Economist,* August 4, 1951.

Scott, M. F. "Investment Policy in a Nationalised Industry," *Review of Economic Studies,* No. 44, 1949–1950.

"Sphere of the Cabinet," *The Economist,* January 21, 1950.

"The Dividend Monstrosity," *The Economist,* August 4, 1951.

"The Public Corporation," *The Times* (London), January 20, 21, 22, 1947.

"The Rights of the Subject," *The Economist,* November 25, 1950.

Thornton, R. H. "Nationalisation: Administrative Problems Inherent in a State-Owned Enterprise," *Public Administration,* Spring 1947.

Tress, R. C. "The Practice of Economic Planning," *Manchester School of Economic and Social Studies,* May 1948.

"TUC on Public Ownership," *The Economist,* August 26, 1950.

"What Must Be Kept?," *The Economist,* November 18, 1950.

Wilson, T. "Programmes and Allocations in the Planned Economy," *Oxford Economic Papers* (New Series), January 1949.

II. NATIONALIZATION: COAL

A. GOVERNMENT PUBLICATIONS

Annual Report and Statement of Accounts (for the years 1947–1950), National Coal Board, H.M.S.O.

Coal Industry Nationalisation, Ministry of Fuel and Power, Cmd. 6716, H.M.S.O., 1945.

Plan for Coal, National Coal Board, 1950. The Board's proposals for industry investment and reorganization during 1950–1965.

Report of the Technical Advisory Committee Appointed by the Minister of Fuel and Power, Cmd. 6610, H.M.S.O., 1945. A basic report underlying the nationalization undertaking.

B. BOOKS AND MONOGRAPHS

Cole, G. D. H. *National Coal Board* (revised edition), Gollancz, London, 1949. The problem of organization and incentives.

Cole, M. *Miners and the Board,* Gollancz, London, 1949.

Court, W. H. B. *Coal,* H.M.S.O., 1951.

Foot, R. *A Plan for Coal,* Mining Association, London, 1945. An alternative proposal.

Heinemann, M. *Coal Must Come First,* Frederick Muller, Ltd., London, 1948. An analysis by the Labour Research Department.

Neuman, A. M. *Economic Organization of the British Coal Industry,* Routledge, London, 1934.

Report on The British Coal Industry, Political and Economic Planning, London, 1936.

The British Fuel and Power Industries, Political and Economic Planning, London, 1947. A basic report.

Wilson, H. *New Deal for Coal,* Contact Publications, London, 1945.

Zweig, F. *Men in the Pits,* Gollancz, London, 1949.

C. ARTICLES

Beacham, A. "The Present Position of the Coal Industry in Great Britain," *The Economic Journal,* March 1950.

Burn, D. "The National Coal Board," *Lloyds Bank Review,* January 1951.

"Desperation in Coal," *The Economist,* December 16, 1950.

"How Many Miners?" *The Economist,* January 27, 1951.

Moos, S. "The Statistics of Absenteeism in Coal Mining," *Manchester School of Economic and Social Studies,* January 1951.

"Plan for Coal," *The Economist,* November 18, 1950.

Reid, C. "The Problem of Coal," *The Times* (London), November 22, 23 and 24, 1948. The problem of organization as seen by an ex-member (resigned) of the National Coal Board.

"The Coal Board Looks Ahead," *The Economist,* June 25, 1949.

"The Coal Board's Profits," *The Economist,* July 8, 1950.

"The Next Coal Board," *The Economist,* June 9, 1951.

"The Second Coal Board," *The Economist,* July 7, 1951.

"What Price Coal?" *The Economist,* February 3, 1951.

III. Nationalization: Transport

A. GOVERNMENT PUBLICATIONS

British Air Services, Ministry of Civil Aviation, Cmd. 6712, H.M.S.O., December 1945.

Integration of Freight Services by Road and Rail, British Transport Commission, 1950.

Report and Accounts (for the years 1948–1950), British Transport Commission, H.M.S.O.

B. BOOKS AND MONOGRAPHS

Dimock, M. E. *British Public Utilities and National Development,* Allen & Unwin, London, 1933; University of Chicago Press, Chicago, 1934.

Morrison, H. S. *Socialisation and Transport,* Constable, London, 1933.

Walker, G. J. *Road and Rail* (2d edition), Allen & Unwin, London, 1947; Macmillan, New York, 1949.

C. ARTICLES

"Can Transport Pay?" *The Economist,* March 3, 1951.

Cropper, R. "Road Freight Transport and the Act of 1947," *Manchester School of Economic and Social Studies,* September 1950.

Hurcomb, C. W. "The Development of the Organisation of the British Transport Commission," *Public Administration,* Autumn 1950.

Milne, A. M. "Passenger Road Transport and the Transport Act 1947, with Particular Reference to the North-East of England," *The Economic Journal,* June 1951.

"Public and Private Enterprise," *The Economist,* December 2, 1950.

"The Cost of Transport," *The Economist,* January 21, 1950.

"Transport and Costs," *The Economist,* July 14, 1951.

"Transport in Trouble," *The Economist,* September 23, 1950.

"Trucks and the Act," *The Economist,* November 25, 1950.

Walker, G. J. "The Transport Act 1947," *Economic Journal,* March 1948.

Wilson, G. L., and Plowman, E. G. "An Appraisal of Nationalized Transport in Great Britain," *American Economic Review* (Papers and Proceedings), May 1950.

IV. NATIONALIZATION: ELECTRICITY AND GAS
A. GOVERNMENT PUBLICATIONS

First Report and Accounts, July 1948–March 1950, Gas Council, H.M.S.O., 1951.

Report and Accounts (for the years 1947–1950), British Electricity Authority, H.M.S.O.

Report of the Committee on Electricity Distribution [*McGowan Committee*], Ministry of Transport, H.M.S.O., 1936.

The Gas Industry, Report of the Committee of Enquiry, Cmd. 6699, H.M.S.O., 1945.

B. BOOKS AND MONOGRAPHS

Chantler, P. *The British Gas Industry,* Manchester University Press, Manchester, 1938.

Dimock, M. E. *British Public Utilities and National Development,* Allen & Unwin, London, 1933; University of Chicago Press, Chicago, 1934.

H., G. *The Socialization of the Electrical Supply Industry,* Gollancz, London, 1934.

Report on the Gas Industry in Great Britain, Political and Economic Planning, London, 1939.

The British Fuel and Power Industries, Political and Economic Planning, London, 1947.

C. ARTICLES

"British Electricity's Horizon," *The Economist,* December 9, 1950.

Coase, R. H. "Nationalization of Electricity Supply in Great Britain," *Land Economics,* February 1950.

de Chazeau, M. G. "The Rationalization of Electricity Supply in Great Britain," *Journal of Land and Public Utility Economics,* August and November 1934.

"Economics of Electricity," *The Economist,* October 13, 1951.

"Electricity Economics," *The Economist,* July 1, 1950.

Houthakker, H. S. "Electricity Tariffs in Theory and Practice," *Economic Journal,* March 1951.

"Report on Gas," *The Economist,* March 24, 1951.

"Report on Power," *The Economist,* January 21, 1950.

V. NATIONALIZATION: IRON AND STEEL
A. GOVERNMENT PUBLICATIONS

Iron and Steel Industry, Cmd. 6811, H.M.S.O., May 1946. The industry's plan.

B. BOOKS AND MONOGRAPHS

Burn, D. L. *The Economic History of Steelmaking, 1867–1939,* Macmillan, New York, 1940; Cambridge University Press, London, 1940.

Cole, G. D. H. *Why Nationalise Steel?,* New Statesman & Nation, London, 1948.

Fienburgh, W., and Evely, R. W. *Steel Is Power,* Gollancz, London, 1948.

Gumbel, W., and Potter, K. *The Iron and Steel Act, 1949,* Butterworth, London, 1951.

"Ingot" (pseud.). *The Socialisation of Iron and Steel,* Gollancz, London, 1936.

Iron and Steel Bill: Discussion in Committee, British Iron and Steel Federation, London, April 1949.

Iron and Steel Bill: Some Arguments For and Against, British Iron and Steel Federation, London, June 1949.

Organisation in the Steel Industry, British Iron and Steel Federation, London, 1948.

Progress of the Steel Development Plan, British Iron and Steel Federation, London, 1949.

Robson, W. A. (Editor). *Problems of Nationalized Industry,* Allen & Unwin, London, 1951.

The Federation and Its Work, British Iron and Steel Federation, London, 1949.

C. ARTICLES

Langley, S. J. "The Iron and Steel Act, 1949," *Economic Journal,* June 1950.

"State Steel," *The Economist,* February 17, 1951.

"Steel in 1951," *The Economist,* January 13, 1951.

"Will the Steel Act Work?," *The Economist,* September 23, 1950.

VI. TOWN AND COUNTRY PLANNING

A. GOVERNMENT PUBLICATIONS

Advice on Buying and Selling a Site for Building a House, Central Land Board, 1948.

Control of Land Use, Cmd. 6537, H.M.S.O., 1944.

Greater London Plan, 1944, H.M.S.O., 1945. Prepared on behalf of the Standing Conference on London Regional Planning by Sir Patrick Abercrombie.

Greater London Plan, H.M.S.O., 1947. Memorandum by the Ministry of Town and Country Planning on the Report of the Advisory Committee for London Regional Planning.

Report of the Central Land Board for the financial year 1949–50, H.M.S.O., 1950.

Report of the Committee on Land Utilisation in Rural Areas [*Scott Report*], Cmd. 6378, H.M.S.O., 1942.

Report of the Expert Committee on Compensation and Betterment [*Uthwatt Report*], Cmd. 6386, H.M.S.O., 1942.

Report of the Royal Commission on the Distribution of the Industrial Population [*Barlow Report*], Cmd. 6153, H.M.S.O., 1940. These three reports, the Barlow, Scott and Uthwatt, are classics in the field. They are basic to an understanding of present-day issues of town and country planning.

Reports of the Ayecliffe, Crawley, Harlow, Hatfield, Hemel Hempstead, Peterlee, Stevenage and Welwyn Garden City Development Corporations for the period ending 31st March, 1949, H.M.S.O., July 1949.

Town and Country Planning Act, 1947 (Part I: General Notes; Part II: Notes on Sections), H.M.S.O., 1947 and 1948.

Town and Country Planning Bill, 1947: Explanatory Memorandum, Ministry of Town and Country Planning, Cmd. 7006, H.M.S.O., 1947.

Town and Country Planning in Britain (I.D. 920), British Information Services, May 1949.

Town and Country Planning, 1943–1951, Ministry of Local Government and Planning, Cmd. 8204, H.M.S.O., 1951. Includes, besides an analysis and survey, a list of reports and plans published since 1939, a list of orders and regulations made under planning acts since 1943, and a list of Command papers and other publications issued by the Ministry up to January 31, 1951.

B. BOOKS AND MONOGRAPHS

Abercrombie, L. P. *Town and Country Planning,* Oxford University Press, Oxford, 1943.

Doble, R. L., and Mann, H. *A Guide to the Town and Country Planning Act, 1947* (2d edition), Sweet & Maxwell, London, 1949.

Fogarty, M. P. *Town and Country Planning,* Hutchinson, London, 1948; Longmans, New York, 1950.

Sharp, T. *Town Planning* (reprint), Penguin, West Drayton, 1949.

C. ARTICLES

Monson, D., and Monson, A., "The Development and Practice of Compensation and Betterment in Present English Planning Law," *Land Economics,* May 1949.

Osborn, F. J. "Planning and Its Critics," *Town and Country Planning,* May 1950.

Plant, A. "Land Planning and the Economic Functions of Ownership," *Journal of the Chartered Auctioneers' and Estate Agents' Institute,* May 1949.

Sharp, E. "Town and Country Planning," *Public Administration,* Spring 1948.

"The Approach to Land-Use Planning," *Planning,* June 4, 1951.

"The 1947 Act: The First Year," *Journal of the Town Planning Institute,* September–October 1949. A symposium.

"The Town Planners' Dream," *The Economist,* March 3, 1951.

"The Working of the Town and Country Planning Act," *Journal of the Royal Institute of British Architects,* July 1950. A symposium.

"The Working of the Town and Country Planning Act, 1947," *Town and Country Planning,* February 1950.

"Town Planners' Apology," *The Economist,* May 12, 1951.

Wendt, P. F. "Administrative Problems Under the British Town and Country Planning Act of 1947," *Land Economics,* November 1949.

———. "A Reply from England on the Effects of the British Town and Country Planning Act, 1947," *Land Economics,* November 1950.

VII. DISTRIBUTION OF INDUSTRY

A. GOVERNMENT PUBLICATIONS

Distribution of Industry, Cmd. 7540, H.M.S.O., October 1948.

First Report of the Commissioner for the Special Areas (England and Wales), Cmd. 4957, H.M.S.O., 1935; *Second Report,* Cmd. 5090, H.M.S.O., 1936; *Third Report,* Cmd. 5303, H.M.S.O., 1936; *Report for the year ended 30 September, 1937,* Cmd. 5595, H.M.S.O., 1937.

Industrial Building: Notes for the Guidance of Industrialists who wish to carry out Building Work, Economic Information Unit, The Treasury, 1949.

Industrial Survey of the Lancashire Area (Excluding Mersey-side); . . . of Merseyside; . . . of the North East Coast Area; . . . of South Wales; . . . of the South West of Scotland, Board of Trade, H.M.S.O., 1932.

Notes for the Guidance of Applicants for Building Licenses (3d edition), Ministry of Works, November 1948.

"Part Played by the Location of Industry Planning Room," *Board of Trade Journal*, H.M.S.O., June 18, 1949.

"Progress in the Development Areas in the Post-War Years," *Board of Trade Journal*, H.M.S.O., December 2, 9, 16, 30, 1950 and January 6, 13, 1951.

Report of the Royal Commission on the Distribution of the Industrial Population [Barlow Report], Cmd. 6153, H.M.S.O., 1940.

Reports of Investigations into the Industrial Conditions in Certain Depressed Areas of I—West Cumberland and Halt-whistle, II—Durham and Tyneside, III—South Wales and Monmouthshire, IV—Scotland, Ministry of Labor, Cmd. 4728, H.M.S.O., 1934.

B. BOOKS AND MONOGRAPHS

Dennison, S. R. *The Location of Industry and the Depressed Areas*, Oxford University Press, Oxford, 1939.

Report on the Location of Industry, Political and Economic Planning, London, 1939.

C. ARTICLES

Heatherington, D. F. "Location of Industry," *Foreign Commerce Weekly*, May 4 and May 11, 1946.

Sykes, J. "Postwar Distribution of Industry in Great Britain," *Journal of Business*, July 1949.

VIII. NATIONAL HEALTH SERVICE

A. GOVERNMENT PUBLICATIONS

Health Services in Britain (I.D. 753 Revised), British Information Services, August 1948.

Medical Services in Great Britain (No. R.1237), Central Office of Information, London, 1946.

Remuneration of Doctors Under the National Health Service (I.D. 906), British Information Services, September 1950.

Report of the Central Health Services Council for the period ending December 31, 1949, H.M.S.O., 1950.

Report of the Inter-departmental Committee on the Remuneration of Consultants and Specialists, Cmd. 7420, H.M.S.O., 1948.

Report of the Inter-departmental Committee on the Remuneration of General Dental Practitioners, Cmd. 7402, H.M.S.O., 1948.

Report of the Inter-departmental Committee on the Remuneration of General Practitioners, Cmd. 6810, H.M.S.O., 1946.

Report of the Ministry of Health for the year ended 31st March, 1949, Cmd. 7910, H.M.S.O., 1950.

Seventh Report from the Select Committee on Estimates (Session 1948–1949), H.M.S.O., 1949.

Social Insurance and Allied Services, Report by Sir William Beveridge, Inter-departmental Committee on Social Insurance and Allied Services, H.M.S.O., and Macmillan, New York, 1942. The first, and most important, of the Beveridge reports.

Some Statistics on the National Health Service (I.D. 1002), British Information Services, March 1950.

Third Report from the Select Committee on Estimates (Session 1950), H.M.S.O., 1950.

Twentieth Report from the Select Committee on Estimates (Session 1948–1949), H.M.S.O., 1949.

B. BOOKS AND MONOGRAPHS

Hill, C., and Woodcock, J. *The National Health Service,* Christopher Johnson, London, 1949. An excellent factual survey.

Institute of Public Administration. *The Health Services: Some of Their Practical Problems,* Allen & Unwin, London, 1951.

National Service for Health, The Labor Party, London, 1943.

Rappleye, W. C. *The National Health Service of Great Britain,* Josiah Macy, Jr. Foundation, New York, 1950. The health service as seen by the Dean of Columbia University's College of Physicians and Surgeons.

Report on the British Health Services, Political and Economic Planning, London, 1937.

C. ARTICLES

"Financing the Hospitals," *The Economist,* July 1, 1950.

Martin, H. E. "The Transition to the National Health Service," *Public Administration,* Autumn 1946.

"The Hospital Service: System of Management" [and] "The Patient Is Human," *Planning,* September 26, 1949 and February 13, 1950.

"The N.H.S. Through American Eyes," *The Lancet,* November 4, 1950. *The Lancet* is a weekly journal of British and foreign medicine, surgery, obstetrics, physiology, pathology, pharmacology, public health and news.

"The National Health Service Act in Great Britain: A Review of the First Year's Working," *The Practitioner,* Autumn 1949.

IX. Housing

A. GOVERNMENT PUBLICATIONS

Housing in Britain (R. 1901), Central Office of Information, London, March 1950.

Housing Return for England and Wales, 31st March, 1950, Ministry of Health, Cmd. 7938, H.M.S.O., 1950.

Housing Return for Scotland, 31st March 1950, Ministry of Health, Department of Health for Scotland, Cmd. 7939, H.M.S.O., 1950.

Housing Summary, 30th November, 1950, Ministry of Health, Cmd. 8114, H.M.S.O., 1950.

Housing Summary, 31st August, 1950, Ministry of Health, Department of Health for Scotland, Cmd. 8056, H.M.S.O., 1950.

Rent Control in England and Wales, Ministry of Health, H.M.S.O., 1946.

Report of the Inter-departmental [Ridley] Committee on Rent Control, Cmd. 6621, H.M.S.O., 1945.

Report of the Ministry of Health for the year ended 31st March, 1949, Cmd. 7910, H.M.S.O., 1950.

B. BOOKS AND MONOGRAPHS

Bowley, M. *Housing and the State, 1919–1944,* Allen & Unwin, London, 1945; Macmillan, New York, 1948.

C. ARTICLES

"A New Policy for Housing Subsidies," *Planning,* April 24, 1950.

"After the Millionth House," *The Economist,* January 7, 1950.
"Economics of the Council House," *Planning,* January 23, 1950.
"Houses in the Air," *The Economist,* October 21, 1950.
"Housing Costs," *The Economist,* January 14, 1950.
"Housing Figures," *The Economist,* February 17, 1951.
Paish, F. W. "The Economics of Rent Restriction," *Lloyds Bank Review,* April 1950.
"Rent Control Policy," *Planning,* November 7, 1949.
"The Assessment of Housing Needs," *Planning,* January 10, 1949.

X. AGRICULTURE

A. GOVERNMENT PUBLICATIONS

Agriculture in Britain (I.D. 945 Revised), British Information Services, 1951.
Explanatory Memorandum on Agriculture Bill, Cmd. 6996, H.M.S.O., 1946.
First Report of Smallholdings Advisory Council, H.M.S.O., 1949.
Journal of the Ministry of Agriculture, H.M.S.O. Monthly.
Report of the Committee Appointed to Review the Working of the Agricultural Marketing Acts [*Lucas Report*], Ministry of Agriculture and Fisheries, H.M.S.O., 1947.

B. BOOKS AND MONOGRAPHS

Astor, W., and Rowntree, B. S. *British Agriculture,* Penguin Books, Harmondsworth, 1939.
Stamp, L. D. *The Land of Britain: Its Use and Misuse* (2d edition), Longmans, New York, 1950.

C. ARTICLES

"Food Stocktaking," *The Economist,* February 24, 1950.
"Farming Merry-Go-Round," *The Economist,* April 7, 1951.
"Inquest on Agriculture," *The Economist,* May 26, 1951.
Skilbeck, D. "War-Time Changes in British Farming," *Lloyds Bank Review,* July 1947.

Index

ILL HEALTH: relation to poverty, 188
Imperial Airways, Limited, 49
Import Duties Act (1932), 251
Imports: importance, 8; licensing, 18; projected for 1949, 28
"Inducement" payments to doctors, 199, 200n
Industrial Coal Consumers' Council, 58
Industrial goods: allocation, 18
Industrial insurance, see Insurance, industrial
Industry: control of, 17; inducements to locate in Special Areas, 170
Industry, distribution of, 166–86; criticisms of government's policy, 183–85; lack of national plan, 185; report of Barlow Commission on, 172
Inflation: control in 1948, 25; fight against, 32
Ingots and castings: output, 126n
Insurance, industrial: mutualization, 43; nationalization proposed, 42
Inter-departmental Committee on the Remuneration of General Dental Practitioners, 205
Inter-departmental Committee on the Remuneration of General Practitioners, 198
Interdepartmental committees: estimates and recommendations, 22; importance in planning machinery, 14, 15
Investment: program for 1949, 27; rate in 1948, 24
Investments, foreign: prewar imports paid by, 260
Iron and Steel Act (1949), 127; repeal proposed by Conservatives, 133n
Iron and Steel Board: functions, 125
Iron and Steel Consumers' Council, 132
Iron and Steel Corporation, 127, 128, 129–33; decentralization policy, 131
Iron and steel industry: arguments for and against nationalization, 123; claims for equipment, ma-

terial, and manpower, 22; government supervision welcomed, 126; nationalization, 43, 122–33, 279; opposition to nationalization, 122–24, 127–29; production, 126; self-government, 124; statistics under public ownership, 130(t); unemployment in, 167

JARROW: unemployment in, 167

LABOR: position in nationalized industry, 135; shortages, 230; see also Agricultural labor; Coal miners; Management and labor; Railroad workers; Wages
Labor government: activities for industrial expansion in Development Areas, 181–82; agricultural policy, 260–62; appraisal of accomplishments, 275–85; attack on poverty, 188; attempt to combine a free democracy and a planned economy, 11; attitude toward Lucas committee recommendations, 266; food distribution program, 264–66; health program, 191–93; housing accomplishment, 242–47; housing program, 230; land planning measure, 146; political status, 282; pronouncements on planning, 5; provisions for distribution of industry, 178
Labor party: attitude toward land nationalization, 273; nationalization program, 42–52; nationalization record consistent with program, 46
Labor relations: electric industry, 113; railroads, 85, 91
Labour Believes in Britain, 42
Land: agricultural use, see Farm holdings; compensation for public use, 137–40, 148–50; compulsory public purchase of land, 146, 160; cost of development for public use, 138–40; free individual use traditional in Great Britain, 136; nationalization prospects, 272–74; public ownership, 42; see also Tenants

Nuffield Trust, 171
Nursing services, 210

OATS: production, 250
Oil, 14
Ophthalmic services, 206–7
Ophthalmic Services Committee, 207
Optical appliances, see Ophthalmic services
Organisation for European Economic Co-operation: memoranda submitted to, 9
Overseas trade: improvement in 1948, 24

PAYMENTS, balance of, see Balance of payments
Passenger rates, see Railroads: passenger rates
Pharmaceutical committees, 208
Pharmaceutical services, 207
Pigs, see Hogs
Planning, economic, see Economic planning
Planning machinery, 12–21
Planning Staff: responsibility for Survey, 23
Political and Economic Planning: quoted on electric power nationalization, 108
Postmaster General: responsibility for telecommunications, 51
Post Office, 47
Potatoes: marketing scheme, 3; production, 250; production goals, 267
Poultry: production goals, 267
Poverty: relation to health, 188
Power industry: claims for equipment, material, and manpower, 22
Practices Compensation Committee, 201
Price controls, 19; government desire to remove as soon as possible, 19
Prices, 134; of farm products, 249, 257, 261, 265
Private enterprise: in providing housing, 229, 245
Production: increase in 1949, 32
Production Committee, 12

Public health: government concern with, 187–89; statutes (1911–46), 189; see also National health service
Public ownership (British): history, 47
Public purchase of land, compulsory, see Land: compulsory public purchase of

RAILROADS, 14; combination, 76; compensation for, 79; costs, 94; financial aspects of nationalization, 82–87; freight rates, 87–91, 94; nationalization problems, 81; passenger rates, 91, 94
Railroad workers: changes in working conditions, 92n; wage negotiations, 91–93; wages, 85, 92
Railway Executive, 79, 80
Railway Rates Tribunal, see Transport Tribunal
Railway Road Transport Act (1928), 76
Railways Act (1921), 76
Rationing, 19
Raw materials: allocation, 18
Regional Hospital Boards, 212n
Regional planning, see Town and country planning
Reid, Sir Charles: member National Coal Board, 59, 65, 71n
Reid Commission, see Technical advisory (Reid) commission
Rent control, 239–42
Rents, see Housing: rents
Residential hostels, 237
Resource budgeting, 277
Road haulage: compensation for, 79; competition with railroads, 76; nationalization, 78, 95–99, 103, 279; review for 1951, 98, 99
Road Haulage Executive, 96
Road Passenger Executive, 96, 100
Road passenger service, 99–100
Roads, 14
Road Transport Executive, 79, 81; trucking organization, 96
Royal College of Obstetricians and Gynaecologists, 194